KU-606-181

## Dedication

*In memory of Peter Bain (1941–2007).*
*Socialist, working-class militant and scholar.*

'What happened to those workers in the public sector when New Labour came into office? This book tells us, systematically, on the basis of sound empirical research and across the public sector as a whole. Essential reading, not just for academics, but for trade unionists and anyone interested in both the reality described and in doing something about it.' *David Byrne, University of Durham*

014117199

University of Liverpool

Withdrawn from stock

# NEW LABOUR/HARD LABOUR?

## Restructuring and resistance inside the welfare industry

Edited by Gerry Mooney and Alex Law

First published in Great Britain in 2007 by

The Policy Press
University of Bristol
Fourth Floor
Beacon House
Queen's Road
Bristol BS8 1QU
UK

Tel +44 (0)117 331 4054
Fax +44 (0)117 331 4093
e-mail tpp-info@bristol.ac.uk
www.policypress.org.uk

© Gerry Mooney, Alex Law 2007

British Library Cataloguing in Publication Data
A catalogue record for this book is available from the British Library.

Library of Congress Cataloging-in-Publication Data
A catalog record for this book has been requested.

ISBN 978 1 86134 833 3 (paperback)
ISBN 978 1 86134 834 0 (hardback)

The right of Gerry Mooney and Alex Law to be identified as the editors of
this work has been asserted by them in accordance with the 1988 Copyright,
Designs and Patents Act.

All rights reserved: no part of this publication may be reproduced, stored in
a retrieval system, or transmitted in any form or by any means, electronic,
mechanical, photocopying, recording, or otherwise without the prior
permission of The Policy Press.

The statements and opinions contained within this publication are solely those
of the editors, and not of The University of Bristol or The Policy Press. The
University of Bristol and The Policy Press disclaim responsibility for any injury
to persons or property resulting from any material published in this publication.

The Policy Press works to counter discrimination on grounds of gender, race,
disability, age and sexuality.

Cover design by Qube Design Associates, Bristol.
Front cover: photograph supplied by kind permission of Jess Hurd at Report
Digital, showing UNISON strikers and their families marching through Merry
Hill, Dudley, August 2000, in protest against the privatisation of the NHS.
Printed and bound in Great Britain by MPG Books, Bodmin.

# Contents

# Acknowledgements

Just as this book was nearing completion we received the tragic news that one of our contributors, Peter Bain, had died. As well as being a personal blow for his family, friends, comrades and colleagues, Peter's death represents a profound loss for those concerned with the serious study of workers and their conditions. We hope that this book does some justice to his memory.

There are a number of people who provided unfailing support and encouragement to us as we worked on this project. At The Policy Press we would like to offer our sincerest thanks and gratitude to Philip de Bary, Emily Watt and Jessica Hughes as well as to The Policy Press team in general. Producing collections such as this is hard work, or perhaps more aptly, hard labour and therefore we would like to extend our thanks to all the contributors for their work for this book and for their willingness to respond to our demands. We appreciate only too well that they produced their chapters in the context of increasing demands on their time and space in their respective institutions. Thanks also to Jess Hurd at Report Digital for allowing us to use the excellent photograph on the front cover of striking health workers and their families in Dudley in 2000.

We were both fortunate to present a paper emerging from this book at the annual conference of Historical Materialism in London in December 2006 and would like to thank contributors to the panel discussion on 'Hard Labour in the UK and US', in particular Colin Leys for his helpful feedback and advice.

This has been a collective effort and there are other colleagues who, in ways that perhaps they do not appreciate, have also made contributions. In particular Gerry would like to extend his thanks to Jenny Robertson and Michelle Hynd at The Open University in Scotland for all their patience and their support to him in this endeavour. Likewise he would like to offer thanks too to John Clarke and Allan Cochrane and other colleagues in the Social Policy Department in the Faculty of Social Sciences at The Open University for their encouragement and for the constant flow of ideas and good advice that, as they appreciate only too well, he often ignores! Alex is indebted to Stuart Fairweather and Gill Motion for their friendly but critical discussion of some of the issues in this book with him in various forums such as the Dundee Social Forum, and in the same critical spirit to Owen Logan, Duncan Forbes and Leigh French, who have advanced the debate about neoliberal cultural politics and welfare reform in discussions around the free arts magazine *Variant*.

This book has also caused much hard labour on the part of our respective families. Gerry would like to express his thanks and love to Ann, Claire and Hilary. For his part, Alex is especially grateful for all the endurance and forbearance shown over the years by Jan, Kerrie and Natalie.

Finally, we hope that this book will help in some small way to encourage further resistance to New Labour's neoliberal agenda. As this book was going to press (August 2007) 600 care workers in Glasgow were involved in strike action over a dispute brought about by a 'single status' pay review which would leave some of them up to £1,000 a year worse off. We offer our support and best wishes to all workers engaged in such resistance.

Gerry Mooney and Alex Law
Paisley and Dundee
August 2007

# List of abbreviations

| | |
|---|---|
| AfC | Agenda for Change |
| ASHE | Annual Survey of Hours and Earnings |
| AUT | Association of University Teachers |
| BASW | British Association of Social Workers |
| BEd | Business Education |
| BMA | British Medical Association |
| CCT | Compulsory competitive tendering |
| CMS | Customer management system |
| CoSLA | Convention of Scottish Local Authorities |
| CPD | Continuing professional development |
| CPSA | Civil and Public Services Association |
| DWP | Department for Work and Pensions |
| EIS | Educational Institute of Scotland |
| EU | European Union |
| FE | Further education |
| GMB | General and Municipal Workers Union |
| GP | General practitioner |
| GTC | General Teaching Council |
| HE | Higher education |
| HMI | Her Majesty's Inspectorate (Scotland) |
| HMIC | Her Majesty's Inspectorate of Constabulary |
| HRM | Human resource management |
| HSE | Health and Safety Executive |
| ICT | Information and communication technology/ies |
| IFSW | International Federation of Social Workers |
| ILO | International Labour Organization |
| IT | Information technology |
| NAS/UWT | National Association of Schoolteachers/Union of Women Teachers |
| NATFHE | National Association of Teachers of Further and Higher Education |
| NHS | National Health Service |
| NPM | New public management |
| NUS | National Union of Students |
| NUT | National Union of Teachers |
| Ofsted | Office for Standards in Education |
| PCS | Public and Commercial Services Union |
| PCT | Primary care trust |
| PDS | Performance development scheme |

PGDE — Professional Graduate Diploma of Education
PISA — Programme for International Student Assessment
PFI — Public finance initiative
PPP — Public–private partnership
PR — Public relations
QAA — Quality Assurance Agency
QCA — Qualifications and Curriculum Authority
RAE — Research Assessment Exercise
RCN — Royal College of Nursing
RoE — Retention of Employment
SATS — Standard Attainment Tests
SCVO — Scottish Council for Voluntary Organisations
SMT — Senior management team
SPRU — Science and Technology Policy Research Unit
SSP — Scottish Socialist Party
STUC — Scottish Trades Union Congress
TGWU — Transport and General Workers Union
TIMSS — Trends in International Mathematics and Science Study
TRAC — Transparent Approach to Costing
TUC — Trades Union Congress
TUPE — Transfer of Undertakings (Protection of Employment)
UCEA — Universities Employers Association
UCU — Universities and Colleges Union
UKCC — United Kingdom Central Council
WERS — Workplace Employment Relations Survey

# List of contributors

**Peter Bain** was Senior Lecturer, Department of Human Resource Management, University of Strathclyde.

**Peter Kennedy** is on the editorial board of *Critique, Journal of Socialist Theory* and lectures in sociology and social policy in the School of Law and Social Sciences, Glasgow Caledonian University.

**Carole Ann Kennedy** teaches part time in sociology and social policy in the School of Law and Social Sciences, Glasgow Caledonian University.

**Alex Law** is Lecturer in Sociology, School of Social and Health Sciences, University of Abertay Dundee.

**Michael Lavalette** is Senior Lecturer in Social Policy, School of Sociology and Social Policy, University of Liverpool.

**Tricia McCafferty** is Lecturer in Sociology, Department of Geography and Sociology, University of Strathclyde.

**Henry Maitles** is Reader in Education and Head of Department of Curricular Studies, Faculty of Education, University of Strathclyde.

**Gerry Mooney** is Senior Lecturer in Social Policy and Staff Tutor, Faculty of Social Sciences, The Open University.

**Lynne Poole** is Lecturer in Social Policy, School of Social Sciences, University of Paisley.

**Sally Ruane** is Deputy Director of the Health Policy Research Unit at De Montfort University, Leicester.

**Phil Taylor** is Professor of Work and Employment Studies, Department of Human Resource Management, University of Strathclyde.

**Hazel Work** is Lecturer in Sociology, School of Social and Health Sciences, University of Abertay Dundee.

# ONE

# New Labour, 'modernisation' and welfare worker resistance

*Gerry Mooney and Alex Law*

## Introduction

> My work was not only relatively lower paid than thirty
> years ago, it was also entirely insecure, day-to-day agency
> employment. Back then at least I had the security of joining
> the staff of the NHS from day one: it was a safe job for life
> if I wanted it, but everything is shifting sands for the low
> paid. It is called 'flexibility', and in the name of flexibility
> the hospital had shed or 'outsourced' all its ancillary workers.
> I was about to learn the full meaning of contracting out.
> (Toynbee, 2003, pp 56-7)

Polly Toynbee's comments here will be familiar to the many who work
in the lower reaches of public services work in the UK today. As a
high-profile and well-respected journalist, Toynbee had the luxury of
knowing that her involvement in this particular work, here as a hospital
porter employed by a large private firm, was not a permanent feature
of her day-to-day life but allowed her the opportunity to explore for a
short period of time some of the experiences of the most poorly paid
and vulnerable workers in New Labour's Britain. In *Hard work: Life in
low-pay Britain* (2003), she embarked on a similar journey to *A working
life* (Toynbee, 1971), allowing for an informed comparison to be made
between key aspects of working lives in the public sector in the 1970s
and now. Clearly both studies are located in very different economic,
political, social and cultural contexts. In short, and of importance for
us in this particular collection, the world of public sector work has
been transformed in crucial ways. Toynbee continues:

> It so happened that on the day I left Tony Blair was
> making an important speech about public services. It was
> another of his ambivalent muddled messages. He praised

public-service workers but then called for more 'reform' and 'flexibility', which from the ground floor felt like a threat. The government always speaks with several agendas. And they are often contradictory. The low-paid public workers consist of the working poor, the deserving poor, many of them women and mothers, the very people the Working Families' Tax Credits are designed to help. These are the very families whose poverty the government has pledged to abolish. But that springs from the part of the government's brain labelled 'poverty targets'. It is the contrary part of its brain that calls for higher productivity and more 'flexibility' in the public sector, making sure pay doesn't rise too much, squeezing every last penny of efficiency out of each worker, whatever the human cost to them and their children. For the government the great advantage of privatisation and PFI [private finance initiative] deals is that they can get the Carillions to do the Gradgrind work for them on the one hand, while still worrying about how to overcome poverty with the other hand. (Toynbee, 2003, p 73)

Many of the issues raised here are reflected in the key themes that run through this book. *New Labour/hard labour?* is primarily concerned with the world of public sector work under New Labour in the late 20th and early 21st century and how this is being experienced by key groups of workers engaged at the 'frontline' in producing and delivering public services. In particular the focus is on those workers located in what we have termed the 'welfare industry', who are involved in the production and delivery of social welfare. The term 'welfare industry' is used to capture what is generally referred to as the 'mixed economy' of welfare providers but also those working at the frontline as well as 'backroom' staff. The idea of a 'welfare industry' also encompasses non-state sectors, such as the voluntary sector and private provision.

Much has been written about different aspects of New Labour's social and public policies and of the organisational changes that have been wrought as a result of public sector 'reform'. However, with relatively few exceptions, this is primarily from a 'top-down' perspective, with a focus on policy making and/or governance. Much less attention has been given to how this reform process is impacting on the welfare workforce, particularly from the standpoint of the workers who are actually involved in service delivery. In this collection we begin to redress the balance by considering some of the struggles that are taking place around the 'frontier of control' (Goodrich, 1975) in the UK welfare industry.

Many welfare workers are involved in supporting and delivering services to some of the most vulnerable and disadvantaged groups in society. In some respects there is little that is new in this. Such work has long been central to the aims and goals of the welfare state, but also in informing the general ethos and culture of public sector employment (see McDonough, 2006). In this respect there is a general moral economy of effort from a workforce that has traditionally been highly committed and dedicated. However, while acknowledging the myriad of contradictions that permeate New Labour's policy making in relation to public sector work and social policy objectives, what Toynbee overlooks is that it is often poorly paid workers (sometimes referred to as 'the working poor') who are key to delivering and maintaining key 'heartland' public services and in the process 'supporting' other disadvantaged groups, including sections of the working and non-working poor. Here, however, public sector workers, and in particular those involved in the welfare sectors, are not simply delivering services, administering benefits and managing the poor and disadvantaged in ever increasing and often, thanks to government demands and strictures, punitive ways; they are also tasked with the delivery and implementation of key New Labour social policy objectives that involve forcing those in poverty into the very low-paid employment and vulnerable forms of work highlighted by Toynbee. Work underpins New Labour's vision but public services are central to achieving the goals that this vision generates. In turn, public servants are then crucial to delivering not only services but also the implementation of key New Labour political and ideological objectives.

In this chapter we consider some of the main ways in which welfare work is being affected by the neoliberal onslaught of recent decades (see Harvey, 2003, 2005; Saad-Filho and Johnston, 2005). Neoliberalism permeates the UK economy, society and culture today. The new common sense that there is 'no alternative to the market' has become widely accepted. Neoliberalism attempts to reconstruct work, welfare and the role of the state to redefine public and private, and, above all, celebrates market relations and 'freedom' of trade. However, it is important to note that neoliberalism is far from being the coherent and universal process that it is widely assumed to be. Further, neoliberalism does not work on a blank canvas but has to cope with and struggle against other ideas, competing forces, different historical, economic, spatial, political and national contexts. Thus, as one example, the celebration of the market by New Labour struggles against widespread popular support for 'the welfare state' and state provision, and work-based conflicts are at the core of the struggles around neoliberalism.

From the outset it is important for us to make it clear that this book is not informed by a desire to romanticise either the working conditions that prevailed for significant numbers of (although far from all) public sector workers in the so-called 'golden age' of the Beveridgean welfare state. Nor is there a desire to glorify that welfare state itself. However, it is argued throughout that as a result of many of the changes that have been brought about by successive governments in the UK since the mid-1970s, against a backdrop of a growing commitment to market-driven policies at the heart of neoliberalism, few public sector workers' lives have not been significantly and adversely affected. New Labour has pushed the institutional 'reform' of the welfare state to much deeper levels than even the Thatcher and Major governments, bringing increased market exposure and worker insecurity. Indeed, despite their overt ideological commitments, the limits to Thatcherite reform of the welfare state created huge divisions within successive Conservative governments. It is perhaps surprising then that New Labour have been more dogmatic and more determined than even the Conservatives in pursuing neoliberal agendas in the context of public service modernisation.

## New Labour and public sector 'modernisation'

'Work' lies at the heart of the New Labour project. It is seen to provide the key means through which poverty as 'social exclusion' can be alleviated and as such is said to represent the 'best' form of welfare (Mooney, 2004; Levitas, 2005). In this sense work was constructed as 'salvational', its morally uplifting properties celebrated by a host of leading New Labour politicians (see Bevir and O'Brien, 2001; Grover and Stewart, 2002) as the key to transforming welfare dependants into model citizens able to participate in society by taking up the opportunities on offer to them.

Welfare-to-work, workfare and other labour market 'activation' programmes have become core elements in social policy making across a range of European societies as well as in North America. In the UK they have been widely discussed and subjected to far-reaching critical interrogation within the social policy literature (see, for instance, Fairclough, 2000; Grover and Stewart, 2002; Lister, 2004; Mooney, 2004; Bevir, 2005; Byrne, 2005; Levitas, 2005; Prideaux, 2005).

However, as New Labour has sought to valorise work, work as a central dimension of daily life and existence has to some extent fallen from focus as an object of social scientific study. This is a generalised claim and in some areas of the social sciences 'work' remains a crucial area of concern. The study of 'industrial relations' remains an obvious area of investigation wherein work in different ways continues to occupy centre stage. Arguably, however, by contrast, the sociology of work occupies a much less central position in sociology as a field of study today compared with the 1970s and 1980s. In social policy analysis, there is a more complex picture. It is right that many social policy researchers have sought to develop critical analyses of different aspects of New Labour's emphasis on work (as entering paid labour through welfare-to-work/labour activation strategies). These are supplemented by a general awareness that much of the work that the 'socially excluded' have entered is, following Toynbee above, 'flexible' in terms of both pay and duration, leading to a general view that the kind of work that has been opened up to many disadvantaged groups is of poor quality, low paying and often temporary or casualised, or in other words, highly vulnerable forms of employment. And there is widespread recognition that much of this work is gendered and racialised in particular ways, with migrant labour playing a particular role in the provision of low-paid care work and ancillary labour across the public and private sectors (see Cox, 2006; May et al, 2006). However, alongside this, we would argue, there is a general neglect in the research of the conditions of paid labour in the workplace. In particular, that work is an exploitative social relation tends to be overlooked, and this is especially so in relation to labour in the welfare and wider public sectors. (We return to this in Chapter Two.)

Work has increasingly become the focus for much of social policy intervention and a concern with 'work' underpins important and contentious areas of social policy making today: welfare 'reform', public sector 'modernisation', and for tackling poverty as social exclusion. What serves to link all of these areas of concern for New Labour is the overriding objective of transforming the UK into a 'modern' efficient economy, able to compete on the global stage. In this respect New Labour's policy agendas and the overall project within which they are located are informed by a 'Third Way' understanding of a world that has changed. As Blair stated in New Labour's 1997 General Election manifesto, 'the policies of 1997 cannot be those of 1947 or 1967' (Labour Party, 1997). Together with Giddens, probably the leading UK architect of the Third Way, Blair shares a view of the world as one gripped by the constraints of globalisation. A world in which the UK is only able to survive on the basis of an increasingly lean and flexible economy, with, of course, an increasingly flexible labour force (see

Blair, 1998; Giddens, 1998, 2000). Flexible labour markets and flexible workers are the order of the day. Education and lifelong learning, reskilling and upskilling are seen as key tools through which the UK labour force could meet the challenges of the new information and knowledge economy. However, as is already apparent, in New Labour's perspective the development of a competitive economy depends on the development of a competitive society. Herein, then, the drive for a 'national renewal' that encompasses both welfare 'reform' and the 'modernisation' of key institutions, including the welfare state:

> Reform is a vital part of rediscovering a true national purpose, part of a bigger picture in which our country is a model of a 21st century developed nation: with sound, stable economic management; dynamism and enterprise in business; the best educated and creative nation in the world; and a welfare state that promotes our aims and achievements. But we should not forget why reform is right, and why, whatever the concerns over individual benefits, most people know it is right. Above all, the system must change because the world has changed, beyond the recognition of Beveridge's generation….We need a system designed not for yesterday, but for today. (Blair, quoted in IPPR, 1998, pp iii-iv)

Through this, New Labour has attempted to reconcile the irreconcilable: economic prosperity and social justice or, in another perhaps more common phrase, 'competition and cohesion' (Boddy and Parkinson, 2004).

The Third Way approach has been widely and critically discussed elsewhere (see Jones and Novak, 1999; Glennerster, 1999; Hay, 1999; Lavalette and Mooney, 1999; Powell, 2000; Bevir and O'Brien, 2001; Callinicos, 2001; Newman, 2001; Barnett, 2002; Ferguson et al, 2002; Finlayson, 2003; Arestis and Sawyer, 2005; Bevir, 2005; Byrne, 2005; Levitas, 2005). Importantly, for our purposes, welfare 'reform' and the 'modernisation' of public services are presented as central aspects of the drive for national competitiveness (for a general discussion, see Finlayson, 2003). This involves not only a wide-ranging attack on the aforementioned 'welfare dependency', involving the provision of in-work benefits such as tax credits to increase incentives to work, but also a drive towards employability and the 'modernisation' of workplace labour relations (which has involved the introduction of a National Minimum Wage, 'flexible' forms of working and work–life balance initiatives) (see Gilman and Arrowsmith, 2001). Central to this modernisation agenda is the reform of public service labour, involving regular attacks by leading New Labour politicians on what have been constructed as bureaucratic or producer 'interests' in public sector work.

## Welfare, welfare labour and welfare workers

Before proceeding further it is important to acknowledge the difficulty of attempting to arrive at a precise definition of 'welfare work', or indeed of disentangling welfare work from other sectors of public sector employment (see Newman and Mooney, 2004). This is increasingly problematic given the ever-changing organisational structures and boundary 'blurring' taking place, alongside the growing role of sectors not traditionally associated with the welfare realm. The increasing use of call centres to access care services in some areas of the health and social services is an obvious case in point (see Chapter Nine).

Public sector workers represent a significant group within the UK labour force today (see Table 1.1). In 1999 public sector workers represented 19% of the UK labour force, rising to 20.2% in 2006 (Livesey et al, 2006). (This is the UK-wide picture but it hides marked differences across the UK, with many of the northern English cities, Scotland, Wales and Northern Ireland showing a higher proportion of the workforce engaged in the public sector.) Clearly the figure of 5.84 million workers (in 2006) includes many who are not employed in areas that could be viewed as coming under the welfare industry umbrella. However, it does include workers within the NHS, Europe's largest employer, with some 1.55 million workers in 2006 (plus an additional 384,000 in other health and related services), 2.94 million local government workers and 1.4 million education workers (Livesey et al, 2006). That said, those who work for the non-profit sector as well as those in private firms providing public services, are largely excluded from these figures. Further, a massive proportion of welfare work is

**Table 1.1: Numbers of public sector workers (1991–2006)**

| Year | Million |
|------|---------|
| 1991 | 5.98 |
| 1998 | 5.16 |
| 1999 | 5.85 |
| 2006 | 5.84 |

*Source:* Livesey et al (2006, p 425)

also provided in the home, unpaid, carried out primarily by women, and this is not accounted for in these figures.

The notion of welfare itself is by no means uncontested and this adds to the problems of defining and counting welfare workers. The term 'welfare', as Clarke points out (Clarke, 2005; see also Clarke, 2004, pp 20-1), pre-dates its institutionalisation as a set of state organisations, policies and practices in the 20th century. It has a much longer history embracing charity, various forms of philanthropy and mutualism, as well as 19th-century state interventions such as the Poor Laws and early state housing provision. Welfare today encompasses all of these as well as newer forms of state provision. This is a much wider definition than the narrower and more specific meaning of welfare as 'public assistance' that dominates in the US and which has gradually entered political discourse in the UK also.

Public sector workers and the services they help to provide have been subjected to far-reaching and dramatic changes in recent decades. From the late 1970s through to the first half of the 21st century different groups of public sector workers have experienced assorted forms of privatisation:

- contracting out or outsourcing of public sector work to for-profit firms
- wage freezes and constraints
- 'public' funding through both the private finance initiative (PFI) and public–private partnerships (PPPs)
- marketisation, 'best value'
- attacks on collective bargaining and constraints on trade union rights and organisation
- redundancies and job cuts
- performance-related pay
- increasing pressures to 'self-manage'
- regrading and reclassification
- casualisation
- new forms of public managerialism
- increased workplace regulation, audit and inspection
- work intensification and extensification
- a declining sense of job security and increasing levels of workplace stress and related illnesses.

Alongside deskilling and the loss of autonomy there have also been employer-led demands for reskilling, upskilling and retraining, often leading to 'qualification inflation', while engagement in lifelong learning has equipped workers with the human capital that would make them marketable assets. These assorted forms of privatisation have been discussed by a range of authors who have focused on particular aspects of change or on specific groups of workers (see Monbiot, 2000; Green, 2001; Leys, 2001; Whitfield, 2001, 2006; Beynon et al, 2002; Harris, 2003; Wills, 2003; Bunting, 2004; Pollock, 2004; Innes et al, 2006). And then there are the growing number of cases of the substitution of caring labour through the use of new technologies and information and communication technologies (ICT), for instance in National Health Service (NHS) call centres (Fairbrother and Poynter, 2001, pp 314-15; see also Chapter Four, this volume).

Further, as highlighted and explored in several of the chapters in this collection, government social policy agendas have been demanding 'more and more' from public sector workers as they struggle to meet the myriad of objectives and service the multiple strategies that New Labour has developed since 1997. As Fairbrother and Poynter (2001, p 319) argue:

> State employees are increasingly entreated to take on tasks that their occupation previously did not require – teachers are engaged in health promotion activities, university lecturers are encouraged to ensure the employability of their graduates and doctors are called upon to advise on healthy life styles rather than specifically treating illnesses.... In this sense, the social and moral dimensions of the customer-oriented approach have been deployed to reform the relationships between professionals and their various publics and erode the monopolies of skill and discretion over decision-making and job content that professional staff traditionally exercised.

It is a central argument of this book that these developments are the product of the increased marketisation of welfare in the UK. Market modes of delivery and market-influenced forms of practice, together with newer forms of managerial practice, are working to restrict the 'space' that many welfare professionals once enjoyed to provide the services and support they perceived service users to require, often resulting in a significant deskilling of work tasks. Routinisation and work degradation is contributing to what Richard Sennett calls 'the spectre of uselessness' that is now gripping increasing numbers of professional workers, as it had manual workers before them (Sennett, 2006). This calls into question the changing nature of 'professionalism' and the different requirements that are now made of 'professionals' in the welfare and public sectors. In several of the chapters in this collection (for instance, Chapters Six, Eight and Nine) the issue of professionalism occupies centre stage, highlighting that there is a struggle between notions of professionalism generated by workers themselves and government and employer-led ideas of what professionalism should be about. In turn this raises important questions about the notion of 'skill' itself, and how this is being deployed as part of the ongoing conflicts between employers and employees that characterise many welfare workplaces today. This issue is taken up in Chapter Two.

Further, we must also show some awareness that in the devolved UK such developments have not been uniform across the different constituent nations. Thus far, although there are clear trends in such a direction, marketisation in the NHS in Scotland, for instance, is not as developed as in England or in Wales. In the Scottish education sector, thanks in part to the overwhelming dominance of secondary schooling, the private sector has yet to penetrate school management to the extent it has in parts of England, even if PFI/PPP appears to be more prevalent north of the border (see Poole and Mooney, 2006). We should be cautious, however, and avoid the suggestion that public service work in Scotland is immune in some ways to the radical Blairite reform agenda unfolding in England (see Mooney and Poole, 2004; Mooney and Scott, 2005). As the authors of the different case study chapters that comprise this book highlight, across the UK there is, perhaps at times and in places at different speeds, something of a general 'race to the bottom'.

The unevenness of managerialism, work intensification and modernisation as well as worker responses do not detract from the point that public sector work in the UK has undergone far-reaching change, change that has all too frequently been detrimental to workers. Yet again we need to be alert that managerialism is contested and not always successful in meeting its objectives (see Clarke et al, 2000; Kirkpatrick, 2006).

The changing nature of public sector work is part and parcel of New Labour's Third Way reconstruction of the idea of the 'public' itself, a process that crucially involves blurring the boundaries between public and private forms of provision (see Clarke, 2004, pp 121-2). In general, as we have noted above, this has involved a shift towards the privatisation of public goods and services and the greater involvement of the private sector in 'public' service provision.

In addition, as part of its wider reform of the welfare and modernisation agendas, New Labour has sought to emphasise the role and responsibilities of family and community in the provision of welfare services. Such agendas are part of a wider project of renewing the 'contract' between the state, on the one hand, and the individual as a worker-citizen, on the other. Alongside this there is also an attempt to reconstruct the ideal citizen both as a worker *and as a citizen-consumer* (Clarke et al, 2007). Here the overarching context is one of consumerism and the extension of 'choice', and these are key to the restructuring of public services.

> In reality, I believe that people do want choice, in public services as in other services. But anyway, choice isn't an end in itself. It is one important mechanism to ensure that citizens can indeed secure good schools and health services in their communities. Choice puts the levers in the hands of parents and patients so that they as citizens and consumers can be a driving force for improvement in their public services. We are proposing to put an entirely different dynamic in place to drive our public services; one where the service will be driven not by the government or by the manager but by the user – the patient, the parent, the pupil and the law-abiding citizen. (Blair, 2004)

The promotion of choice reflects a desire to reconstruct the role of the state, no longer always and everywhere the provider of services but as an 'enabler' and regulator of services provided by other 'partners' and 'stakeholders'. In repeated speeches and announcements, in successive Green Papers, in government select committees and across many government departments, the emphasis on choice at the heart of New Labour's project is all too evident (Blair, 2001, 2002; Brown, 2006; for a fuller discussion of choice in New Labour's public service reform programme see Clarke and Newman, 2006). However, it is also all too noticeable from the quote from Blair above that the promotion of choice and the consumerist vision carry with them particular consequences for public sector workers. It is also evident that workers do not feature here, except as an 'absent presence'. Implicit in this comment is a stark warning to public sector workers that they have to become more customer focused, which involves extensive changes in the working lives of those concerned.

For Blair and other leading New Labour politicians, including Gordon Brown (Brown, 2006), public sector workers are generally viewed as an obstacle to modernisation and reform, and seen as hindering the delivery of key New Labour social policy objectives.

For example, at Labour's Spring Conference in Cardiff in February 2002, Blair drew a distinction between 'reformers' and 'wreckers', the latter category including public sector workers who were resisting New Labour's modernisation package. Speaking to the British Venture Capital Association in London in 1999, the Prime Minister talked of bearing 'the scars on my back' from trying to reform welfare (Blair, 1999a). This was followed up at the Labour Party Conference in the same year where Blair made his now infamous 'forces of conservatism' speech in which he identified some groups of education and health professionals as holding back the government's reform programme (Blair, 1999b). And on 21 October of that year Blair attacked what he saw as a 'culture of excuses' among schoolteachers who were resistant to aspects of his reform agenda (http://news.bbc.co.uk). Such comments played an important role in helping to ferment the growing disillusionment with New Labour among public sector workers after the first few years of Labour government, and in fuelling more recent opposition to the government's 'permanent revolution' in public services (TUC, 2006).

As a consequence of government policies and objectives, the pressures on public sector workers connect in many different and at times hidden or complex ways with wider social, economic, political, cultural and geographical changes in UK society, and at a global level. However, in attemping to win the 'reform' battle, New Labour has faced many difficulties, as did the Conservatives before them. As indicated, there is widespread worker opposition and also continuing and popular support for key welfare state institutions, such as the NHS (see Chapter Four). There has been widespread opposition to housing stock transfer, to the closure of schools, hospitals, community services, swimming pools and so on across the UK with numerous campaigns mounted, drawing in wide public support (see, for example, Chapters Four and Ten).

We turn next to focus specifically on those workers involved in struggles in what we are calling here the 'welfare industry'.

## Welfare workers: resisting New Labour

Privatisation, or the threat of privatisation, has hung over large sections of the public sector workforce since 1997. But even where privatisation has not taken place, or in those sectors where the penetration of the market has been much more limited, the spread of increasingly aggressive forms of managerialism, including 'new public management' (NPM), with its emphasis on flexible forms of work, performance-related pay, the individualisation of contracts and so on, has clearly been in evidence (see Clarke et al, 2000; Fairbrother and Poynter, 2001; Newman, 2001). This has worked to take managerial agendas, often although not always or everywhere borrowed from the private sector, into the core areas of the public sector, in the process marginalising worker and trade union concerns (see Chapter Three).

There is also another dimension here. The increased diversification of welfare providers, increasingly drawing in the private sector on the one hand, and informal female labour on the other, has major implications for worker solidarity and unionisation. For example, the experience of women engaged in informal caring in the home, often providing childcare for family members, neighbours and friends in paid work, differs significantly from the experiences of previous generations of women who benefited from an expanding welfare state and consequently increased work opportunities. This provided opportunities for unionisation and more general involvement in workplace struggles and negotiations. However, in the current context, such workers are often individualised and unable to pursue their collective interests. Indeed, union density remains higher in the public sector than in the economy more generally. In the early 2000s around 59% of public sector workers were in unions, compared with 19% in the private sector (Bach and Givan, 2004, p 89; see also Chapter Three, this volume).

Many of these public sector workers, together with their unions, are challenging many of the core ideological assumptions of New Labour. Arguably there are signs of a re-emergence of new forms of political unionism with unions and their members all too ready to make links between cuts in jobs and services, privatisation and market agendas and, in some cases, with the government's commitment to war in Iraq, Afghanistan and elsewhere, in part to exemplify the redirection of state funding.

A key objective of this book is to highlight the resistance and opposition to New Labour from the public sector/welfare workplace. In this respect we have gone beyond the somewhat narrow remit of simply detailing the impact of public sector modernisation and welfare reform on the workforce involved. In much of the available literature, there has been little substantive examination of opposition to and conflict around key elements of New Labour's agendas for the welfare state and public sector, particularly from those workers on the welfare frontline. Of course opposition to New Labour's policies varies considerably across different areas of the public sector and between workforces within particular welfare sites, like the NHS. However, since the mid to late 1990s, there have been continual and recurring episodes

**Table 1.2: Resistance in the public and welfare sector (1998-2007)**

|  | Industrial action |
| --- | --- |
| Care workers/home helps | 1998 |
| Library workers | 1998 |
| Social workers | 1998 |
| Care workers | 1998; 1999; 2000; 2007 |
| Teachers | 1999 |
| FE college lecturers | 2001; 2006 |
| Local government workers | 2001; 2006; 2007 |
| Hospital ancillary staff | 2002 |
| University lecturers | 2004; 2006 |
| Civil servants (PCS) | 2004; 2005; 2006; 2007 |
| Nursery nurses | 2004 |
| Social workers | 2004; 2005 |
| Housing association workers | 2006 |
| School ancillary staff | 2006 |
| NHS logistics workers | 2006 |

*Note:* PCS = Public and Commercial Services Union

of industrial action of various kinds involving social workers, teachers, lecturers (both in further and in higher education, FE and HE), nurses, hospital ancillary staff, nursery nurses, home helps and care workers, and local authority librarians, among others (see Table 1.2). Welfare delivery has become a central point of industrial relations disputes in the UK today (see Chapter Three, this volume).

We do not claim that this is a full or in any way a complete listing of disputes, strikes and other episodes of 'industrial action' that have taken place in different areas of the welfare industry since 1998. However, it indicates the range of localised disputes, such as those among Glasgow care workers in 1998 and Liverpool social workers in 2004-05, as well as the generalised nature of resistance to New Labour. For instance the list includes nation-specific (although country-wide) strikes, such as with nursery nurses in Scotland in 2004, as well as national (in a UK sense) disputes around pensions and, in 2006 and 2007 in the local government sector in particular, around 'single status', job regrading, pay and privatisation (see www.unison.org.uk; www.pcs.org.uk). We acknowledge here but do not Jinclude disputes involving other public service workers, such as firefighters, passport agency staff and different groups of transport workers. Importantly, however, and this is particularly the case in the Department for Work and Pensions (DWP), strikes and other forms of industrial action were not only concerned with pay and conditions, but also in protecting services (see Chapters Nine and Ten, this volume).

As was widely documented at the time, during its first two years in government (1997-99) New Labour remained committed to the tight public sector spending constraints put in place by the previous Conservative administration. The fact that this did not lead to widespread resentment and anger among public sector workers is largely due to the 'honeymoon' period that Labour enjoyed during its first few years in office, subsequently helped by the easing of public sector spending restrictions from 1999 and after. The promise that New Labour would deliver, however, was soon followed by a growing disillusionment with the new government among some groups in the public sector workforce, traditionally among Labour's core voters. It was to become increasingly evident that although there would be considerable increases in public expenditure, especially for education and the health service, this would not signal an end to privatisation but would be accompanied by the increasing penetration of the market (and in some cases also by the voluntary or third sectors) into heartland areas of public and welfare services provision. Pay would increase for public sector workers, that is, for those who were not transferred to private firms through outsourcing, but the growing pay differentials of the 1980s and 1990s between public and private sector employees would remain largely unaffected. Public services became a major issue in the 2001 election campaign and an important part of New Labour's second term agenda thereafter (see Timmins and Cox, 2001).

## The organisation of the book

The main aim of this book is to explore the impact of New Labour's welfare 'reform' and public sector 'modernisation' agendas on different groups of workers in the welfare industry across the UK. A related aim is to bring together for the first time in one collection the experiences of different groups of workers engaged in the frontline of welfare and social policy delivery. The book aims to explore some of the working experiences of different groups of welfare workers and in the process to highlight key issues of union and worker mobilisation and resistance.

While the book does not seek to provide a comprehensive account of the particular situations affecting the many different groups of welfare workers, it brings together case studies, chosen to illustrate the wide-ranging impact of government policies on workers, industrial relations and the labour process, in order to facilitate a degree of comparison between the experiences of different groups.

Many of the contributors draw on their own, in some cases ongoing, research with groups of workers at the frontline of service delivery and welfare reform, and make use of qualitative data generated through a variety of interview techniques. All too often the 'voices' of these workers have been marginalised in both official discourses and in academic study. Several chapters also call on surveys and empirical research conducted by trade unions and other relevant groups as well as the growing body of literature exploring the impact of PFI/PPPs on the delivery of welfare and public services (see, for instance, Monbiot, 2000; Whitfield, 2001; Pollock, 2004), the role of managerialism and new forms of governance (for example, Clarke et al, 2000; Newman, 2001; Clarke, 2004). However, where secondary sources have been utilised, care has been taken to reframe key findings with reference to the impact welfare changes have had on those involved in delivering them. We have sought to illuminate the ways in which macro-level policy shifts have affected the day-to-day working lives of those engaged in delivering social inclusion and a multitude of new health and new educational initiatives.

The focus throughout the book is on welfare at the point of its production. Several of the chapters utilise a labour process framework of analysis, drawing on insights from labour process theory. The book seeks to be innovative insofar as it synthesises arguments and understandings, as well as drawing on research from across the social sciences. One of the strengths of this transdisciplinary approach is that it enables us to bring together and integrate ideas from social policy, the sociology of work, labour process theory and industrial relations in particular. Only through integrating debates and materials from a wide spectrum such as this is it possible to make sense of the changing world of welfare work/workers in the UK today.

In Chapter Two Alex Law and Gerry Mooney outline an analytical framework developed to facilitate a critical understanding of the restructuring of the welfare labour process. In the next chapter, 'A "Third Way"? Industrial relations under New Labour', Peter Bain and Phil Taylor provide the general industrial relations context as it relates to public sector work in the UK today, and in particular they offer an account of New Labour's approach to the question of workplace relations, highlighting the ways in which this is couched in terms of a Third Way agenda. Chapter Four by Sally Ruane, entitled 'Acts of distrust? The experiences of support workers in PFI hospital schemes', explores the key ways in which New Labour's privatisation and marketisation programmes are impacting on some of the most vulnerable groups of public sector workers. Here, Sally Ruane examines how outsourcing and contracting out are, together with the intensification of work, seriously eroding the hard fought-for pay and conditions structures of key groups of health service workers. The next chapter maintains the focus on developments in the NHS. In 'Control and resistance at the ward-face: contesting the nursing labour process', Peter Kennedy and Carole A. Kennedy examine how a changing organisational context is combining with different managerial strategies to enforce control over the labour process of nursing. They highlight the 'frontier of control' that is at the centre of nursing in the NHS today and argue that management has been unsuccessful in securing this frontier entirely for their own ends.

Chapters Six and Seven consider one of the key areas of worker mobilisation in recent times, education. In his chapter entitled "'I didn't come into teaching for this!" The impact of the market on teacher professionalism', Henry Maitles focuses on some of the ways in which the work of schoolteachers is being intensified as a result of recent market-focused reforms. Maitles offers a particular understanding of the ways in which these reforms relate to the continuation of educational inequalities in the state school sector. In Chapter Seven, Alex Law and Hazel Work focus on HE lecturers. In 'Ambiguities and resistance: academic labour and the commodification of higher education', they describe some of the tensions in an increasingly bureaucratised, or proletarianised, academic labour process. Industrial action among university lecturers indicates some of the ways in which even relatively autonomous kinds of labour such as academic work are being subjected to an externally imposed managerialism that is sometimes internalised by academics themselves. Like other workers, the control exercised over academics is far from total, yet many identify an erosion of professional self-organisation at work.

One of the most notable episodes of strike action in recent years was the all-out national strike by local authority-employed nursery nurses in Scotland in 2004. In Chapter Eight Gerry Mooney and Tricia McCafferty examine what they term the paradox of 'professionalisation and degradation' of welfare work. Against a simple deskilling thesis, they argue that there are contradictory trends in evidence, which nevertheless work to intensify the labour of nursery nurses. In particular, it is argued that nursery nurses, like many other groups of welfare workers, are increasingly charged with implementing and delivering important New Labour social policy agendas, without appropriate remuneration. Thus they are being asked to do more and more *for* less and less.

Chapter Nine, 'Social work today: a profession worth fighting for?', offers a different approach from some of the other chapters in that the author, Michael Lavalette, makes an explicit and committed case for a return to a different kind of social work practice. Taking as a case study the Liverpool social work dispute of 2004-05, he outlines some of the main ways in which social work and social workers have been subjected to government-inspired changes, eroding the scope for social workers to act in the best interests of clients, but also how some groups of social workers in different parts of the UK have sought to respond to this, re-asserting in the process the potential for a return to a more radical social work. In Chapter Ten, 'Working "for" welfare in the grip of the "iron" Chancellor?: modernisation and resistance in the Department for Work and Pensions', Tricia McCafferty and Gerry Mooney focus on another key group that have been in the New Labour firing line, civil servants. Focusing in particular on workers in the DWP, they highlight how far-reaching job cuts have impacted on the workforce, arguing that those that are left are being asked to do more and more *with* less and less.

Given the growing importance of the third sector or voluntary sector in the delivery of welfare in the contemporary UK, we thought it important to include some discussion of the ways in which welfare work is also undergoing profound and far-reaching changes. In 'Working in the non-profit welfare sector: contract culture, partnership, Compacts and the "shadow state"', Lynne Poole considers some of the ways in which welfare work in the voluntary sector is subject to the same kinds of pressures as in the public sector and how New Labour's agendas have also worked to fundamentally reshape the voluntary sector. In the final chapter, 'Beyond New Labour: work and resistance in the "new" welfare state', Alex Law and Gerry Mooney bring together the main issues and questions that have arisen from the substantive chapters, drawing out comparisons and points of contrast and outlining some potential research agendas. There are many areas of public sector work that we have been unable to include in this collection and we hope that this book will help to promote more research in this field. Importantly, the contributors also highlight the ways in which key groups of welfare workers are taking action not only to protect jobs, wages and conditions, but also to defend the very services that many of the most vulnerable groups in society depend on. In this respect they are challenging not only New Labour's modernisation agendas and developing social policy objectives, but also, albeit at times implicitly, the division that New Labour, and the Conservatives before them, have sought to open up between producers and service users. Lest we forget, the vast majority of public sector workers and their families are also consumers of welfare services.

We conclude here by recognising that this book is an unfinished but developing project. The issues explored here will have a life beyond Blair, Brown and New Labour, with the main political parties in different parts of the UK cohering around market-based or neoliberal-informed understandings of welfare and public services. The potential for more disputes and struggles around the organisation and delivery of welfare and public services suggests that *hard labour* is likely to be the dominant story for welfare workers for the immediate future, irrespective of the party in government. State policies impact on all workers, on their working and non-working lives. The battles around welfare work in the UK today are thus battles around services but, perhaps more fundamentally, they are also battles around the maintenance of a public sphere or realm that is not subject to market demands and pressures. In other words, it is a battle to maintain de-commodified forms of provision that can help to address the multiple inequalities that characterise UK society today. This is the context for *New Labour/hard labour?*.

## References

Arestis, P. and Sawyer, M. (2005) 'Neoliberalism and the Third Way', in A. Saad-Filho and D. Johnston (eds) *Neoliberalism: A critical reader*, London: Pluto, pp 177-83.

Bach, S. and Givan, R.K. (2004) 'Public service unionism in a restructured public service', in J. Kelly and P. Willman (eds) *Union organization and activity*, London: Routledge, pp 89-109.

Barnett, N. (2002) 'Including ourselves: New Labour and engagement with public services', *Management Decision*, vol 40, no 4, pp 310-17.

Bevir, M. (2005) *New Labour: A critique*, London: Routledge.

Bevir, M. and O'Brien, D. (2001) 'New Labour and the public sector in Britain', *Public Administration Review*, September/October, vol 61, no 5, pp 535-47.

Beynon, H., Grimshaw, D., Rubery, J. and Ward, K. (2002) *Managing employment change: The new realities of work*, Oxford: Oxford University Press.

Blair, T. (1998) *The Third Way: New politics for the new century*, London: Fabian Society.

Blair, T. (1999a) Speech to the British Venture Capital Association, London, 6 July.

Blair, T. (1999b) Speech to the Labour Party Conference, Bournemouth, 28 September.

Blair, T. (2001) Speech at the British Library London on Public Sector Reform, 16 October.

Blair, T. (2002) *The courage of our convictions: Why reform of the public services is the route to social justice*, London: Fabian Society.

Blair, T. (2004) 'Choice, excellence and equality', Speech at Guys and St Thomas' Hospital, London, 23 June.

Boddy, M. and Parkinson, M. (eds) (2004) *City matters: Competitiveness, cohesion and urban governance*, Bristol: The Policy Press.

Brown, G. (2006) Speech at '21st-century Public Services: Putting People First', QEII Conference, London, 6 June.

Bunting, M. (2004) *Willing slaves*, London: Harper Collins.

Byrne, D. (2005) *Social exclusion* (2nd edn), Buckingham: Open University Press.

Callinicos, A. (2001) *Against the Third Way*, Cambridge: Polity.

Clarke, J. (2004) *Changing welfare, changing states*, London: Sage Publications.

Clarke, J. (2005) 'Welfare', in T. Bennett, L. Grossberg and M. Morris (eds) *New keywords*, Oxford: Blackwell.

Clarke, J. and Newman, J. (2006) 'The people's choice? Citizens, consumers and public services', Paper delivered at the 'International Workshop: Citizenship and Consumption', King's College, Cambridge, 30 March-1 April.

Clarke, J., Gewirtz, S. and McLaughlin, E. (eds) (2000) *New managerialism, new welfare?*, London: Sage Publications.

Clarke, J., Newman, J., Smith, N., Vidler, E. and Westmarland, L. (2007) *Creating citizen-consumers: Changing publics and changing public services*, London: Sage Publications.

Cox, R. (2006) *The servant problem: Domestic employment in a global economy*, London: I.B. Tauris.

Fairbrother, P. and Poynter, G. (2001) 'State restructuring: managerialism, marketisation and the implications for Labour', *Competition and Change*, vol 5, pp 311-33.

Fairclough, N. (2000) *New Labour, new language?*, London: Routledge.

Ferguson, I., Lavalette, M. and Mooney, G. (2002) *Rethinking welfare*, London: Sage Publications.

Finlayson, A. (2003) *Making sense of New Labour*, London: Lawrence and Wishart.

Giddens, A. (1998) *The Third Way*, Cambridge: Polity.

Giddens, A. (2000) *The Third Way and its critics*, Cambridge: Polity.

Gilman, M. and Arrowsmith, J. (2001) 'Modernising the workplace: Labour's employee relations agenda', *Competition and Change*, vol 5, pp 291-310.

Glennerster, H. (1999) 'A Third Way?', in H. Dean and R. Woods (eds) *Social Policy Review 11*, University of Luton/Social Policy Association, pp 28-44.

Goodrich, C.L. (1975) *The frontier of control*, London: Pluto.

Green, F. (2001) 'It's been a hard day's night: the concentration and intensification of work in late twentieth-century Britain', *British Journal of Industrial Relations*, vol 39, no 1, pp 53-80.

Grover, C. and Stewart, J. (2002) *The work connection*, London: Palgrave.

Harris, J. (2003) *The social work business*, London: Routledge.

Harvey, D. (2003) *The New Imperialism*, Oxford: Oxford University Press.

Harvey, D. (2005) *A brief history of neoliberalism*, Oxford: Oxford University Press.

Hay, C. (1999) *The political economy of New Labour*, Manchester: Manchester University Press.

Innes, A., MacPherson, S. and McCabe, L. (2006) *Promoting person-centred care at the front line*, York: Joseph Rowntree Foundation.

IPPR (Institute for Public Policy Research) (1998) *Leading the way: A new vision for local government*, London: IPPR.

Jones, C. and Novak, T. (1999) *Poverty, welfare and the disciplinary state*, London: Routledge.

Kirkpatrick, I. (2006) 'Taking stock of the new managerialism in English social services', *Social Work and Society*, vol 4, no 1, pp 14-24.

Labour Party (1997) *New Labour: Because Britain deserves better: 1997 General Election manifesto*, London: Labour Party.

Lavalette, M. and Mooney, G. (1999) 'New Labour, new moralism: the welfare politics and ideology of New Labour under Blair', *International Socialism*, vol 85, pp 27-47.

Levitas, R. (2005) *The inclusive society* (2nd edn), London: Palgrave.

Leys, C. (2001) *Market-driven politics*, London: Verso.

Lister, R. (2004) *Poverty*, Cambridge: Polity Press.

Livesey, D., Machin, A., Millard, B. and Walling, A. (2006) 'Public sector employment 2006: seasonally adjusted series and recent trends', *Labour Market Trends*, December, pp 419-38.

McDonough, P. (2006) 'Habitus and the practice of public service', *Work, Employment and Society*, vol 20, no 4, pp 629-47.

May, J., Wills, J., Datta, K., Evans, Y., Herbert, J. and McIllwaine, C. (2006) *The British state and London's migrant division of labour*, London: Department of Geography, Queen Mary College, University of London.

Monbiot, G. (2000) *Captive state: The corporate takeover of Britain*, London: Macmillan.

Mooney, G. (ed) (2004) *Work: Personal lives and social policy*, Bristol: The Policy Press.

Mooney, G. and Poole, L. (2004) 'A land of milk and honey?: social policy in the "new" Scotland', *Critical Social Policy*, vol 24, no 4, pp 458-83.

Mooney, G. and Scott, G. (eds) (2005) *Exploring social policy in the 'new' Scotland*, Bristol: The Policy Press.

Newman, J. (2001) *Modernising governance*, London: Sage Publications.

Newman, J. and Mooney, G. (2004) 'Managing personal lives: doing "welfare work"', in G. Mooney (ed) *Work: Personal lives and social policy*, Bristol: The Policy Press, pp 39-72.

Pollock, A.M. (2004) *NHS plc: The privatisation of our health care*, London: Verso.

Poole, L. and Mooney, G. (2006) 'Privatizing education in Scotland? New Labour, modernization and "public" services', *Critical Social Policy*, vol 26, no 3, pp 562-86.

Powell, M. (2000) 'New Labour and the Third Way in the British welfare state', *Critical Social Policy*, vol 20, no 1, pp 39-60.

Prideaux, S. (2005) *Not so New Labour: A sociological critique of New Labour's policy and practice*, Bristol: The Policy Press.

Saad-Filho, A. and Johnston, D. (eds) (2005) *Neoliberalism: A critical reader*, London: Pluto.

Sennett, R. (2006) *The culture of the new capitalism*, London: Yale University Press.

Timmins, N. and Cox, B. (2001) 'A public realm', *Prospect*, vol 65, July, pp 20-5.

Toynbee, P. (1971) *A working life*, London: Hodder and Stoughton.

Toynbee, P. (2003) *Hard work: Life in low-pay Britain*, London: Bloomsbury.

TUC (Trades Union Congress) (2006) *TUC response to the UK government's approach to public service reform*, London: TUC.

Whitfield, D. (2001) *Public services or corporate welfare*, London: Pluto.

Whitfield, D. (2006) *New Labour's attack on public services*, Nottingham: Spokesman Books.

Wills, J. (2003) *On the front line of care: A research report to explore home care employment and service provision in Tower Hamlets*, London: UNISON/ Queen Mary College, University of London.

# TWO

# Strenuous welfarism: restructuring the welfare labour process

*Alex Law and Gerry Mooney*

## Introduction

Chapter One provided a substantive outline of the neglected relationship between New Labour's modernisation agenda for public services and the responses of different kinds of welfare workers. The purpose of this chapter is to stand back a little from the empirical detailing of this relationship to focus on the crucial sphere of what might be called the 'welfare labour process'. Like other kinds of waged labour, welfare services are produced as well as distributed through the social organisation of different kinds and amounts of labour. However, unlike other kinds of waged labour, welfare services are produced to serve predetermined social and public policy objectives involving the relief of some unwanted personal or social state. As highlighted in Chapter One, the main focus in this book is on welfare work in the public sector, that is, publicly provided and (not always well) paid labour. We also recognise that there is a suppressed tension between specific capitals bringing welfare work, previously performed without pay and mainly by women, into the marketplace as commodities, such as private nursing homes, and the wider national economy, or 'capital-in-general', that continues to rely on the unpaid work of female labour in the home. Rather than collapsing the distinction between waged and unwaged work, our focus in this book is on the specific nature of the relationship between welfare and employment.

As neoliberalism has emerged as an ideological doctrine and the neoliberal state as a governing structure, commodities, accessed in the marketplace by means of the cash (or credit) nexus, have increasingly serviced the fulfilment of social need. In the process, the relationship between capital accumulation and the welfare state has been reconfigured. This has been widely discussed, as Chapter One demonstrated in the case of the 'modernisation' of welfare governance in the UK by New Labour in the late 1990s and the 2000s. Clearly, the neoliberal welfare state is an unsteady, chaotic and contradictory creature, reflecting the tension between the ideological clarity of neoliberalism as an abstract model and the pragmatic realities involved in implementing market-facing institutional change (Pierson, 2006). As ever such developments are uneven in and between different areas of the public sector and welfare state, at times affecting different groups of workers in different ways. These are incomplete processes and, as indicated in Chapter One and throughout this book, they are also deeply contested processes.

There are complex, often contradictory and multitangled trends and developments unfolding here. It must also be acknowledged at this point that the public sector labour force is a highly stratified one: the conditions and position of professionals such as some high ranking doctors, civil servants and university employees are worlds removed from the low-grade, low-paid, low-status service work delivered across the UK by growing numbers of migrant workers. From the start the National Health Service (NHS) has been dependent on migrant labour, with around a quarter to a third of doctors and nurses from overseas occupying jobs in unpopular specialisms and areas of the UK for the past four decades. As neoliberalism has internationalised welfare labour markets the British welfare state has enjoyed a 'perverse subsidy' through the employment of nurses and doctors trained in Africa and elsewhere, a global redistribution of welfare resources from the poorest countries to the richest (Mackintosh et al, 2006).

It is also well known that the medical division of labour has been deeply stratified historically on gender lines, with male doctors seen as highly qualified, authoritative functional experts concerned with medical treatment, while female nurses have been pictured as lower-qualified, all-round carers carrying out 'sentimental work' (Strauss et al, 1982) or 'emotional labour' (Hochschild, 1983; Witz, 1986; Chapter Five, this volume). Even here, though, the situation is not static. Nurses have more recently become increasingly 'professionalised' and have deployed counter-claims of formal rationality in an attempt to usurp the status of the predominantly male medical profession.

Yet there has been a lack of detailed research and analysis on the changing nature of work and the workers who service the welfare face of neoliberalism. Perhaps one reason for this is that it sits on the boundary of a number of different academic disciplines such as social policy, welfare economics, organisational sociology and industrial relations. Unfortunately, there has been little concern in social policy with theory, analysis and empirical detailing of the varied nature of the labour process that underlies paid welfare work. At best, where the employment relationship within the welfare state has been examined, the focus tends to be on empirical case studies of specific sectors or individual workplaces. Within welfare economics the accent has been less on the organisation of work itself than on the optimal allocation and distribution of politically determined wants and desires. Even in more critical studies of the postwar welfare state and welfare state restructuring, for example O'Connor's *The fiscal crisis of the state* (1973) or Gough's *Political economy of the welfare state* (1979), while welfare labour is present it is rarely central to the analysis. More broadly based studies of political economy, the labour process and industrial relations have also tended to neglect the welfare sector. Compared to 'the Ugly Sisters' of the car factory, the office, and, more recently, the call centre, welfare work has been traditionally seen in terms of a 'Cinderella' service function, with no serious lessons for understanding the wider political economy of workplace restructuring. Taken together, academic social policy, welfare economics and organisational studies have had precious little engagement with the condition of welfare workers *qua* workers, waged labourers of a certain kind. There are of course salutary exceptions to this and contributors to this volume call on this subsidiary literature.

This chapter therefore outlines an analytical framework for understanding the restructuring of the diversified welfare labour process. It does not claim that this is the only way to think about the welfare employment relationship, or even that there is one in the singular. Rather, this is approached as a preliminary sketch, one that is selective in its focus and argument. For instance, much more could be said about the nature of the welfare employment relationship in general theories of the 'post-Fordist welfare state' (Fitzpatrick, 2001), the 'Schumpeterian workfare state' (Jessop, 1999), or 'the managerial state' (Clarke and Newman, 1997). As it stands, we focus more narrowly on the key problem of productive efficiency in neoliberal critiques of the welfare state and show how a certain behaviourist model of X-inefficiency underpins this. Such behaviourism is evident in the twin critique of 'welfare as bureaucracy' and 'welfare as profession' in neoliberal claims about the 'producer group capture' of the welfare state.

More recent restructuring of the welfare state labour process in Britain has been characterised by Pollitt (1993) as 'neo-Taylorist' and, while we accept some of the force of that analysis, it does not adequately explain the marketisation and managerialisation of welfare organisations (see also Harris, 1998). Instead, the new levels of flexible intensity demanded of labour in the welfare sector are described as 'strenuous welfarism'. In the final section of this chapter, we attempt to set this restructuring within the wider political economy of neoliberal capitalism, one that marks an attempt to more intensively subordinate labour to X-efficiencies in the overriding drive to simplify work and cheapen outputs, with the goal of enhancing national competitiveness.

## Models of X-inefficiency

At the heart of the restructuring of the welfare labour process is the neoliberal problem known as 'X-inefficiency' (Leibenstein, 1966). 'X' here stands for an unknown magnitude of failure within the production process to minimise inputs and maximise outputs in organisations that are not engaged directly in market competition. X-inefficiency is concerned with relative measures of productivity rather than the allocative inefficiency that is more usually levelled at the welfare state by neoliberal critics (Comanor and Leibenstein, 1969). For such critics, allocative inefficiency occurs when markets do not function, typically due to incomplete information represented by the absence of an explicit price signal. Consumer preference or 'choice' is unable to be spontaneously aligned with a preferred supplier. This is the more typical sense of 'welfare inefficiency', or 'sub-optimal disequilibria', one that has led to the appearance of various distributional mechanisms like targeting, selection, rationing and means testing. However, neoliberal critics of state welfare argue that such efforts to create 'allocative efficiencies' conceal inefficiencies within the production or provider side of the relationship. Neoclassical economics tends to treat organisational efficiency as a 'black box' on the premise that inputs to the production process will be rationally consumed. For the Chicago school of neoliberal economics the behaviour of individuals can be manipulated through normative reconstructions of the atomised rational self, responding self-interestedly to environmental signals and commands (Lemke, 2001).

This has some affinity with Leibenstein's (1976) attempt to impart behavioural micro-foundations for productive activity typically neglected in the unreal neoclassical assumptions of homo economicus. At the same time, Leibenstein retained something of neoclassical economics' methodological individualism in identifying the motivational psychological structure of individual workers as crucial to X-inefficiency. Individual workers were thought to be 'selectively rational', torn between the rational conformism of the superego to objectify itself in the efficient performance of tasks and the rebellion of the id to spontaneously resist external directives (Leibenstein, 1979). The psycho-dynamic struggle between superego and id within the individual was therefore devastating for the neoclassical assumption that individuals were always efficiently rational utility-maximisers. Workers have a complex of individual motivational structures that affect work performance, including submission to group norms. Norm-governed effort levels tend to stabilise below 'utility-maximising' levels of performance unless management practices establish higher group norms for 'optimal' levels of efficient performance (Shen, 1985). Workers and their organisations routinely function within what Leibenstein calls 'inert areas' of effort based on routine, habit and norms, which they will only leave under internal psychological pressure and external managerial and market pressures once the benefits of remaining at a given level of effort declines and costs increase.

An absence of competitive pressures, risk and adversity results in an indulgent management regime that is 'sub-optimal' in its use of resources, thus increasing the unit cost of outputs. Productive inefficiencies emerge from the exercise of worker discretion over judgements and diligence in the performance of work tasks. Only effective market pressures will compel management, and in turn its subordinates, within organisations to optimise rational psychological and economic outcomes. Yet managerial control over production efficiency is always fraught with uncertainty since contracts for labour are always incomplete, production involves non-marketed goods and services, many aspects of production cannot be fully specified, and firms in a sector tend to collaborate and imitate each other. In such ways, sub-optimal practices become diffused throughout the organisation and the sector. Managers and workers lack 'proper motivation' and 'permit a considerable degree of slack' that leaves them unable 'to bestir themselves' (Leibenstein, 1966) to produce at near-optimal levels and reduce unit costs, as identified, for instance, by management consultants:

> In situations where competitive pressure is light, many people will trade the disutility of greater effort, of search, and the control of other people's activities for the utility of feeling less pressure and of better interpersonal relations. But in situations where competitive pressures are high, and hence the costs of such trades are also high, they will exchange less of the disutility of effort for the utility of freedom from pressure, etc. (Leibenstein, 1966, p 413)

Hence the nature of management, a competitive environment and incentive systems are significant for X-efficient outcomes.

Such behaviourist assumptions are now widely held in the economics profession. Economists like George Akerloff and Joseph Stiglitz were awarded the Nobel Prize for their work on the social and psychological micro-foundations of economic activity, extending the earlier work of Leibenstein to bolster the neoclassical image of market efficiencies (Frantz, 2004; Lapavitsas, 2005). From such behaviourist micro-foundations, the absence of a profit imperative within a competitive market environment and comparative measures of productive efficiency, publicly provided welfare services fall into the category of X-inefficient. As non-market monopoly producers welfare workers may still be low paid relative to the private sector and therefore work even longer hours than the wages they are paid actually cover. But instead of this extra labour time being converted into a surplus product for the employer, according to neoliberals the state as both producer and (surrogate) consumer allows its employees to re-appropriate surplus labour time through under-work, over-employment, 'feather-bedding', work rigidities, disguised managerial incompetence and abuses, and a host of other working time indulgences. Such alleged X-inefficiencies derive from two sources in the 'producer capture' of the welfare state: the bureaucracy and the professions. These are often conflated together, with the distinctive way that they apparently contribute to X-inefficiency to be remedied by the same neoliberal managerialism. Here we will deal with their supposedly characteristic self-interested failings separately.

## Bureaucratic X-inefficiencies

In various ways X-inefficiency came to be identified with a malfunctioning, self-serving bureaucratic welfare apparatus. Bureaucracy operated far from the ideal-type classically envisaged as a super-efficient machine by Max Weber (1958). For Weber, bureaucracy was a highly efficient form of legitimate rational-legal authority. Authority was enshrined in explicit rules and procedures that were expected to displace arbitrary, lawless forms of power and personal domination. An impersonal, rule-bound management hierarchy separated ownership of the means of production from control over the work process. Records were maintained impartially and rules were followed with probity and discretion. Workplace subordinates were trained to accept the legitimacy of rule by an objective culture based on the credentialed status of superordinate officials. For large-scale organisations like the welfare state, therefore, bureaucracy expressed the *most*, not the least, X-efficient form of public administration. Weber (1958, p 214) put this explicitly in terms of bureaucratic technical efficiency and economic value compared to the vagaries of professionalised administration:

> The fully developed bureaucratic apparatus compares with other organisations exactly as does the machine with non-mechanical modes of production. Precision, speed, unambiguity, knowledge of the files, continuity, discretion, unity, strict subordination, reduction of friction and of material and personal costs – these are to be raised to the optimum point in strictly bureaucratic administration.... As compared with all collegiate, honorific, and avocational forms of administration, trained bureaucracy is superior on all these points. And as far as complicated tasks are concerned, paid bureaucratic work is not only more precise but, in the last analysis, it is often cheaper than even formally unremunerated honorific service.

For Weber (1958), the public servant was engaged in a 'vocation', 'devoted to impersonal and functional purposes' from which they derived 'an ideological halo' for selfless public service. More prosaically, public servants received the 'grant of a secure existence', what used to be known technically as 'tenured employment' or, more colloquially, as 'a job for life'. Officials were appointed on the basis of their expertise and training. Wages, or rather 'salaries', were not expected to be 'competitive' in the market for bureaucratic labour. Indeed the idea of 'service' – the 'service ethos' – was deeply embedded in the habitus of the public servant (McDonough, 2006), with its own intrinsic rewards in kind such as high prestige in the community combined with the extrinsic rewards of a demarcated career structure, job security and a relatively generous pension. All this sets the official up with a lifelong, meritocratic career ideal, to move 'through the ranks' from the bottom of the ladder upwards based, above all, on the evidence of educational qualifications. Weber (1958) cautioned that those at the very top of the apex effected status group closure by relegating formal qualifications as a measure of their own superordinate status and indeed often escaped any accountability to the rule-governed procedures exacted through the rest of the bureaucracy. Through such pure forms, Weber thought that the 'rationalised inner structure' of bureaucracy would lessen class conflict and make revolution 'impossible'. However, Weber also noted that the formal rationality of bureaucracy could end up dominating society itself in the form of an 'iron cage' if it escaped the specialised sphere of administration to become society's overriding principle.

The abstract nature of Weber's taxonomy and his ideal-typical method (which shared certain rationalising features in common with the bureaucratic abstractions being analysed) unsurprisingly differed in marked ways from the empirical reality of actual bureaucracies. Critics of bureaucracy objected to the substantive failure of bureaucracy to humanise welfare services and its standardised capacity to show an indifference towards human suffering, let alone respond efficiently to consumer preferences (Beetham, 1987). An extreme example of this indifference was the role of the bureaucratic apparatus in efficiently administering the complex system of concentration camps across Europe to carry out the mass murder of the Holocaust (Bauman, 1989). Neoliberals drew less extreme examples from the routine practices of the bureaucratic welfare state. Weber's notion of formal rationality out of control was captured and accentuated in numerous studies, from Michels' (1921) 'iron law of oligarchy' through to Hayek's (1944) critique of 'totalitarianism', models of bureaucratic despotism that, more recently, neoliberals have drawn from freely. Hayek was less interested in X-efficiency, in the actual nature of large-scale organisations like welfare services, than in mystifying market freedom as a neutral zone that spontaneously coordinated the multiple and diffuse decision making of individual producers and consumers.

More recently productive inefficiencies have become as central to the critique of bureaucratic welfarism as the neoliberal loss of individual freedom (Niskanen, 1973). Creating systems of rules and records is a time-consuming and resource-wasteful practice. In the process, a culture of compliance evolves. Employees protect themselves from hierarchical opprobrium by conforming to the formal letter of the law regardless of the immediate problem in hand. Low-paid workers in public services may rationally insist on 'working to contract', which is operating only within the explicit rules that they are paid to observe. Bureaucratic workers engage in what Merton (1949) called 'trained incapacity', ritualistically following the rules to the letter as a mode of self-protection and career advancement. Rather than seeing bureaucracy as a 'vocation' they fatalistically conform to the decisions of others or merely pay lip service to centralised decision making. Either way, over-commitment or under-commitment to formal rules ensures that the outcome for neoliberals will be X-inefficient. Welfare administrators may adopt 'work to rule' as a specific bargaining tactic against their employer, who is well aware that all organisations depend on subordinates performing 'extra-legal' duties 'beyond contract' simply to get the job done. Indeed, contemporary organisations attempt to get round such prohibitions by writing into their 'operating manuals' statements such as 'the employee will carry out any reasonable demand made by their manager', which merely helps to undermine the force of explicitly stated rules and procedures.

## Professional X-inefficiencies

If publicly provided welfare became for neoliberals an inefficient bureaucratic monolith that stifled individual initiative then it was aided and abetted by the position of the professional within or contiguous to the bureaucracy (see Harris, 1998, 2003). In some ways professionalism cuts across bureaucracy, creating numerous points of friction; in other ways it supplements and reinforces bureaucracy. However, although welfare employees at various levels of bureaucratic organisations may imagine themselves as 'professionals', it is important to make an analytical distinction between welfare *administrators* and welfare *professionals*. Indeed, 'horizontal' relations of professional autonomy may in fact sharply contradict and come into conflict with 'vertical' relations of bureaucratic hierarchy, compliance and proceduralism (Foster and Wilding, 2000). Professionals owe their first obligation to an externally organised professional body while bureaucrats are legitimated by the particular nature of the internal organisational structure. Professionals have previously entered on a prescribed course of accreditation and professional practice and not only are deeply versed in the competencies of technical knowledge but are socialised into professional cultures and values of appropriate conduct, diligence, trust and so on. Professional identity is established through the mutual evaluation of expertise by peers rather than primarily through internal measures of organisational efficiency. This in turn determines the manner in which work is performed, ideally free from external interference, with the expert nature of the complex problems selected and delineated by the professional's own specialised field of activity. Professionals feel themselves accountable to their professional body, their clients, and perhaps only in the last instance to their immediate employer. Whereas administrators are subject to standard detailed rules that govern working practices professionals contend with loose sets of guidelines and protocols, and work under broad strategic goals that leave them with considerable operational autonomy.

The architects of the welfare state from the Webbs, R.H. Tawney through to Keynes, Beveridge and, later, T.H. Marshall, were in their different ways much enamoured by the professional ideal (Perkin, 1989). For them the capitalist speculator and rentier were rapidly becoming a redundant class, in the process of being replaced by a superior middle class of functional specialists. Self-organised professions would overcome the wasteful, inefficient practices of market capitalism, and make it more functionally efficient as well as engendering social unity and ethical justice. In other words, professional autonomy was viewed as necessarily efficient for the welfare state. More power was placed progressively in the hands of welfare professionals as the welfare state took shape in the 1940s and was consolidated in the decades that followed. Through the British Medical Association, for instance, doctors exerted considerable power to shape the NHS, demanding deference to their expert knowledge from patients, politicians and bureaucrats alike. Regardless of sensational cases of malpractice the medical profession continued to assert that self-regulation was the most secure method for guaranteeing expertise and ethical standards of conduct. Since welfare could no longer be viewed in individualistic and moralistic terms institutionally secure professional expertise defined social need and how resources were used rather than the other way around. For some, like the founder of the NHS, Anuerin Bevan, this could sound like self-serving cant. Suspicions were further voiced in the 1950s by social democrats like Richard Titmuss that narrow sectional interests were being advanced by such professional bodies to treat only 'the symptoms of need' over the public interest in 'curing or preventing the causes of need', and that social services were 'being artificially developed by the professional, administrative and technical interests upon whose skills the services depend' (cited in Perkin, 1989, p 344). Not all professions enjoyed the elevated status of the medical profession. Some professions were creatures of the welfare state and, unlike doctors and teachers, had no organised base outside of it. Such welfare professions could be imposed on 'clients', that is, the poor and the vulnerable, by statutory fiat in a way that doctors' services were not. Some professions like social work and teaching grew almost by stealth as new social problems were uncovered and new social objectives identified, stimulating new forms of expertise and the creation or expansion of institutional systems.

Professionalism and bureaucracy marched together step by step through the institutions of the postwar welfare state. Behind each expansion of the professions went a concomitant growth in public administration, legitimated by claims to functional knowledge, expressed in professional accreditation and qualifications. Neoliberals saw the professionalisation of the welfare state in terms of a self-interested 'monopolisation of trade', which artificially restricted the supply of services and made them more expensive by inefficient practices, was unaccountable for resource use, and interfered with the individual freedom. On this basis neoliberal theory urged successive governments to tackle inefficient, special interest 'producer groups'. The first 'producer group' to be taken to task were the trade unions, although the Conservative governments of the 1980s promised to rein in the professions and rationalise public services. For some organisational sociologists like Glenn Morgan (1990, p 124), professional appeals to formal rationality made it difficult, perhaps impossible, to resist 'more efficient' forms of public service 'rationalisation':

> Although these same professionals may in certain respects dislike and resist the implications of rationalisation, eg doctors and their feelings about 'value for money' in the National Health Service, their general commitment to expertise makes a wholesale opposition to rationalisation impossible.

Such arguments over-extend insights from Foucault about how deeply the discursive logic of formal rationality constitutes professionals as subjects who are then unable to defy the absolute imperative of rationalisation. But, as the following chapters demonstrate, there is also a point beyond which the intrinsic nature of welfare work cannot be formally rationalised without degrading or destroying the specific welfare capacity being produced by professionals. As the welfare state comes under ever renewed pressure to 'rationalise' its cost base, it risks counterproductively eroding professionals' commitment to perform their recognised welfare function as embodied 'sentimental' or 'emotional' or 'intellectual' labour. In community nursing, for instance, the managerial drive for flexible, ambivalent forms of social control over client groups like children, older people and people with mental ill health interferes with the autonomy and the professional identity of nurses as carers (Kelly, 2003).

## A neo-Taylorist welfare labour process?

As recent changes in the organisation of various labour processes in the welfare state in this book show, professionalisation is not so clear-cut an alternative to bureaucratisation as these organisational models suggest. For one thing, many workers are neither professionals nor administrators but routinised workers carrying out relatively straightforward tasks and commands. Just as nurses historically specialised in patient care and left all other 'household chores' to ancillary staff who came under their expert supervision, so a detailed, gendered medical division of labour emerged, simplifying tasks at the bottom of the hierarchy. At the bottom of the welfare sector hierarchy an increased reliance has been placed on part-time and hourly-paid, mainly female under-labourers, whose exploitation helps keep afloat the vestiges of professional autonomy for the 'core' welfare workforce. Such women suffer the worst pay and the worst conditions but are expected to carry the burden of under-labouring for more secure 'core' staff and to contribute emotional labour to the welfare users with empathy, conviction and sincerity (see Innes et al, 2006). They are also too often treated as an after-thought for trade union representation and collective bargaining. Yet, as the example of the nursery workers strike in Scotland (see Chapter Eight, this volume), the disputes in the NHS (see Chapters Four and Five), and the university lecturers' industrial action in 2006 (see Chapter Seven) show, discontent is fuelled throughout the welfare sector not only by pay levels but by work intensification, functional flexibilities and job insecurity.

At the other end of the hierarchy, animosity between administrators and professional bodies led some to embrace the new managerialist powers to control and subordinate independent groups of social workers, doctors, teachers and lecturers. As they emerged in the 1980s and deepened under New Labour, the range of new, 'business-focused', 'entrepreneurial' managerial powers over welfare workers – 'the new public management' (NPM) – were meant to solve the problem of X-inefficiency and transcend the professional-administrative welfare fix by concentrating on 'frontline' services while reducing or 'outsourcing' 'back office' functions (Flynn, 2001). In 2004, the Gershon Review of public services identified more than £20 billion departmental costs that could be saved by 2008 in order to 'release resources to the frontline' (Gershon, 2004; see also Chapter Ten, this volume). However, what emerged instead was a cost-cutting exercise that imposed further managerial controls on the remaining public service workers and cuts in areas like adult social care and housing services. As the Trades Union Congress (TUC) (2006, p 13) summed up the impact of the Gershon cuts on public service workers:

> Across the UK, sick leave, sick pay and unsocial hours payments have been targeted, with large numbers of staff made redundant or their working hours reduced, while others are being forced to work longer hours to cover vacant or deleted posts. Unions are concerned about the

impact on the workforce, especially of deskilling and de-motivation. We are not convinced that savings will be fully reinvested in frontline services or in workforce training and development.

Despite this gloomy prognosis some argue that the New Labour emphasis on 'partnership' and 'joined-up government' has moderated the worst excesses of the contract-driven X-efficiency agenda (Newman, 2000). But, as later chapters in this book amply demonstrate, neo-Taylorist conceptions of efficiency measures and the internal impact on workplace relations have, if anything, intensified under New Labour. In 2006 New Labour published its reform agenda for public services, *The UK government's approach to public service reform* (Cabinet Office, 2006). This promised to extend and deepen the use of the private and voluntary sectors, customer choice and 'competition and contestability' mechanisms across the welfare state. For the NHS, New Labour's White Paper *Our health, our care, our say* (DH, 2006) proposed that general practitioners (GPs) and primary care trusts (PCTs) move away from a 'provider model' to adopt a 'commissioning model' by purchasing care and health services from a variety of competitive and approved providers. This, it is assumed, would constantly improve the quality and efficiency of services. However, the 'commissioning model' implies the further hollowing-out of the NHS through a 'flatter' organisational architecture. Yet this is beset with self-contradiction. Leaner and fragmented service provision undermines the organisational capacity of the NHS to rationally plan and develop the mix of workforce skills necessary for managing such a complex labour process. Similarly, schools are being encouraged to drop out of local authority control in England (see Chapter Six, this volume). The National Agreement of School Remodelling in 2003 embraced the concept of the 'school team', with poorly paid support staff taking on enhanced roles inside and outside the classroom, in the process narrowing the scope of qualified teachers.

NPM is less a single, coherent ideology than a self-contradictory managerialist zeitgeist, peppered with jargon like 'robust', 'quality', 'best practice', 'roll out' and 'fit for purpose'. Rhetorically, the purposive solidity of NPM is perhaps more accurately captured in the equally leaden prose of audits, contracts and procedures, which are difficult to separate from public relations (PR) exercises. Audit and inspection is a key way of embedding neoliberal priorities of performance competition among service units. New Labour promised a softer, 'lighter touch' for regulating health and education through audit and inspection, in part due to its costly (and inefficient) nature. However, there was no real departure from the philosophy of regulatory inspection systems that assumes, first, that the nature of institutions and services can be made transparent and visible through numerical values and, second, that individual self-interest and competition are compatible with improved public services (Rustin, 2004).Various forms of calculable quantification appear in the NPM, although this is less about public probity and due procedure of bureaucracy than about delivering comparative performance information for 'the public' such as league tables as proxies for market efficiency. Little sense exists that auditisation assumes the paradoxical status of representing little more than an index of itself. Self-presentation through audits sails perilously close to self-deception, the thing itself being confused with the measurement of some proxy. Audits may stimulate organisational games designed to meet the audit's own indicators for grading but it is less clear that they contribute to directly improving public services as such.

Through such self-referential mechanisms many welfare professions suffered further bureaucratisation and deskilling within a quasi–market environment. In response, professions began to codify their 'mission' and procedures in documents like 'professional guidelines' or a 'code of ethical conduct'. Deskilling as a formally rational technique of scientific management rubs up against certain limits inherent to professionalism as the basis for job control, performative discretion and task autonomy. Within managed markets professional duty rests increasingly with the direct employer rather than the service user or the peer body. For example, Leys (2001, pp 197-8) described the shifting 'structure of professional motivation' for medical consultants:

> The NHS made consultants into senior partners in a huge sort of monopolistic guild, deriving satisfaction from a distinctive blend of high social status, professional autonomy, unchallenged administrative authority, a sense of vocation and relatively high salaries (for most of them only modestly supplemented by private practice). From the mid-1980s onwards, however, this structure of motivations was progressively undermined by subordinating consultants to general managers, curtailing the time allowed for research, forbidding the sharing of information with either the 'purchasers' or even their colleagues in other – competing – hospitals, and in many other ways. One NHS Trust chairman notoriously said a doctor's duty to the employer (the Trust) came 'before the professional duty to the patient'.

Such examples could be extended across the various sectors of professional welfare service (see Chapters Seven and Nine, this volume). Here a strange 'hybrid' of bureaucracy and market, 'managed markets', has been created, often combining the worst of both models for welfare professionals and routinised workers alike (Pollitt, 1993; Clarke and Newman, 1997). In NPM, managers have acquired considerable operational power and become more directive of professionals in their employment. Specialist knowledge is displaced by managerial 'competencies'. Under New Labour, as Fairbrother and Poynter (2001, p 320) claim, tensions emerge 'between the exercise of professional judgement and the necessity to conform to a new ethical or social agenda that operates within a tight framework of financial or performance targets, [which] has tended to be resolved in favour of the latter'. Contracts and indicators are used to control and manipulate the autonomy of welfare professionals, who are now seen negatively as potentially disruptive of the authority of managers. In contrast, other professionals like accountants and human resource specialists are viewed positively as allies of managerial regimes. This new emphasis on contracts and performance indicators is helping to deskill professionals in two ways. First, drawing up detailed management contracts and protocols commits to paper the professional's area of obligations. Second, at the margins of 'core activities' less qualified staff are used by managers to nibble away at the more routine tasks of professionals, fragmenting work tasks further and cheapening the overall rate for the job.

Hence the 'frontier' between public and private provision, bureaucracy and market, has been eroded, if not fully dismantled quite yet, and the welfare values of universalism and equity supplanted by values of efficiency and competitive individualism. All this is driven by a managerialist neurosis, expressed as an obsession with measurement, calculation, audit, quantification and the PR management of public perception. The main features of this shift are well known:

- a new emphasis on accountancy techniques for measuring inputs and outputs to derive the ratio of efficient use of resources;
- welfare users re-designated as 'customers' to which welfare providers are 'responsive';
- increased employee surveillance through performance indicators, staff reviews, Quality Assurance documentation and inspection regimes;
- increased use of management consultants and legal experts to draw up and enforce contractual compliance;

- an enhanced role for personnel departments, now re-titled after the private sector fashion as 'human resource management' or HRM;
- devolved and 'full cost' budgets and strict financial regimes;
- creation of more specialised, 'lean', 'flat' and autonomous structures replacing large, multifunctional bureaucracies;
- the heightened use of marketing and PR to 'interface' with the consumer.

(See Pollitt, 1993; Clarke and Newman, 1997; Flynn, 2001; Clarke et al, 2000.)

What at first in the late 1980s may have felt phoney, contrived and short-term to public servants still committed to some idea of the 'service ethos' has since become entrenched as the organisational reflex of insurgent managerialism. Pollitt (1993) described it as a neo-Taylorist form of labour process. Frederick Winslow Taylor's theory of 'scientific management' provided a set of management principles for exercising control over the labour process by fragmenting labour tasks to the simplest measurable operation, deskilling tasks within a defined workshop division of labour. In such ways control over working practices would pass to work engineers who designed the overall operation. Labour becomes tightly circumscribed, monitored and controlled by incorporating human discretion and skill into machinery designed and maintained by a growing layer of management and technocratic experts (Braverman, 1974). Technical substitution, for instance, is making itself felt across the welfare sector, even in the 'caring professions', despite the difficulty of modelling social care in terms of technical rationality. Thus the Department of Health's 'modernisation' agenda has information and communications technologies (ICT) at the centre of computerising performance, records and monitoring through 'integrated management systems' (Gould, 2003). Such technological substitution has given rise to the post-Fordist idea that welfare organisations can take the new form of flatter structures, networked together by ICTs, as particularly suited to the cultural ethos of the caring professions. Despite claims for a benign view of ICT as enhancing welfare organisational capacities through 'interconnectivity' and 'horizontal networks', as with the wider debate about the Network Society (Castells, 2001), such arguments obscure the relations of power and the value imperative within which such technologies are embedded.

Ideas of interconnectivity, horizontal networks and responsive management are suggestive of the reconfiguration of organisational structures within the welfare state from pyramidical bureaucracies to looser, 'flat' regimes. Flat organisations strip out many of the middle management layers that mediated between top and bottom levels of the hierarchy. This means that communication flows from top to bottom more quickly and precisely. Moreover, the bottom can be surveilled more directly and intensively, without the 'interpretative modulation' of intervening layers amending the command on its way down or the reporting data on its way up. For Sennett (2003, p 188) this makes social relations more unequal and less respectful, both within welfare organisations and between service providers and users: 'Hollowing out a welfare bureaucracy reduces, as in business, the interpretative communication between layers which marks the bureaucratic pyramid. "Need" becomes an abstraction, a number, a datum instantly assessed from the top rather than a negotiable human relationship'. Littler (1982, p 53) makes the often overlooked point that Taylor also wanted to limit the control of lower and middle levels of the management hierarchy. In terms of its lessons for bureaucracy, Taylorism sought to rationalise and refine the structure of control over the job but, unlike classical bureaucracies, offered no organisational commitment to career structure or fixed salaries (Littler, 1982, p 58). Pollitt (1993, p 56) identified similar principles at work in a quite different context from that envisaged by Taylor of NPM:

> The central thrust, endlessly reiterated in official documents, is to set clear targets, to develop performance indicators to measure the achievement of those targets, and to single out, by means of merit awards, promotion or other rewards, those individuals who get 'results'. The strengthening and incentivizing of line management is a constant theme. There is far less (if any) official acknowledgment of the complexities of workplace norms, beliefs and aspirations ('human relations' or 'culture') or of the equally complex issues of cognitive and motivational biases in decision making (decision-making approach) and inter-institutional interdependencies (systems perspective).

With their shared interest in defining and measuring work-time economies, Taylorism and formal public administration have always evinced a special affinity. In this sense, the shift to neo-Taylorism in public services was not a revolutionary leap at the level of operational practices. But the shift has involved more than a straightforward adoption of a fully controlled, industrialised labour process on Taylorist lines (Newman, 2000). The refashioned welfare division of labour has been implemented more pragmatically and flexibly than that. It has been adapted to take into account existing organisational design, service function, socio-technological mixes, union resistance and even geographical region. Managerial control functions in the new public services are less strictly separated from work content than in the classical Taylorist model. Control more often operates through self-disciplined subjects 'buying in', literally, to the prevailing managerialist culture of flexibly intensive work effort captured in measurable outputs (Rose, 1990).

Such shifts form part of what we call 'strenuous welfarism'. This refers to the multiple demands placed on welfare labour to raise the intensity of effort within the service unit. Strenuous welfarism registers the shift in the shared perception of the employment relationship in what Baldamus (1961) called the 'wage/effort exchange'. Sustained attempts have been made to transform a customary understanding among workers of the 'moral economy of effort', embodied in the trade-off of low pay in the public services for a 'stabilised effort' of steady but manageable work loading, to the imposition of 'functional flexibility' in more versatile 'effort intensity' controls to raise the rate at which varied work tasks are accomplished, all the while holding wages steady. The shift to flexible intensity controls results in continual X-efficiency gains in the more intensive and extensive labour effort performed.

But strenuous welfarism puts at risk such residual levels of worker commitment to the service ethos as remain and which restructuring sets out to flexibly subordinate (Webb, 1999). Where this fails to be replaced by higher wages, and additional tasks are added to the flexible intensity controls, worker resentment surfaces and duties are undertaken reservedly and dutifully. A withdrawal of sentimental work or emotional labour and its replacement with 'surface' commitment spreads among public service professionals. They may elect in the face of flexible intensity controls to take refuge in 'core activities', and, where they still can, in the legal-rational defensive measure of 'working to contract', or alternatively exercise 'trained incapacity'. Detailed controls over work performance are exercised through hierarchical line management at more routine ends of the welfare function while professionals and quasi-professionals are subject to rigid indicators and targets, on the one hand, and the flexible managerialist redefinition of professional values, on the other. Some roads seem to lead back to the under-commitment of 'trained incapacity' of the routine administrator, others to the over-commitment of the 'service ethos' of the 'professional habitus'. Elsewhere in this volume our contributors argue that a demand for a renewed professional autonomy for social workers (Chapter Nine, this volume), the deepening professionalisation of nursing (Chapter Five), or the acquisition of professional status for the first time for nursery nurses (Chapter Eight) show how entrenched the felt sense of service to their respective clients, patient and infant groups remains (McDonough, 2006). The demand for professionalisation or for legal-rational work refusal depends on the concrete conditions in different types of welfare workplaces, practices and customary economy of effort that applies in specific settings.

## Neoliberalism and strenuous welfarism

Just as Harry Braverman (1974) situated his classical account of the labour process at a particular point in the development of what he called 'monopoly capitalism', so more recent shifts in the welfare labour process need to be situated within a wider political economy of neoliberal capitalism. The delivery of welfare services by a seemingly ever-diverse assortment of forms of provider has restricted the scope and range for state welfare, what post-Fordist theorists term the 'hollowing-out' of the state. This foregrounds our concern to redress the missing dimension of labour in the political economy of welfare, particularly within the context of neoliberal capitalism. Such developments have given rise to claims that a distinctive form of state has emerged, alternatively termed the 'post-Fordist welfare state', 'the workfare state', 'the managerial state', 'the contractual state' and 'the new market state' (see Jessop, 1999; Clarke, 2004, pp 12-14). We seek to emphasise the embeddedness of the welfare state within capitalist social relations and institutions: work in the welfare state is premised on waged labour and value relations. In this way we want to emphasise that state welfare is a crucial part of the capitalist economy, a sector of it, rather than something completely separate and only externally related to it. For some the widening range of 'welfare providers' has led to the idea of a 'mixed economy of welfare'. We believe that there are a number of problems in deploying this notion uncritically. First, it is redolent of the Keynesian context within which it was first minted more than 30 years ago. Second, non-state providers were then viewed as supplementary to state provision. Today, as Lynne Poole argues in Chapter Eleven, the voluntary and third sectors have become much more central in the delivery of welfare. Third, there is today an overarching emphasis on market models and quasi-market mechanisms that, as noted above, have had profound effects for the nature of the core welfare state. Rather than a mixed economy of welfare, which tends to obscure the exploitative social relations and the specifically capitalist dynamics of welfare in the contemporary UK, it seems preferable to talk instead about the 'welfare sector' of the capitalist economy.

This moves away from the idea, advanced most recently by David Harvey (Harvey, 2003, 2005), that there are wholly separate logics of accumulation that may bisect each other in places but are essentially distinct. In the UK the welfare state has been subject to what Harvey has called 'accumulation by dispossession' (Harvey, 2003). By this he refers to a new round of 'primitive accumulation' in the private confiscation of public capital to further extend the profit base of capital that has become less and less capable of sustaining its own preconditions for renewed accumulation.

> Since privatization and liberalization of the market was the mantra of the neo-liberal movement, the effect was to make a new round of 'enclosure of the commons' into an objective of state policies. Assets held by the state or in common were released into the market where overaccumulating capital could invest in them, upgrade them, and speculate in them. New terrains for profitable activity were opened up, and this helped to stave off the overaccumulation problem, for a while. (Harvey, 2003, p 158)

Such forms of 'deflected welfarism' in the granting of public subsidies to private capital are bolstered by 'strenuous welfarism' in the form of more intensive use of labour and constant capital within the service unit. With the transfer of assets a concerted effort is made by private capital to 'sweat' constant capital through the exploitation of space in the more intensified use of facilities and the practices of rent racking in private finance initiative (PFI) deals. One example of this has been the LIFT programme in England, which centralised services like GP surgeries, dentistry, social services and the police, in an attempt to make PFI investment attractive to private health firms like Prime plc on the premise that GP surgeries alone are not profitable enough. The centralisation of multiple services has had a particularly damaging impact on care services in deprived areas, echoing concerns in Sally Ruane's Chapter Four that PFI/public–private partnership (PPP) built and maintained hospitals and other premises may prove profitable for private sector asset management companies but fail to meet the expressed needs of service users.

Accounts like Harvey's tend to stay focused on 'capital–capital' relations in the transfer of public assets. Account also needs to be given of the restructured 'capital–labour' relationship in the neoliberal welfare sector, or 'accumulation by exploitation' as well as 'accumulation by dispossession'. Where deflected welfarism in the shape of a direct and comprehensive redistribution of public capital to private ownership and control cannot be readily effected, as has been the case with many areas of welfare, the wider institutional framework is restructured to place labour power more firmly under the coercive power of managerialism and the pseudo-market to effect more intensive, strenuous forms of welfarism. Welfare services are exposed to various types of 'productivity' measurements, which are used to impose on labour the need for further and deeper self-capitalisation. Publicly provided welfare must justify its existence in terms of improving 'value for money' or X-efficiency, that is, employing workers at a lower cost to produce the same or greater level of output for clients and customers. Since the 1980s tighter managerial controls have spread like a virus through the metabolism of publicly provided welfare services. Work 'performance' must be made convertible against a universal measure, that is, qualitative judgements made subject to quantification through placing a numerical value on it.

As argued above, claims about X-inefficiency and the efficacy of managerialism rest on the relatively indeterminate nature of professional labour power and the over-determinate labour power of administrators. In the latter case, labour power is over-controlled by rules and procedures; in the former, it is insufficiently controlled. Managerialism therefore consists of a weak convergence of professional and administrative labour power. Here we mainly focus on professional labour power since it defines welfare services in ways that administration, which extends to other parts of the state and large private corporations, simply does not. Converting the indeterminate labour power of welfare workers like nurses, educators and social workers, into concrete labour performed in line with predetermined outcomes is the central problem that welfare managerialism addresses. Welfare managers attempt to transform the tacit knowledge embedded in particular disciplines and organisational settings into the kind of codified knowledge that could be made subject to generic managerial measurements and controls. Unless welfare work performance can somehow be regulated, calibrated, canalised and controlled its subordination will remain at the purely formal level. Examples of standardisation under the watchwords of 'transparency' and 'accountability' abound in health, education and social work to give welfare labour the semblance of being rationally X-efficient.

But in the absence of a universal equivalent imposing socially necessary labour times on the welfare sector there is no way of registering its relative performance. Productive efficiency remains an unknown (and unknowable) X-factor. The concept of productive labour refers not merely to the production of commodities as such but to the production of surplus value for capital. Self-valorisation is *not* therefore identical to material production. Marx gave the well-known example from 'outside the sphere of material production' of an educational worker who is considered 'productive' in comparison to a 'material' worker in a sausage factory:

> In addition to belabouring the heads of his pupils, he works himself into the ground to enrich the owner of the school. That the latter has laid out his capital in a teaching factory rather than a sausage factory makes no difference to the relation. The concept of a productive worker therefore implies not merely a relation between the activity of work and its useful effect, between the worker and the product of his work, but also a specifically social relation of production, a relation with a historical origin which stamps the worker as capital's direct means of valorisation. To be a productive worker is therefore not a piece of luck, but a misfortune. (Marx, 1976, p 644)

It makes little difference that the enterprise is owned by the state, by public–private coalitions or is wholly privately owned so long as capital is laid out to animate 'the worker as capital's direct means of valorisation'. However, welfare workers contribute only indirectly to the extraction of surplus value. A commodified product is created in the transformation of the 'raw material' of patients, claimants and students, into labour power that will re-enter the circuit of accumulation, labour power previously held in reserve or temporarily withdrawn. In the welfare service industry it is the *process* of producing welfare users, rather than a discrete *product*, that is bought and consumed for its distinctive use value. As such, capitalised forms of welfare also suffer from crises of over-production where a socially useful product – healthy, educated, adaptable labour power – circulates within the labour market but fails to find a buyer. Through commodification processes, average levels of socially necessary labour times – 'X-efficiencies' – must somehow be imposed on welfare services in the interests of 'national competitiveness'. This takes two forms. First, the costs of social reproduction in the wider economy rely on the welfare functions of maintaining as cheaply as possible an educated, healthy, versatile labour force and maintaining surplus and redundant labour power. Second, relatedly, the costs of social reproduction of labour power in the welfare sector itself contribute to these wider costs and so need to be cheapened relative to average levels. In this double movement of 'devalorising' labour power through strenuous welfarism, the costs of subsistence and training decline generally. Branch-specific, collective labour is made commensurable to other branches of the economy using marketised measurements, league tables and other proxy figures.

However, as Jacques Bidet (2007, p 65) recounts, 'value is not "measured" but *established* in the confrontation of the market' (emphasis in original). In pseudo-market recognition of this, stricter pricing regimes attempt to establish in imperfect ways the 'full economic costs' of welfare work. Such costing regimes assume that labour is paid at an average ideal of its 'full' value, something contradicted by the higher than average levels of trade union organisation in the welfare state, whose entire raison d'être is to prevent wages from falling below their value (Marx, 1976, p 1069). Hence the devalorisation of labour power in strenuous welfarist regimes meets its point of resistance in the collective struggle to maintain the value of labour power, that is, in class struggle.

Table 1.2 in Chapter One registered the general pattern of industrial action in and around the welfare state. Later chapters further amplify sector-specific labour struggles to compel employers to pay wages at something approaching its estimable value. Variations in the value of labour power within the welfare state and against other branches of the national economy can therefore be explained in terms of the specific nature of the altercation between workers and the state and private capital. As such the welfare industry is also being made commensurable to other branches of the national economy in relation to the average intensity of labour. Marx argued that classical political economists were simply wrong to define productive work exclusively in terms of the specific nature of surplus value. Instead it should be defined as a specific kind of social relation.

If we accept that much welfare labour may be understood as indirectly productive for the (de)valorisation of capital, *how* this is achieved through strenuous flexi-welfarism will shed light on the degree to which later chapters elucidate the uneven proletarianisation of such labour power. Even under strenuous welfare regimes, work typically retains something of the character of an artisanal labour process where some discretion is retained over how to carry out predetermined tasks. This varies across the complex and developing division of labour in welfare/public services work. Such work generally remains at a level of the formal subordination to capital. Increasingly, we argue, aspects of a more substantive subsumption of labour are being experienced throughout the sector. A fully proletarianised form of valorisation depends on the real subsumption of labour through a re-ordering of the organisational and technical relations of production:

> Assuming that labour power is paid for at its value, we are confronted with this alternative: on the one hand, if the productivity of labour and its normal degree of intensity is given, the rate of surplus-value can be raised only by prolonging the working day in absolute terms; on the other hand, if the length of the working day is given, the rate of surplus value can be raised only by a change in the relative magnitudes of the components of the working day, ie necessary labour and surplus labour, and if wages are not to fall below the value of labour power, this change presupposes a change in either the productivity or the intensity of the labour. (Marx, 1976, p 646)

This, we would argue, is what the strenuous welfarism of the past 20 years or so represents: a circular (as it constantly relapses towards failure) attempt to intensify the effort controls over welfare workers while holding constant or reducing the relative value of wage levels. New Labour has continued and deepened strenuous welfarism in the workplace. Its overriding objective has been to augment the national basis for accumulation in the new 'globalised knowledge economy' by lowering traditionally high levels of socially necessary labour times in the welfare state in the training and maintenance costs of complex forms of professional labour power.

## Conclusions

In this chapter we have agreed that a critical examination of social relations in the welfare sector in the UK points to some of the key points of contradiction and fissure in neoliberal capitalism. It is around welfare services that some of the major conflicts, both in the workplace on the frontline of service delivery as well as around the provision of services in general, are taking place. Collective resistance to what we call 'strenuous welfarism' is, in part, because the neoliberal reform of the welfare state asserts itself in a more 'extra-ordinary', stark and explicit form than the ceaseless but apparently 'ordinary' restructuring of capital to which private sector employees have become inured over the past three decades. The welfare state, by comparison, represented a stable point of reference, a fixed pivot of de-commodified social relations within the broader compass of generalised market scarcity, uncertainty and risk for workers. This sense of relative security and stability even appeared to hold during the onslaught of the Thatcher/Major years of the 1980s and early 1990s. With the election of New Labour in 1997, it seemed to many that the welfare state would now be protected from the encroachments of private capital and market forces. While New Labour has transferred significant resources into the welfare sector through the Exchequer and has had some success in lifting some of the very poorest out of complete abject conditions, hopes for a more comprehensive and egalitarian welfare state have proven illusory.

Disillusion with the reformed welfare state is not simply because of accumulation through dispossession, where public assets and funds have been re-routed into private channels ('deflected welfare'), typified by arrangements such as 'partnerships' through to increased costs of accounting, marketing and PR, as well as 'management fees'. It is also one of 'strenuous welfarism'. Here workers within the orbit of the welfare state have been paradoxically expected to produce more and more intensively 'quality' welfare 'outputs' with fewer or, at best, constant resource 'inputs', accumulation through workers' subordination to capital. This is in response to critiques of the X-efficiency type, although often without the qualifications advanced by Leibenstein that individual worker motivations are complex and dynamic. Rather, the restructuring of welfare organisations in the UK bolts a vulgar motivational model for individuals and organisations onto more fanciful neoclassical theories of allocative efficiency.

The self-imposed necessity to reduce socially necessary times and simplify the reproduction of labour power through strenuous welfarism is an essential component of New Labour's programme for national economic competitiveness. Claims about unproductive or inefficient welfare labour thus rest on conflicting notions of welfare as administration and welfare as profession. Despite differences in the nature of each, both have been subjected to similar solutions: managerialism, privatisation and marketisation. Like Harvey's 'accumulation by dispossession', this demands permanent ontological insecurity through the systematic transfer of public services into the clammy hands of the market. Notwithstanding such transfers of welfare services into the marketplace – deflected welfarism – and the intensification and proletarianisation of welfare work – strenuous welfarism – that have occurred, these are not uncontested, unqualified or irreversible shifts. Indeterminate labour power, its necessarily incomplete subordination, and the strategies and tactics of worker resistance, mean that New Labour's project for UK welfare X-efficiency is condemned to fall backwards, Sisyphus-like, into perpetual failure.

## Further sources

In his pioneering study *The social work business* (2003), John Harris has provided a detailed account of the impact of Thatcherism and New Labour on social work in the UK.

In *Social theory at work* (2006), Marek Korczynski, Randy Hodson and Paul Edwards offer a detailed examination of some of the main ways in which work has been theorised. Stephen Edgell's *The sociology of work* (2006) offers an accessible introduction to many of the key issues in the sociology of work today, including a critical discussion of labour process theory.

## References

Baldamus, W. (1961) *Efficiency and effort: An analysis of industrial administration*, London: Tavistock.

Bauman, Z. (1989) *Modernity and the Holocaust*, Cambridge: Polity Press.

Beetham, D. (1987) *Bureaucracy*, Buckingham: Open University Press.

Bidet, J. (2007) *Exploring Marx's capital: Philosophical, economic and political dimensions*, Lieden: Brill.

Braverman, H. (1974) *Labor and monopoly capital: The degradation of work in the twentieth century*, New York, NY: Monthly Review Press.

Cabinet Office (2006) *The UK government's approach to public service reform*, London: Prime Minister's Strategy Unit.

Castells, M. (2001) *The internet galaxy: Reflections on the internet, business and society*, Oxford: Oxford University Press.

Clarke, J. (2004) *Changing welfare, changing states*, London: Sage Publications.

Clarke, J. and Newman, J. (1997) *The managerial state*, London: Sage Publications.

Clarke, J., Gewirtz, S. and McLaughlin, E. (eds) (2000) *New Labour, new managerialism*, London: Sage Publications.

Comanor, W. and Leibenstein, H. (1969) 'Allocative efficiency, X-efficiency and the measurement of welfare losses', *Economica*, vol 36, pp 304-9.

DH (Department of Health) (2006) *Our health, our care, our say: A new direction for community services*, Cm 6737, Norwich: The Stationery Office.

Edgell, S. (2006) *The sociology of work: Continuity and change in paid and unpaid work*, London: Sage Publications.

Fairbrother, P. and Poynter, G. (2001) 'State restructuring: managerialism, marketisation and the implications for labour', *Competition and Change*, vol 5, pp 311-33.

Fitzpatrick, T. (2001) *Welfare theory*, Houndsmill, Basingstoke: Penguin Books.

Flynn, N. (2001) *Public sector management* (4th edn) Hemel Hempstead: Prentice-Hall.

Foster, P. and Wilding, P. (2000) 'Whither welfare professionalism?', *Social Policy and Administration*, vol 34, no 2, pp 143-59.

Frantz, R. (2004) 'The behavioural economics of George Akerloff and Harvey Leibenstein', *Journal of Socio-economics*, vol 33, no 1, pp 29-44.

Gershon, P. Sir (2004) *Releasing resources to the frontline: Independent review of public sector efficiency*, Norwich: The Stationery Office.

Gough, I. (1979) *The political economy of the welfare state*, London: Macmillan.

Gould, N. (2003) 'The caring professions and information technology: in search of a theory', in E. Harlow (ed) *Information and communication technologies in the welfare services*, Philadelphia, PA: Jessica Kingsley Publishers, pp 29-48.

Harris, J. (1998) 'Scientific management, bureau-professionalism, new managerialism: the labour process of state social work', *British Journal of Social Work*, vol 28, pp 839-62.

Harris, J. (2003) *The social work business*, London: Routledge.

Harvey, D. (2003) *The new imperialism*, Oxford: Oxford University Press.

Harvey, D. (2005) *A brief history of neoliberalism*, Oxford: Oxford University Press.

Hayek, F.A. (1944) *The road to serfdom*, London: George Routledge and Sons.

Hochschild, A. (1983) *The managed heart: The commercialization of the human feeling*, Berkeley, CA: University of California Press.

Innes, A., MacPherson, S. and McCabe, L. (2006) *Promoting person-centred care at the front line*, York: Joseph Rowntree Foundation.

Jessop, B. (1999) 'The changing governance of welfare', *Social Policy and Administration*, vol 33, no 4, pp 348-59.

Kelly, A. (2003) *The social construction of community nursing*, Gordonsville, VA: Palgrave Macmillan.

Korczynski, M., Hodson, R. and Edwards, P.K. (eds) *Social theory at work*, Oxford: Oxford University Press.

Lapavitsas, C. (2005) 'Mainstream economics in the neoliberal era', in A. Saad-Filho and D. Johnston (eds) *Neoliberalism: A critical reader*, London: Pluto, pp 30-40.

Leibenstein, H. (1966) 'Allocative efficiency versus X efficiency', *The American Economic Review*, vol 56, pp 392-415.

Leibenstein, H. (1976) *Beyond economic man*, Cambridge, MA: Harvard University Press.

Leibenstein, H. (1979) 'A branch of economics is missing: micro-micro theory', *Journal of Economic Literature*, vol 17, pp 477-502.

Lemke, T. (2001) 'The birth of bio-politics: Michel Foucault's lecture at the College de France on neoliberal governmentality', *Economy and Society*, vol 30, no 2, pp 190-207.

Leys, C. (2001) *Market-driven politics: Neoliberal democracy and the public interest*, London: Verso.

Littler, C.R. (1982) *The development of the labour process in capitalist societies: A comparative study of the transformation of work organization in Britain, Japan and the USA*, London: Heinemann Educational Books.

Mackintosh, M., Raghuram, P. and Henry, L. (2006) 'A perverse subsidy: African trained nurses and doctors in the NHS', *Soundings*, vol 34, pp 103-13.

McDonough, P. (2006) 'Habitus and the practice of public service', *Work, Employment and Society*, vol 20, no 4, pp 629-47.

Marx, K. (1976) *Capital: A critique of political economy, Volume One*, Harmondsworth: Penguin Books.

Merton, R.K. (1949) *Social theory and social structure*, Glencoe, IL: Free Press.

Michels, R. (1921) *Political parties*, Chicago, IL: Free Press.

Morgan, G. (1990) *Organizations in society*, Basingstoke: Macmillan Education Ltd.

Newman, J. (2000) 'Beyond the new public management? Modernising public services', in J. Clarke, S. Gewirtz and E. McLaughlin (eds) (2000) *New Labour, new managerialism*, London: Sage Publications, pp 45-61.

Niskanen, W.A. (1973) *Bureaucracy: Servant or master?*, London: Institute for Economic Affairs.

O'Connor, J. (1973) *The fiscal crisis of the state*, New York, NY: St Martin's Press.

Perkin, H. (1989) *The rise of professional society: England since 1880*, London: Routledge.

Pierson, P. (2006) *Beyond the welfare state? The new political economy of welfare*, Cambridge: Polity Press.

Pollitt, C. (1993) *Managerialism and the public services: Cuts or cultural change in the 1990s?* (2nd edn), Oxford: Blackwell.

Rose, N. (1990) *Governing the soul: The shaping of the private self*, London: Routledge.

Rustin, M. (2004) 'Rethinking audit and inspection', *Soundings*, vol 26, pp 86-107.

Sennett, R. (2003) *Respect: The formation of character in an age of inequality*, London: Allen Lane.

Shen, T.Y. (1985) 'Worker motivation and X-efficiency', *Kyklos*, vol 38, no 3, pp 392-411.

Strauss, A., Fagerhaugh, S., Suczek, B. and Weiner, C. (1982) 'Sentimental work', *Sociology of Health and Illness*, vol 4, no 3, pp 254-78.

TUC (Trades Union Congress) (2006) *TUC Response to the UK government's approach to public service reform*, London: TUC.

Webb, J. (1999) 'Work and the new public service class', *Sociology*, vol 33, no 4, pp 747-66.

Weber, M. (1958) 'Bureaucracy', in H.H. Gerth and C.W. Mills (eds) *From Max Weber: Essays in sociology*, New York, NY: Oxford University Press.

Witz, A. (1986) 'Patriarchy and the labour market: occupational control strategies and the medical division of labour', in D. Knights and H. Willmott (eds) *Gender and the labour process*, London: Gower.

# THREE

# A 'Third Way'? Industrial relations under New Labour

*Peter Bain and Phil Taylor*

## Introduction

New Labour's standard defence of its record in the sphere of industrial relations is to refer trade union critics to its legislative achievements. Government apologists point to the 1999 Employment Relations Act, the 1998 National Minimum Wage Act and to endorsement of the European Union (EU) Social Chapter soon after the 1997 electoral victory. While these Acts marked a distinct break from the Conservatives' repudiation of any form of statutory union recognition, and the limited protection afforded the lowest-paid workers by the Wages Councils, many regard the legislation as limited – indeed, minimalist – measures (McKay, 2001; Smith and Morton, 2001, 2006). These strictures also applied to the government's attitude to the EU directives on working time, part-time workers and information and consultation. Similarly, the introduction of the National Minimum Wage was designed to bring the UK into line with other EU countries, and the composition of the Low Pay Commission appointed by New Labour 'guaranteed that the level would be set well below what trade unions were asking for' (Howell, 2004, p 7).

Notwithstanding the Labour Party's long-standing organisational links to the trade unions, the Blair government's legislative approach has been characterised by a determination to do nothing that might be perceived to favour them or detract from the overall pro-business agenda. The government has paid the weakest form of lip service to the EU concept of permitting (if not promoting) formal, orderly dialogue between union and employer 'social partners' in order to discourage adversarial relations. In practice, UK legislation has been framed so as neither to disadvantage the employer nor to undermine the far-reaching effects of the battery of coercive anti-union laws imposed by Conservative governments between 1980 and 1993. The role of labour law, in Blair's words, is 'to put a very minimum infrastructure of decency and fairness around people in the workplace' (Howell, 2004, p 14).

Insofar as it can be argued that workers' rights have been advanced, then these have been concerned mainly with the position of the *individual* employee. Thus, legislation has been designed to eschew the use of collectivist terminology that might conceivably enhance the influence of trade unions (Undy, 1999). Indeed, obstacles placed in the way of unions seeking to utilise the limited employee grievance and disciplinary clauses introduced under the Employment Relations Act severely constrain their ability to defend even individual rights (McKay, 2001; Smith and Morton, 2001). Furthermore, employers with 20 or fewer workers – 8.1 million people, 31% of the workforce – are excluded from the Act's recognition provisions (Smith and Morton, 2001, p 124); as Waddington plaintively asked, 'why "fairness at work" should be a feature only of workplaces where more than 20 people are employed remains a puzzle' (2003, p 342). At the time of its enactment, Towers (1999) showed how the Act's approach drew heavily on employer-favouring procedures long established in US labour law. When collective bargaining is addressed, the Employment Relations Act – in defiance of International Labour Organization (ILO) standards – privileges 'common law individualism' (Smith and Morton, 2001, p 129).

Union density has stabilised at around 30%, from a high point of 50%-plus, following precipitous decline during the 1980s, and 40% of employees have their pay and conditions determined through collective bargaining (Kersley et al, 2005, p 30). The 2004 Workplace Employment Relations Survey (WERS) calculated that 64% of the public sector workforce were union members, and 82% were covered by collective bargaining (pp 12, 19). The most recent government statistics estimate membership density at 59% and collective agreement coverage at 71% (Grainger, 2006). As stated earlier, New Labour refuses to repeal the array of legislation imposed by the Thatcher and Major governments, which was avowedly anti-union and anti-collectivist in intent. The cumulative effects have been, on the one hand, to make it increasingly difficult for workers to take effective, legal, industrial action while, on the other, strengthening the role of unions as centralised corporate bodies in order to ensure that national and local officials stringently 'police' the activities of their members in any dispute with the employer. Official strike statistics, at historically low levels in the 1990s, have risen slightly (Waddington, 2003, p 351), while individual applications to employment tribunals have grown exponentially (McKay, 2001, p 298).

The government's approach to the law as it affects workers' rights to defend and improve conditions has been subject to trenchant criticism. Comparing the situation in other countries, McKay argued, 'the UK legal regime regulating industrial action is the most restrictive of all the EU states' (2001, p 297). Undy said that the UK exemplified 'the most extreme regulation of trade unions to be found in G7 countries' (1999, p 321). By way of contrast, regarding British employers' treatment of their workers, Blair's foreword to *Fairness at Work* (DTI, 1998) boasted that the UK had 'the most lightly regulated labour market of any leading economy in the world'. This, Hay argued, was to allow employers to hire and fire as the vagaries of the market dictated (2002, p 19).

The theoretical approach of this chapter, as elsewhere in this book, is grounded in the totality of the political economy of capitalism, and also draws on labour process theory. The government's approach to employment legislation has so far been considered. This chapter argues that it will be argued that New Labour's embrace of the 'Third Way' – policies associated with the perceived hegemony of neoliberalism and 'globalisation' (Callinicos, 2001; Hay, 2002) – has helped to generate a sustained managerial offensive across both public and private sectors. A main focus of the chapter is the intensification of work and a related aim is to analyse how workers in the public services and their unions experienced these developments, and to what extent they opposed and resisted them.

The chapter is divided into three sections, with a further concluding section. First, the genesis, content and purpose of the 'Third Way' is analysed, and its implications for New Labour's industrial relations policies considered. Arguably, the most visible manifestation of these policies in the employment relationship has been heightened tension between government and unions over public sector 'reform' (Bach and Winchester, 2003). Indeed, union opposition to private finance initiative (PFI) programmes and 'modernising government' agendas prompted Blair to describe public service workers as 'wreckers' (Waddington, 2003, p 335).

Second, focusing on work intensification, changes imposed at the point of service delivery, in the workplace, are analysed. Introduced under the banner of 'reforming government/best value' criteria (Cabinet Office, 1999), such policies have impacted massively on work content and organisation (Bach and Winchester, 2003). These 'reform' agendas, it will be argued, have increased the intensification of work that has occurred in the economy generally, and in the public sector particularly. For many, reduction in the 'porosity' of the working day (Green, 2001) has been accompanied by an 'extensification' of working time (Bunting, 2004). A notable trend is the extent to which employees, not least in public services, are increasingly compelled to comply with a plethora of targets and performance indicators.

Third, while we present evidence of the intensification of work from diverse sources, nothing is more emblematic of government policy than the adoption of the private sector call centre model in public services. The authors draw on their own research into call centres, focusing on workers' experiences in what is commonly regarded as a hitherto quiescent, 'ring-fenced' area of public service employment – call-handling in police control and communication rooms. If this (increasingly civilianised) workforce, employed to respond to '999' and other vital public safety calls, can be shown to be subject to government-driven intensification of work and deteriorating conditions, then this clearly has serious implications for all areas of the public and welfare services.

## The 'Third Way' and the employment relationship

While proclaiming the uniqueness of 'Third Way' philosophy, which New Labour says lies at the heart of its decision making, proponents offer differing interpretations (Undy, 1999; Hay, 2002). Anthony Giddens, New Labour's 'intellectual guru' and author of *The Third Way* (1998), referred to his book as 'a framework for thinking and policy-making that seeks to adapt social democracy to a world that has changed fundamentally over the past two or three decades' (1998, p 26). Underpinning his perspective is the assertion that Marxism has been finally discredited (p vii), and that 'no one any longer has any alternatives to capitalism' (p 41). In the economic sphere, Blair claimed 'Third Way' policies were 'neither laissez-faire nor state control and rigidity' (1998, p 27). Howell criticised New Labour's method of positioning 'Third Way' industrial relations policies as 'classic triangulation' – neither, it is asserted, Thatcherite nor 'Old Labour' (2004, p 13).

In terms of industrial relations, the most significant implications of Giddens' analysis are related to what are seen as irreversible trends towards globalisation and individualism. Regarding the former, Hay argued that New Labour presented what was seen as the non-negotiable character of globalisation 'as an external constraint', while 'Third Way' philosophy, and its invocation of globalisation, was simply 'post hoc rationalisation for a reform trajectory established long before' (2002, p 4). Although Giddens said that collectivism had been losing ground to individualism since the 1970s, and that this required 'a new balance *between* individual and collective responsibilities' (p 37), he then referred to Third Way politics as having *abandoned* collectivism (p 65). So, the irresistible tide of globalisation reigns supreme, with societal focus on the needs of the de-collectivised individual.

However, Giddens was not very helpful on work and employment relations. In what might be expected to be the most fully developed exposé of the Third Way, Giddens' only discussion of whether, or how, his espoused democratic societal principles should apply to the workplace, or to the citizen as employee, is confined to one fleeting reference to employee participation (1998, p 79). Furthermore, although Giddens discussed the role, and advocated the participation, of environmental, community and voluntary groups in their related social spheres, any suggestion that trade unions constitute similar legitimate, workplace-based organisations was notable only by its absence. Similarly, Blair's 1998 Fabian pamphlet on the 'Third Way' (Blair, 1998) did not mention trade unions (Howell, 2004, p 12). The majority of the UK adult population spend most of their waking hours at work, so the absence of discussion or policy related to employee rights is clearly a lacuna in Giddens' societal thesis, and in New Labour's 'guiding principles'. Furthermore, it raises the question – *why* is there no consideration of the world of work and industrial relations in the 'Third Way'?

In practice, New Labour's approach to industrial relations was 'more wary of the European Social model than of [the] contemporary American mixture of hyper-individualism and social authoritarianism' (Marquand, quoted in Undy, 1999, p 316). This assessment would support those characterising New Labour's implementation of EU legislation as minimalist since 'unilateral rule-making by management, as opposed to joint or legal regulation, retained its central position' (Undy, 1999, p 322). And, after a year of the new government, the General Secretary of the Trades Union Congress (TUC) complained bitterly:

> We are cast in the role of stooge – to be used as a contrast to New Labour – not modern, not new or fashionable, old, in decline, in hock to sectarian politics which resonate with only a tiny proportion of the British people. (TUC, 1998)

Thus, despite the claimed novelty of the government's Third Way approach, their industrial relations policy amounted to little more than acceptance of employer dominance inherited from the Thatcherite era, albeit leavened by measured amounts of European 'partnership' rhetoric. In essence, it amounted to a rather crude, unitaristic, 'happy families', rather than a pluralistic (far less Marxian), conflict-recognising approach to the world of work (see Smith and Morton, 2001, 2006).

While the political–economic content of *The Third Way* (Blair, 1998; Giddens, 1998) was 'decidedly thin' (Hay, 2002, p 1), little doubt existed about the government's determination to proceed with public sector reform as a central aspect of their programme. This was regarded as more than a symbolic shift from reliance on state provision of welfare and other services, towards greater involvement with what was seen as the more efficient private sector. In a 'globalised' world, welfare expenditure was 'no longer justified principally in terms of its contribution to social justice but in terms of its contribution to competitiveness' (Hay, 2002, p 19). Such a strategy clearly had significant implications for employment relations, not least in the public sector, where trade unions retained a presence in 93% of workplaces (Kersley et al, 2005, p 12), with public sector trade union density at 58.6%, according to the most recent government statistics (Grainger, 2006). As well as partially privatising the National Air Traffic Service and opening up areas of the National Health Service (NHS), state education, prisons and roads to private sector companies, the government pushed ahead with more PFI/public–private partnership (PPP) schemes to build and operate public sector projects and services. Rejection of PFI/PPP at the 2002 TUC and Labour Party conferences indicated that working-class disillusionment with New Labour's policies continued in the aftermath of the 2001 electoral victory (Waddington, 2003, p 345; UNISON, 2004a).

Rising discontent was reflected in a rise in both the number of strike ballots in favour of action, and in actual strikes, in the public services (albeit from historically low levels) (Waddington, 2003, p 351). Among the strikers in 2002 were workers in the post office, further education (FE) and local government and, increasingly, a contributory factor was workers' determination to oppose further cuts in staffing and to defend the quality of the services they provided. Although public service strike statistics were not comparable to those of the 1978-79 'winter of discontent', some workers shared 'a similar desire to reverse relative long-term pay decline' (Waddington, 2003, p 351). The Prime Minister, having denounced public service strikers as wreckers, reserved particular opprobrium for what he called the 'Scargillite' firefighters (Waddington, 2003, p 335).

If proof were needed of New Labour's intrinsic antipathy to effective trade unionism, then Blair's terminology, combined with evidence of government intervention in November 2002 compelling the employers to withdraw a pay offer to the firefighters, resolved matters for some

(Waddington, 2003, p 352). By this time, several unions had reduced their contributions to the Labour Party, including the Communication Workers Union, Fire Brigades Union, General and Municipal Workers, Rail, Maritime and Transport Workers, Transport and General Workers Union and the Transport Salaried Staff Association; a survey of Labour-affiliated union branches revealed that support for the government had fallen massively, in protest against PFI and New Labour's lack of commitment to public services; and leading Blairite union leaders, such as Jackson (Amicus) and Reamsbotton (Public and Commercial Services Union), were defeated in elections (Waddington, 2003, pp 355, 339). It was anticipated that the related emergence of the so-called 'awkward squad' of new union leaders might result in a mounting tide of industrial action to match their anti-government rhetoric (Charlwood, 2004, p 387). However, the relative failure of the firefighters' dispute dampened hopes that other public service workers might follow in their wake. Nonetheless, when Royal Mail management pushed too hard in the aftermath of a vote narrowly accepting a national pay offer, 30,000 postal workers took 'unofficial' (and illegal) strike action in late 2003 (Charlwood, 2004, p 388). The possibility of widespread industrial action also loomed early in 2005, when the government announced changes to public sector workers' pensions. Seven unions embarked on UK-wide action, including a proposed one-day strike, until the government partially retreated in the run-up to the general election (TUC, 2005).

Undoubtedly, an overarching factor in the growing discontent among public sector workers was the widespread perception that, as workloads increased and pay and conditions were held down, the quality of service they provided was becoming impossible to sustain. Managerial restructuring at workplace level, driven by Blair's 'modernising government' agenda, showed few signs of abating. Thus, the effects of work intensification generated by New Labour policies loomed larger on workers' industrial, social and political antennae, and it is this issue that we now address.

## 'Modernising government': work intensification the New Labour way

> In its first four-year period of office ... many public sector employees and their trade unions ... strongly criticized the government's initial caution in its public expenditure plans, the proliferation of performance targets and, in many public

services, the widespread demoralization of staff arising from increases in work intensity. (Bach and Winchester, 2003, p 292)

Between 1992 and 1998, growing numbers of UK workers experienced increases in both work *intensification* (effort while at work) and work *extensification* (time spent at work) (Green, 2001, p 56). Based on extensive research, Green showed that this work pressure was greater in the public than in the private sector, and was greatest of all in education (2001, p 73). Increases in work intensification were broadly experienced across the whole economy. However, in terms of extensification, while the *average* number of hours worked had fallen, the proportion of employees working at least 48 hours per week had increased from 17% in 1983, to 20% by 1998 – and from 25% to 30% among male workers (Green, 2001, pp 59-60). These statistics cover only the first year of New Labour's term of office, and ended just before the Working Time Directive was introduced. However, Waddington later argued that growing union resistance to government policy was significantly founded in the belief that it had increased 'labour intensification ... particularly in the public sector' (2003, p 346). Furthermore, the Bach and Winchester quotation points to a similar conclusion – under New Labour, work intensification was widely experienced, identified and opposed by public service employees and their unions. UNISON, for example, complained that nursing workplace representatives were increasingly having problems in carrying out their union duties as 'their colleagues cannot cover for them because of work overload' (UNISON, 2002).

The situation New Labour inherited in 1997 was one in which 'large parts of the public sector had been privatised and ... [others] restructured into semi-autonomous "enterprises"' (Bach and Winchester, 2003, p 285); the rise of more assertive managers, with greater discretion to change pay and work organisation, had been encouraged by the Conservatives; organisational structure had been fragmented with, for example, more than 400 NHS trusts and 100 civil service agencies. However, despite the introduction of market disciplines, 'traditional hierarchies and long-standing work practices remained intact in some parts of the sector'. Earlier concepts of the state as a 'model employer', offering institutional support to trade unions and collective bargaining, were shaken under national incomes policies from the mid-1960s, before collapsing during the Thatcherite 1980s (Bach and Winchester, 2003, p 287).

New Labour accepted most of the Conservatives' public services restructuring but, it is argued, their 'modernising government' programme represented a shift away from simply cost minimisation towards 'improved service quality and tight monitoring of service standards' (Bach and Winchester, 2003, p 290). Although Third Way ideology may be detected in the greater role attributed to the private sector in the provision of public services, New Labour justified this approach principally as a means of promoting consumer choice, improving efficiency and providing performance benchmarks. Thus, intrinsic to the 'modernising government' strategy was a necessity for the widespread imposition of targets and monitoring in order to measure the output and quality of the 'reformed' services. Furthermore, each area of the public service subject to new targets was already operating in a general environment in which the government – partly to 'sustain its "business-friendly" credentials' – wished to be seen as being extremely frugal with regards to public expenditure (Bach and Winchester, 2003, p 291).

Close monitoring and measuring of output and performance at the level of the individual workplace was partially enabled by the application of information and communication technologies (ICT). Bunting (2004) argues that New Labour's public sector reform programme was a manifestation of the rise of the 'audit society', in which data could be gathered quickly and put to a range of managerial uses (2004, p 134). Setting targets became an organisational norm, and the logic of the process of transmitting policy from government instruction down to its impact on the individual employee's increased workload demanded that every aspect of public service work was subject to continuous (sometimes 'real time') monitoring and assessment. Frontline managers – themselves subject to top-down imposition of targets – were required to focus on the minutiae of staff performance in order to ensure compliance with a plethora of quantitative and qualitative criteria.

For example, NHS targets ranged from the percentage of Accident and Emergency patients to be seen within a stipulated period of time to ambulance response times; in education, league tables were introduced, based on primary school children's examination results; and Home Office staff had targets to deport a stated number of asylum seekers (Bunting, 2004, pp 125-7). In local government, 'best value' required authorities, instead of periodic market testing, to 'engage in a more continuous process of performance reviews to increase service standards and achieve efficiency gains' (Bach and Winchester, 2003, p 291). Nor were targets confined to the lower occupational grades, as a British Medical Association (BMA) official lamented, 'You can't win with targets. The professions are sick to death of being shackled in this way and feeling that their clinical priorities are being undermined' (Bunting, 2004, p 125). This tension, between government-inspired imposition of a range of targets and the pride that professional employees traditionally took in their work, was increased by additional pressures on public service workers arising from the government setting targets on the one hand, and their (un)willingness to provide funding to achieve their aims on the other.

The successful implementation of targets, and other changes to work content and organisation, partially depends on the extent to which employees see themselves as sharing certain interests with the employer and frontline management. In the delivery of public services, the distinctive sectoral 'ethos', to the extent that it still exists, involves a degree of commitment on the part of the employee in return for decent terms and conditions, and still holds certain sway (Bunting, 2004, p 137). Green differentiates between employees' 'constrained effort', what the job specifically requires them to do, and their 'discretionary effort', the effort workers put into the job *beyond* what is required (2001, p 66). Concerning 'discretionary effort', or working beyond contract, Green found that the proportion of respondents who said this had increased 'a lot' between 1992 and 1997 had risen from 68.4% to 71.8% (females from 69.9% to 75.9%), and those who replied 'some' from 21.0% to 22.5% (Green, 2001, p 67). A survey of managers confirmed these employee responses. Since, as discussed earlier, Green reported that the rise in public sector employees' increased effort exceeded that in the private sector, we can assume that this also applied to discretionary effort. Green also links the rise in worker effort to increased perceived stress (2001, p 76), an issue that has been described as 'the new workplace epidemic' (TUC, 2004) and which will be discussed in the following section. Further evidence that jobs were become more demanding generally was provided by Taylor (2002), who stated that almost half of male employees, and a third of female, frequently worked longer than their basic hours (2002, p 10). When asked why they did so, a majority in every occupational group identified 'in order to meet deadlines and pressures', and most said this was the *most important reason* for working long hours – 90% of higher level professionals/ managers, 80% of lower level professionals/managers, 81% of higher administration/clerical/sales and 77% of both technicians/supervisors and skilled manual workers (Taylor, 2002, p 11).

Additional sources of work intensification may be traced to the human resource management (HRM) agenda, which since the late 1980s has been increasingly adopted by British employers (Guest, 1994).

The broad thrust of HRM is to win workers' unitaristic commitment to the philosophy and 'mission' of the employing organisation so that, henceforth, employees cooperate more fully in the attainment of both organisational and personal aims. De facto, HRM has focused attention on certain workplace practices, such as temporal and functional flexibility and the management of quality, often mediated through the peer pressure aspects of team working (Legge, 1995). While HRM spread throughout the economy, with varying incidence and degrees of success, there is little doubt that New Labour's 'modernising government' agenda gave it particular resonance among public service managers under instruction to improve both efficiency and service (Waddington, 2003, p 346). Indeed, it was argued that, 'the Labour government regards human resource management policies as essential in delivering its modernisation agenda' (Bach and Winchester, 2003, p 292).

'Soft' versions of HRM proclaim the need to involve employees in (usually low-level) 'participation' schemes, an approach that has evinced a mixed response from employers, unions and academics (Kelly, 1996). A recurring argument from critics, such as Kelly, concerning participation as well as more fully developed 'partnership' schemes, is that they can ideologically disarm workers, exposing them to managerial pressure. However, it has been argued that, although partnership agreements remain popular, some unions have moved away from them, on the grounds that it is unclear how employees benefit from these arrangements (Waddington, 2003, p 348). A survey of partnership schemes, operating under 'best value' regimes in local government, concluded that unions had gained neither in terms of fuller consultation by management, nor in better protecting workers' interests generally (Roper et al, 2005, p 646).

As a consequence of New Labour's 'modernising government' agenda, public service workers have experienced work intensification, and this has been succinctly summarised in a motion passed at UNISON's 2004 conference:

> The increasing marketisation of public services brings a threat to the public service ethos and universal services ... cuts in pay and conditions, inequalities, increases in work intensity, and stress.... (UNISON, 2004b)

Injunctions to perform 'beyond contract', sometimes driven by HRM or facilitated by union–employer 'partnership' deals, have eroded terms and conditions previously subject to formal agreement. Thus,

—

many public service workers have found themselves labouring under conditions comparable to the most extreme types of 'lean production' regimes (Delbridge et al, 1992). In such operations, staffing levels are cut to the bone, with workers under constant pressure to meet undeliverable targets.

## Delivering public services: 'best value' in police call handling

> Alongside the emergency services provided by police, fire-fighters and ambulance staff, the funding and organisation of public services was regulated by statute and had no private sector counterpart. The political sensitivity of the quality of public services encouraged stable industrial relations, uniform service standards, and a distinctive orientation to work linked to a commitment to the service provided. (Bach and Winchester, 2003, pp 286-7)

This section aims to present findings drawn from research conducted by the authors into working conditions in an area of public service – call handling in police control rooms – that many intuitively might imagine would be 'ring-fenced' from the effects of government cost-cutting. It might be supposed that this service would prioritise the highest operating standards and practices. However, if the New Labour agenda can be shown to have had far-reaching and deleterious effects on workers in such a vital public service, we can surely conclude that few, if any, other areas of public and welfare provision are likely to be free of similar pressures.

In recent years, much has been written about the massive expansion of call centres in the UK. Although it is not possible to verify the Department of Trade and Industry's (2004) prediction that more than one million would be employed in the sector in the UK by 2007, growth in the domestic sector has continued despite the impact of automation, the rise of the internet and offshoring (IDS, 2005; Taylor and Bain, 2005). As other contributors to this volume show, call centre work is of increasing importance across the public and welfare sectors. Although not applicable to every operation, the present authors have characterised call centre work generally as routine, repetitive and target-driven, resulting in high levels of employee 'burnout' and turnover (Taylor and Bain, 1999; Bain et al, 2002; Deery et al, 2002; Taylor et al, 2003). Call centre models or typologies include Frenkel et al's 'mass customised bureaucracy' (1999), 'mass production, mass customisation or professional service operations' (Batt and Moynihan, 2002), and a quality–quantity continuum (Taylor and Bain, 2001).

There was a perception that the emergence of the call centre in the public sector conformed to the traditional ethos described by Bach and Winchester. It was suggested that staff turnover in public/not-for-profit call centres has been lower than the average for the sector as a whole (IDS, 2004, p 19). This may be attributable to higher levels of customer interaction with better qualified staff in, for example, the NHS (Collins-Jacques, 2004), civil service (Fisher, 2004) and local government (Urwin, 2002). It may also be a consequence of greater union influence over work routines. Nevertheless, it is also possible to chart the more recent transplantation of an intensified private sector call centre model in areas of the public sector (Ellis and Taylor, 2006; Taylor and Bain, 2007). This includes the increasing adoption in the public sector of 'efficiency-enhancing technology' developed in the private sector in the mid to late 1990s and 'aimed at pushing through as many calls as possible' (DTI, 2004, p 140). Further, it is not difficult to identify the ways in which overt commercial pressures have impacted on public sector operations. It is this wider political-economic context that reveals the theoretical flaws in Glucksmann's observations on the nature of emergency helplines. These operations, she argues,

> ... deal in non-traded transactions, are not linked to profit-making business activity (the internal market aside), and are funded by the state, charities or voluntary organizations.... Thus, while emergency operators undertake similar telephone answering work to other call centre workers, both centre and workers occupy a very different (non)-economic space. (Glucksmann, 2004, pp 807-8)

Her assertion is undermined by empirical evidence. In fact, numerous public service helplines – including some dealing with emergencies – have been outsourced to private companies, operating under commercial pressures. Examples include all non-BT '999' calls (Bain and Taylor, 2000), the National Rail Enquiry Service offshored to India (House of Commons Transport Committee, 2004), and national educational and training helplines (Houlihan, 2002). Even the BBC Helplines were outsourced to Capita. The success of dedicated call centre outsourcing companies, like Capita and Vertex, in attracting work from both central and local government also serves as a competitive constraint on the aspirations of public service workers concerning their pay and conditions. Furthermore, overarching budgetary constraints mean that public service call centres have to confront a core contradiction,

> ... which arises on the basis of the conflict between efforts to increase and improve the quality and quantity of service provision, while containing spending on public administration within state expenditure limits. (Fisher, 2004, p 160)

More recent research conducted by the authors into working conditions in police call handling also refutes the idealised picture of public service work, free of cost pressures, described by Glucksmann (UNISON, 2006). The workforce – employed on 24/7 operations seen as vitally important by the government – reported that their terms and conditions of employment were under massive threat. New Labour's 'modernising government' agenda had resulted in the application of 'best value' criteria to the police service, and a rapid expansion in the 'civilianisation' of tasks and roles to free up 'sworn' officers for policing duties (HMIC, 2001). Central to this process was the Home Office decision that, progressively, the main method by which members of the public could contact the police would be by telephone, and that *all calls* would be answered in the first instance by civilian operators. Of 13,000 control room staff, 70% were civilians and 30% 'sworn' officers (HMIC, 2004, p 89); the ratio of female to male employees was also 70:30 (UNISON, 2006, p 24).

Eight other public sector areas were identified as providing 'useful parallels' with reforming the police service – education, health, legal services, customs and excise, and the prison, probation, fire and immigration services (HMIC, 2004, pp 48-51). The common strategic objectives set out for these broad areas of public service and welfare provision by the government included insistence on civilianisation or increasingly using 'non-core professionals', and on utilising 'best value' criteria in determining policy. To these aims, we might add the rapid diffusion of the call centre as a key part of New Labour's 'e-government' targets (Cabinet Office, 2000).

'Best value' will now be considered in terms of its effects on three aspects of call handlers' work in police control rooms: the centralisation of operations, outsourcing and the adoption of the private sector call centre model.

First, the centralisation of control room operations has been implemented in tandem with standardisation of procedures and policies, offering 'economy of scale' savings as local offices were closed (HMIC,

2001, p 19). For example, in one large English county, six geographically scattered control rooms were shut down and replaced by one centralised operation. Managerially recognised disadvantages include the removal of locally based services, public hostility and a probable loss of local knowledge. The outcome, as described by one female senior dispatcher, with 18 years' experience, was:

> 'Having been centralised we now take calls and dispatch to a much larger area. It is difficult when you don't know where they are, and you don't know the local officers or their supervision. At division we had some quiet spells. We don't now.'

Many control room staff also experienced redeployment and longer travel-to-work times, while cohorts of new employees had to be recruited and trained (PSSO, 2003, p 15).

Second, outsourcing of police call handling to private sector organisations has taken place discretely for some time with, for example, emergency boarding up, garage and key holder call-outs provided by the Automobile Association (HMIC, 2001, p 139). Although proposals from the London Metropolitan Police to outsource routine and emergency ('999') calls were postponed, Her Majesty's Inspectorate of Constabulary (HMIC) recommended that policing should engage more in 'the purchaser–provider ethos', including the outsourcing of services and functions (HMIC, 2004, pp 179-80).

Third, as centralisation and standardisation proceeded, clear evidence that the government and police management-preferred model was the 'mass production' call centre is found in the Home Office's *National call handling standards* (2005). Based on idealised accounts of how private sector call centres operate, 'qualitative and quantitative national call handling standards for responding to emergency and non-emergency calls', including targets, are proposed. However, a male dispatch controller, six years in the job, graphically described actual developments in control rooms:

> 'When I started in this job I absolutely LOVED it. I got an immense sense of satisfaction from helping the public and doing a good job. Now I feel I am under constant pressure to exceed targets, usually working on my own and providing the same level of service as a two-person role. I HATE it here now.' (original emphasis)

Comparing these findings with data from the authors' other research, control room staff felt under greater pressure than workers in utilities and finance call centres. The latter were private sector organisations experiencing high levels of attrition and absence, call quantity was prioritised, and stringent targets were imposed under regimented work regimes (Bain et al, 2005). While four in five of the control room staff spent at least 80% of their contracted hours taking calls, the Health and Safety Executive (HSE) suggests 60-70% of working time should be the maximum (HELA, 2001, para 52).

Confirming Green's (2001) findings, many employees related work pressure to rising stress levels:

> 'Volume of calls coming in have far outgrown the number of staff allocated to work per relief. Lack of staff creates further problems for the remaining staff who are then under pressure to cover. This in turn leads to more pressure/stress related illness.' (Female communications officer, 4.5 years' service)

So, control room staff, carrying out vital public service functions, reported chronic under-staffing, work intensification, tight targeting, and a relentless pace of work with few breaks. However, they still endeavoured to engage positively with the challenging, sometimes 'life and death', nature of their duties. When asked to consider what their union's priorities should be, respondents put pay at the top (49%), a choice clearly related to a perceived long-standing injustice and to achieving parity with police officers, within a new national grading structure. Second was staffing levels (39%), followed closely by shift patterns and working time (37%) – two closely linked issues, clearly reflecting a widespread belief that radical changes were essential if the quality of their working and social life was to improve. The question of UNISON's ability to harness, through a national campaign, the undoubted desire of these workers for improvements in working conditions, linked to their deep commitment to assisting the public and providing a high-quality service, is beyond the scope of this chapter.

However, what this brief analysis of the changes to the terms and conditions of the police call-handling workforce has clearly illustrated is that, from the perspective of the government and their cost-cutting agenda, there can be no question of a 'Chinese wall' separating emergency from other public and welfare services.

## Conclusions

Given the vicissitudes of the times, it is perhaps a testament to working-class resilience that two thirds of public sector employees are still union members, with over 80% covered by collective bargaining. Despite low levels of industrial action, according to the TUC almost 9,000 ballots (an under-estimate) were held between 1995 and 2005, and the majority resulted in pro-action votes (Gall, 2006, p 335); actual strikes in these years averaged only 150-250 per annum, as the *threat* of action was used systematically by union negotiators to attempt to leverage concessions from the employer.

This continuing adversarial, pluralistic, approach to the employment relationship was not what New Labour intended. As has been argued, their goal of social partnership 'requires the marginalization of trade unionism as an autonomous force' (Smith and Morton, 2001, p 120). Nowhere was New Labour's desire for union passivity greater than in the public services, lest the 'modernising government' programme be de-railed by 'wreckers'. At certain times, it was conceivable that industrial action might spread across the public sector, notably during the 2002-03 firefighters' dispute (Charlwood, 2004, p 388), and the threatened strikes over the government's attack on pensions before the 2005 General Election (*autLOOK*, 2005). Such eventualities are closely related to the extent to which trade unionists, particularly national leaders, hold to the view that the Labour Party still represents 'the only credible vehicle for establishing a more union-friendly political settlement' and can be reclaimed (Charlwood, 2004, p 391). The continuing importance attached by some union leaders to the 'Warwick agreement' reached with the government in 2004 suggests that the latter perspective is alive and well (TUC, 2006).

Contrary to such views, what this chapter has sought to show is that New Labour's industrial relations policies have been fundamentally pro-employer in character since their inception, more anti-union than those adopted by any right-wing government within the EU, and that the 'Third Way' offers 'no entry' to workers' aspirations. Accompanying the profound neoliberal influence on New Labour's employment relations legislative settlement has been an intensification of work across the public sector as the logic of the market undermines what is left of a public sector 'ethos'. The widespread emergence of the call centre provides one of the most obvious examples of the transformation of workers' experiences at the point of public service delivery.

## Further sources

The following articles provide analyses of the related areas of the 'Third Way' and developments in industrial relations (Waddington, 2003), trends in work intensification (Green, 2001), and the application of the 'modernising government' agenda to a public service (Bain et al, 2005). The websites should enable the reader to comprehend the reasons for policies developed by HMIC and HSE respectively.

Waddington, J. (2003) 'Annual review article 2002: Heightening tension in relations between trade unions and the Labour government in 2002', *British Journal of Industrial Relations*, vol 41, no 2, pp 335-58.

Green, F. (2001) 'It's been a hard day's night: the concentration and intensification of work in late twentieth-century Britain', *British Journal of Industrial Relations*, vol 39, no 1, pp 53-80.

Bain, P., Taylor, P. and Dutton, E. (2005) 'The thin front line: call handling in police control rooms', 23rd International Labour Process Conference, University of Strathclyde, 21-23 March.

ates.homeoffice.gov.uk/hmic/inspect_reports1/thematic-inspections/modernising-police-service/modernising (accessed 4 August 2006).

## References

*autLOOK* (2005) 'Growing opposition to public sector pension changes', London: Association of University Teachers, no 234, p 29.

Bach, S. and Winchester, D. (2003) 'Industrial relations in the public sector' in P. Edwards (ed) *Industrial relations: Theory and practice* (2nd edn), Oxford: Blackwell, pp 285-312.

Bain, P. and Taylor, P. (2000) 'Entrapped by the "electronic panopticon"? Worker resistance in the call centre', *New Technology, Work and Employment*, vol 15, no 1, pp 2-18.

Bain, P., Taylor, P. and Dutton, E. (2005) 'The thin front line: call handling in police control rooms', 23rd International Labour Process Conference, University of Strathclyde, 21-23 March.

Bain, P., Watson, A, Mulvey, G., Taylor, P. and Gall, G. (2002) 'Taylorism, targets and the pursuit of quantity and quality by call centre management', *New Technology, Work and Employment*, vol 17, no 3, pp 154-69.

Batt, R. and Moynihan, L. (2002) 'The viability of alternative call centre production models', *Human Resource Management Journal*, vol 12, no 4, pp 14-34.

Blair, T. (1998) *The Third Way: New politics for the new century*, Pamphlet No 588, London: Fabian Society.

Bunting, M. (2004) *Willing slaves: How the overwork culture is ruling our lives*, London: Harper Collins.

Cabinet Office (1999) *Modernising government*, London: The Stationery Office.

Cabinet Office (2000) *E-government: A strategic framework for public service in the information age*, London: The Stationery Office.

Callinicos, A. (2001) *Against the Third Way*, London: Polity.

Charlwood, A. (2004) 'Annual review article 2003: The new generation of trade union leaders and prospects for union revitalization', *British Journal of Industrial Relations*, vol 42, no 2, pp 379-97.

Collin-Jacques, C. (2004) 'Professionals at work: a study of autonomy and skill utilization in nurse call centres in England and Canada', in S. Deery and N. Kinnie (eds) *Call centres and human resource management*, Basingstoke: Palgrave, pp 153-73.

Deery, S., Iverson, R. and Walsh, J. (2002) 'Work relationships in telephone call centres: understanding emotional exhaustion and employee withdrawal', *Journal of Management Studies*, vol 39, no 4, pp 471-96.

Delbridge, R., Turnbull, P. and Wilkinson, B. (1992) 'Pushing back the frontiers: management control and work intensification under JIT/TQM factory regimes', *New Technology, Work and Employment*, vol 7, no 2, pp 97-106.

DTI (Department of Trade and Industry) (1998) *Fairness at Work*, Cm 3968, London: DTI.

DTI (2004) *The UK contact centre industry: A study*, London: DTI.

Ellis, V. and Taylor, P. (2006) '"You don't know what you've got till it's gone": re-contextualising the origins, development and impact of the call centre', *New Technology, Work and Employment*, vol 21, no 2, pp 107-22.

Fisher, M. (2004) 'The crisis of civil service trade unionism: a case study of call centre development in a civil service agency', *Work, Employment and Society*, vol 18, no 1, pp 157-77.

Frenkel, S., Korczynski, M., Shire, K. and Tam, M. (1999) *On the frontline: Organisation of work in the information economy*, Ithaca, NY: Cornell University Press.

Gall, G. (2006) 'Research note: injunctions as a legal weapon in industrial disputes in Britain 1995-2005', *British Journal of Industrial Relations*, vol 44, no 2, pp 327-49.

Giddens, A. (1998) *The Third Way: The renewal of social democracy*, Cambridge: Polity Press.

Glucksmann, M. (2004) 'Call connections: varieties of call centres and the divisions of labour', *Work Employment and Society*, vol 18, no 4, pp 795-811.

Grainger, H. (2006) *Trade union membership 2005*, London: Department of Trade and Industry

Green, F. (2001) 'It's been a hard day's night: the concentration and intensification of work in late twentieth-century Britain', *British Journal of Industrial Relations*, vol 39, no 1, pp 53-80.

Guest, D. (1994) 'Human resource management in the United Kingdom', in B. Towers (ed) *The handbook of human resource management*, Oxford: Blackwell.

Hay, C. (2002) *Making a virtue of perceived necessity ... and a necessity of a perceived virtue: 'Third Way' political economy, globalisation and economic compulsion*, Paper at Annual conference of the British Universities Industrial Relations Association, University of Stirling, 4-6 July.

HELA (Health and Safety Executive/Local Authority Enforcement Liaison Committee) (2001) *Advice regarding call centre working practices*, Local Authority Circular 94/1 (rev), Sheffield: HSL.

HMIC (Her Majesty's Inspectorate of Constabulary) (2001) *Open all hours*, London: The Stationery Office.

HMIC (2004) *Modernising the police service*, London: The Stationery Office.

Home Office (2005) *National call handling standards*, London: Home Office.

Houlihan, M. (2002) 'Tensions and variations in call centre management strategies', *Human Resource Management Journal*, vol 12, no 4, pp 67-85.

House of Commons Transport Committee (2004) *National Rail Enquiry Service: Eleventh Report of Session 2003-04*, London: The Stationery Office.

Howell, D. (2004) 'Is there a Third Way for industrial relations?', *British Journal of Industrial Relations*, vol 41, no 1, pp 1-22.

IDS (Incomes Data Services) (2004) *Pay and conditions in call centres 2004*, London: IDS.

IDS (2005) *Pay and conditions in call centres*, London: IDS.

Kelly, J. (1996) 'Union militancy and social partnership' in P. Ackers, C. Smith and P. Smith (eds) *The new workplace and trade unionism: Critical perspectives on work and organization*, London: Routledge.

Kersley, B., Alpin, C., Forth, J., Bryson, A., Bewley, H., Dix, G. and Oxenbridge, S. (2005) *Inside the workplace: First findings from the 2004 Workplace Employment Relations Survey (WERS 2004)*, London: Department of Trade and Industry.

Legge, K. (1995) *Human resource management: Rhetoric and realities*, Basingstoke: Macmillan.

McKay, S. (2001) 'Annual review article 2000: Between flexibility and regulation: rights, equality and protection at work', *British Journal of Industrial Relations*, vol 39, no 2, pp 285-303.

PSSO (Police Skills and Standards Organisation) (2003) *Police sector: A thematic skills Foresight Report on communications and call handling 2003*, London: Home Office.

Roper, I., James, P. and Higgins, P. (2005) 'Workplace partnership and public service provision', *Work Employment and Society*, vol 19, no 3, pp 639-49.

Smith, P. and Morton, G. (2001) 'New Labour's reform of Britain's employment law: the devil is not only in the detail but in the values and policy too', *British Journal of Industrial Relations*, vol 39, no 1, pp 119-38.

Smith, P. and Morton, G. (2006) 'Nine years of new labour: neoliberalism and workers' rights', *British Journal of Industrial Relations*, vol 44, no 3, pp 401-20.

Taylor, P. and Bain, P. (1999) 'An assembly-line in the head: work and employee relations in the call centre', *Industrial Relations Journal*, vol 30, no 2, pp 101-17.

Taylor, P. and Bain, P. (2001) 'Trade unions, workers' rights and the frontier of control in UK call centres', *Economic and Industrial Democracy*, vol 22, no 1, pp 39-66.

Taylor, P. and Bain, P. (2005) 'India calling to the far away towns: the call centre labour process and globalisation', *Work, Employment and Society*, vol 19, no 2, pp 261-82.

Taylor, P. and Bain, P. (2007) 'Call centre reflections – a reply to Glucksmann', *Work, Employment and Society*, vol 21, no 2, pp 349-62.

Taylor, P., Baldry, C., Bain, P. and Ellis, V. (2003) '"A unique working environment": health, sickness and absence management in UK call centres', *Work, Employment and Society*, vol 17, no 3, pp 435-58.

Taylor, R. (2002) *Britain's world of work: Myths and realities*, Swindon: Economic and Social Research Council.

Towers, B. (1999) Editorial: '"... the most lightly regulated labour market...": the UK's third statutory recognition procedure', *Industrial Relations Journal*, vol 30, no 2, pp 82-95.

TUC (Trades Union Congress) (1998) *Fairness at Work* conference, London, June.

TUC (2004) *Your rights at work* (2nd edn), London: Kogan Page.

TUC (2005) Press release, London, 21 March.

TUC (2006) *Conference decisions 2006* (see, for example, Composite Motion 4).

UNISON (2002) *Focus*, London: UNISON, 25 October.

UNISON (2004a) *PFI: Against the public interest*, London: UNISON.

UNISON (2004b) *Annual conference motions 2004, Agenda 1D-C, Public services*, London: UNISON.

UNISON (2006) *Working in police control rooms*, London: UNISON.

Undy, R. (1999) 'Annual review article 1999: New Labour's "industrial relations settlement": the Third Way?', *British Journal of Industrial Relations*, vol 27, no 2, pp 315-36.

Urwin, P. (2002) 'The re-organisation of work in the provision of local public services: the introduction of a call centre at a North West local authority', Paper at 20th International Labour Process Conference, University of Strathclyde, 2-4 April.

Waddington, J. (2003) 'Annual review article 2002: Heightening tension in relations between trade unions and the labour government in 2002', *British Journal of Industrial Relations*, vol 4, no 2, pp 335-58.

# FOUR

# Acts of distrust? Support workers' experiences in PFI hospital schemes

*Sally Ruane*

## Introduction

The major determinants of changes to the pay, terms and conditions of health sector support workers during New Labour's occupation of 10 Downing Street have stemmed from a drive to efficiency savings and the commercialisation of service delivery. The commercialisation of service delivery has included the use of market principles mainly through the contracting process and the privatisation of parts of 'public' service delivery. Both of these processes have subjected National Health Service (NHS) support workers, who are the principal focus of this chapter, to competition and to transfer into private sector employment. In health, the specific mechanisms have been the private finance initiative (PFI) and other forms of public–private partnership (PPP). This chapter examines how the PFI procurement process creates pressures on both private consortia and NHS trusts to acquiesce in the depression of terms and conditions of support staff and how those affected have attempted to resist and mitigate these effects.

This chapter draws on accounts of worker experience, notably the qualitative interview data collected in UNISON-commissioned projects, to understand the 'voice from the frontline' (Lister, 2003; UNISON, 2003). The extracts from these interviews, which are in the public domain, form part of two documents examining the impact of PFI, one across several hospitals (UNISON, 2003), the other within the context of the Great Western PFI Hospital in Swindon (Lister, 2003). Although the interview materials reflect a partisan stance, offer no guidance relating to the selection and editing of quotations and cannot be taken as comprehensive, they do offer insights into changing work experience and are rich in practical detail and mundane minutiae. The private consortia or companies and the NHS trusts referred to in this chapter are: SERCO at the Norfolk and Norwich NHS Trust; Sodexho at Hereford Hospitals NHS Trust; Haden at the North Durham Health Care NHS Trust (Durham); Criterion at South Durham NHS Trust (Bishop Auckland); ISS at the Hairmyres Hospital, Lanarkshire; Carillion at the Great Western Hospital, Swindon; Interserve at the Cumberland Infirmary, Carlisle; and Consort at the Edinburgh Royal Infirmary.

The main complaints of workers examined concerned wage levels, other financial terms of service, physical and material conditions of work, control of the labour process, 'belonging' to the wider NHS team and service quality. Individual and collective responses to these complaints are explored in this chapter.

## Contracting out and PFI under New Labour

The compulsory element of compulsory competitive tendering (CCT), the main means by which the Conservative administrations of Thatcher and Major subjected ancillary workers in health to the rigours of market principles, was not retained by New Labour in 1997. However, low funding levels in the late 1990s, various efficiency initiatives and the need to demonstrate that maximum value was being derived sustained a momentum to 'market test'. In addition, competitive market processes acted on health workers in a new and longer-term way through PFI (a point that emerges in a number of chapters in this collection). PFI began life as a Conservative attempt to lever more money into capital investment while avoiding higher levels of public borrowing. Announced in 1992, the policy attracted immediate opposition from the Labour front benches as the 'thin end of the wedge of privatisation' (Crail, 1995). This opposition was reversed, however, prior to Labour's 1997 electoral victory and the successful prosecution of PFI, particularly in the health sector, became one of the most urgent priorities of the New Labour government.

PFI differs from traditional modes of hospital procurement in several respects. First, it entails purchasing from *the private sector* the *use* of hospital amenities and facilities and associated services, not the purchase of a hospital per se. Second, it entails the long-term transfer of substantial sectors of the NHS workforce over to the private companies providing those services. The public authority thus becomes the procurer and regulator rather than the direct provider of services. Third, the public agent, in this case the NHS hospital trust, makes repayments to the consortium of companies, usually millions of pounds each year, for the duration of the contract, typically 30-35 years. These payments are ring-fenced in law and any pressures on the NHS trust budget must be borne by the clinical services on which it spends the rest of its income. PFI is a notoriously expensive form of capital investment (see, for example, Monbiot, 2000; Pollock et al, 2002), and NHS managers have been prepared on occasion to admit that cost-cutting on the ancillary side of the overall deal was considered necessary in order to make 'the affordability stack up' (Ruane, 2002, p 206). By October 2006, there were some 58 operational PFI hospital schemes, 28 of which were classic major district general hospital rebuilds.

Even this very brief sketch of PFI provides sufficient detail for some of the likely consequences for support workers to become obvious. Cleaners, caterers, laundry workers, porters and maintenance staff, at the least, have been forced out of the NHS and into the employment of the companies that constitute the consortium with whom the NHS trust has entered contract. Moreover, they have been transferred in a context of financial 'squeeze'. The services are highly labour intensive and the limited scope for technical, managerial or organisational innovation poses the prospect of cheaper services only through cuts in staffing levels and service quality (Davies, 2005). Compounding earlier dramatic staffing cuts, there was an average annual reduction of 1.5% in hotel, property and estates full-time equivalent staff between 1995 and 2005 (Information Centre, 2006) when almost every other category of staff grew. The experiences of workers described below are shaped by this context.

There is a growing recognition in academic literature that employment relations are shaped, in part, by institutional arrangements, including changes in institutional governance such as the shift towards the presence of multiple employers in circumstances of outsourcing (inter alia, Foss, 1993; McMaster, 1995; Hebson et al, 2003; see also Chapter Three, this volume). McMaster examined the 'differential capacities of governance structures to generate and appropriate benefits' (1995, p 411). Although his work pre-dated PFI, it focused on the development of a model to assess the impact of outsourcing on quality and it continues to offer a valuable set of conceptual tools through which to scrutinise the accounts of workers under PFI. McMaster cited Foss's (1993) conceptualisation of routine as serving two principal functions: first, to preserve and develop an institution's knowledge base; and second, to act as a transmitter of convention. Convention establishes the entitlements ('property rights bundle') of parties, enhancing efficiency by attenuating uncertainty and facilitating a more conducive environment for exchange. Governance changes, such as the arrival of multiple employers, impose costs by requiring the search for new conventions, and run the risk of leaving workers experiencing new patterns of 'entitlement' as inequitable and the governance changes themselves as 'acts of distrust'. These notions of 'acts of distrust' and breached 'entitlements' are evident in the workers' accounts.

## Changes to pay and conditions

The changed 'conventions' and 'entitlements' experienced by workers in PFI schemes have included: hourly pay, overtime and unsocial rates, bonuses, sick pay, annual leave, pension arrangements, hours of work, job descriptions, workload, managerial control of the labour process, control over the physical environment, membership of 'the team' and a sense of 'belonging' in the NHS.

PFI schemes have affected different groups of workers differently. Support services are now provided by groups of workers employed under widely varying terms and conditions despite the fact that they work side by side and perform work of equal value. Staff who were formerly NHS employees will have transferred on protected pay and conditions under TUPE (Transfer of Undertakings [Protection of Employment]) arrangements. This means that they will keep their hourly rate of pay, any overtime rates and any unsocial hours rates of pay they formerly had. They will retain entitlement to bonuses, to sick and holiday pay. They will not remain in the NHS pension schemes but must be offered pension terms that are 'broadly comparable' with those of the NHS scheme. New employees, who are employed from the outset by the company, will typically be on different and poorer terms and conditions. They may take home a lower rate of hourly pay, receive poorer reward for overtime work and for unsocial hours (which will usually be defined in a more restricted way); they will typically enjoy less holiday entitlement and significantly less sick pay.

Workers interviewed (see Lister, 2003; UNISON, 2003) revealed a mass of inequalities and inequities. A UNISON convenor claimed SERCO had been paying new staff 18% less than the Whitley minimum wage in the Norfolk and Norwich NHS Trust. A Hereford porter noted that an employee on an NHS trust contract was paid double time for Sundays, and double time with a day in lieu for Bank Holidays while, on a Sodexho contract, the employees received no extra pay for working on Sundays, and double time but no day in lieu for Bank Holidays. Overtime was paid at only time-and-a-half or time-and-a-quarter. In Durham, a steward reported that the two-tier workforce meant that TUPE porters doing the same hours and the same work as non-TUPE porters were paid £30-£40 per week more because of the two different contracts. By contrast, in catering, two TUPE cooks had had their better paid weekend work taken from them at a cost to each of £50 per week. At Hairmyres, domestics had had their hours cut from eight to six hours per day, despite doing the same job, a loss of £40 per week. In Swindon, managers had tried to eliminate overtime, and domestics worked a 40-hour flat-rate week, including Saturdays and Sundays. Some TUPE workers believed they were being deliberately pushed out of their jobs since their employers altered their hours of work to reduce their ability to benefit from the more 'generous' aspects of their terms. In contrast to comparatively generous NHS sick pay entitlement, many support workers found themselves with one day's pay per month or less for sickness. Some regarded this as particularly ironic given both the risk of infection to new staff in a context of high staff turnover and the continuing risk of workplace accidents and violence from members of the public.

Terms and conditions become ever more divergent over time. For instance, those who transferred from the NHS under TUPE work under pay and conditions that increasingly differ both from those of more recent employees and from those of their former colleagues still employed by the NHS. Additionally, some employers (for example, ISS at Hairmyres) make use of zero hours contracts that give the employer complete flexibility over the hours worked within the terms of the contract. Terms and conditions offered by companies across different hospitals vary significantly.

As well as cuts in financial rewards, staffing levels appeared lower relative to workload after transfer. Some reported absolute cuts; others the same staffing levels but heavier workload. A higher throughput of patients based on more intensive use of available beds could lead to an *increase* in per bed work effort (changing linen, making the bed, cleaning bed area, for instance). This was exacerbated where a promised expansion in community services to complement the new hospital had never been established because of the cost of PFI. Heavier workloads are associated with sickness levels, staff turnover, the physical layout of the premises and the redesign of staff roles.

The material and physical conditions of their work featured prominently in interviewee accounts of their working lives, with problems arising from the layout, scale and design of premises. Extra physical effort arose from both cramped conditions and multisite location since affordability-driven skimping on space in the new development left many trusts having to use a hotchpotch of different buildings, such as rented offices and portakabins. A catering worker at the Norfolk and Norwich NHS Trust said: 'I've never known my legs ache so much at the end of the day' (UNISON, 2003, p 23). In Bishop

Auckland, domestic staff complained that the rooms they were cleaning were too small to enable them to move the furniture enough to clean properly. Lack of daylight was a recurrent problem: according to one nurse, 'lots of secretarial and clerical staff have to spend all day in an office which resembles a cupboard without access to natural light. Many admin staff have left the Trust because of this ...' (Lister, 2003, p 16). In Swindon, the information technology (IT) and finance departments had been located miles from the hospital. In many hospitals, because walls were not weight-bearing, case notes were being stacked in piles across the floor, posing a potential health and safety risk. In Carlisle, medical records were relocated off-site. Lack of storage was frequently reported with the result that ward corridors and floor space were often blocked with papers or stacked linen, an obvious breach of health and safety and infection reduction regulations. Poor architectural design left staff sweltering as temperatures soared at the Edinburgh Royal and Cumberland Infirmaries, while receptionists at the Great Western 'sit there freezing with coats and scarves on' (Lister, 2003, p 17). The design of heavy fire doors could be such that they must be manually opened, making the pushing through of a trolley or wheelchair more difficult. In Swindon, all the lifts had broken down and some were considered dangerous. Workers also complained about the lack of wet-weather wear for outdoor tasks. Some staff incurred additional expenditure through the costs of transport to an out-of-town location or via charges levied on car parking.

Many of the social aspects of work had been adversely affected by the physical constraints of the new premises under the PFI scheme. One instance of this could be found in the isolation of some staff stranded on distant sites, and another in the absence in some PFI hospitals of a 'rest' room for porters and domestics so that there was nowhere to relax or to eat a sandwich or make a cup of tea or store items that needed to be kept cold. Elsewhere such rooms existed but workers complained that they were highly inadequate, sometimes on a basement floor with no natural light; that they were too small for the numbers of staff using them; that no notice boards, pictures or shelves could be erected without permission from the private company or where walls were not load-bearing. The inability to make a cup of tea, store food in a refrigerator and eat in the office or rest room had imposed additional costs on some workers who then found themselves with little choice but to eat in the canteen where prices were high.

As in other areas of the NHS, some workers reported tighter control over the labour process through more oppressive management – taking overtime only with written signed permission; porters having to ask permission to do 'absolutely anything' from their 'controller' meaning 'countless telephone calls from hard-pressed nursing and medical staff for the tiniest of tasks'; domestics having to ring for a supervisor to obtain all their materials from a locked cupboard; having to stick tightly to break times even where the physical layout of the hospital meant that, as a result, there was no opportunity for privacy or a sit-down with a sandwich. In Durham, staff employed by the private company had been forbidden to talk to an in-house driver even though he had worked with some of them for over 25 years. These problems had been posed by the monitoring system in place that put everything on an official basis even though a 'quiet word' might be the best way to put some things right. The existence of two different rooms for these groups of staff amounted to 'segregation': 'there's no teamwork any more'.

## Alienation, belonging and the quality of services

What we see in the talk of the interviewed workers is a perceived interconnectedness between new governance arrangements, conditions of work, reduced quality and a weakened sense of 'belonging', both in terms of team membership and in terms of ownership of the hospital. The limitations and constraints placed on them shaped realistically attainable standards of quality.

Support staff complained that standards had declined because, despite working as hard as possible, they had neither the time nor the resources to do the job properly. A nurse in a specialist unit at the Norfolk and Norwich Hospital observed that, although it was vital for support workers to understand their contribution to patient care through infection control or in more specialist ways, staff turnover meant that they rarely had the chance to become 'members of the ward team'. The effectiveness of support duties was undermined as a result. A UNISON Secretary in Hereford recalled: 'The porters always used to chat with the patients and make them laugh: you could see people smile and feel a little bit better'. Staff compared the past and the present: 'It's just a constant "them and us" with the nursing staff, but it wasn't like that in the old hospital. There we were a team', and 'I worked in the old hospital ... it was like a family and everybody pulled together: porters, domestics, nurses, even the doctors' (UNISON, 2003, p 26). At Hereford, workload among domestics was linked to poor standards of work that in turn created stress, low morale and high staff turnover. A Hairmyres hostess said: 'If you're doing them the way they should be done it takes at least half an hour to do a bed. We are told to do it as quickly as we possibly can. You don't get half an hour'. A cook in

Carlisle lamented the loss of proper cooking since the kitchen system moved to a cook-chill approach: 'I'm not happy with the quality of the food we serve. It comes up from Manchester.... People say: "can you tell me what's in this?" and I have to say: "sorry, I haven't a clue!"' (UNISON, 2003, p 29).

A discernible meanness and lack of generosity pervade the new arrangements. This is manifest in part in conflict over the building itself. In Bishop Auckland, the private company Criterion 'keep telling us it's "their" building', and in Swindon, the 'Carillion boss here says it's his hospital'. The spectre of alienation goes beyond the recognition that workers might not either feel part of the broader team or identify with the values of the public authority. What seems to be being conveyed in these workers' accounts is that the collective values and collective effort of offering a public service were expressed not merely through work content or the employment relationship but were in some way embodied in the building and integral to the physical structure of the workplace. This perhaps reflects the close association in the public mind between the NHS and the local hospital; in one sense, the NHS is visible and made manifest in bricks and mortar.

Legally and symbolically, these now belong to a private company and the declaration or assertion of this transfer has been made through taking away from workers their right to shape and mould and fashion 'their' part of the physical environment to their satisfaction. One waiting list manager reported that 'because the building is privately owned', staff could not eat at their desks, use a kettle in the office or even put up Christmas decorations.

## Class consciousness and individual forms of resistance

Some academics (for example, McMaster, 1995) have speculated that the transfer of workers may lead to a sense among employees that they are no longer part of the wider organisation and no longer share in the overall welfarist or Hippocratic objectives of the contracting authority. He cites Frey (1993), who suggested that perceived inequities could leave workers considering 'shirking' morally defensible. The evidence from these workers does not demonstrate an alienation from the values of the NHS but does point to the corrosive effect of the new arrangements. One widely reported response was to give up the job and look for work elsewhere. Without further research with such workers, it is difficult to know whether this should be understood as a form of resistance through rejection of the exploitation and alienation intrinsic to privatisation or as an *alternative* to resistance. Either way, the result of this over time has been to reduce drastically the numbers of staff covered by TUPE protection. (For a discussion of turnover among cleaning staff across the UK, see Davies, 2005.)

The corrosive effects of PFI have undermined morale, particularly when workers compared the current with their former work environment. On the other hand, some staff at one hospital were reported to resolve the stress and dissatisfaction they felt about workload by coming in half an hour early without pay to make sure the work would be finished. This suggests a coping rather than resistance strategy, an ongoing although potentially unsustainable commitment to the enterprise. A convenor at the Norfolk and Norwich NHS Trust (UNISON, 2003, p 23) observed, 'the original people like me who worked at the old hospital and are still here have come and stayed because we want to look after the patients ... it used to feel good going to work and you had some satisfaction going home at the end of the day. Now there is no more satisfaction for porters than working in a factory or a shop'. This sense of the individual clinging to the moral integrity of the job in the midst of an institutional structure designed to undermine it is found again in the comment of a catering worker: 'Privatisation has taken the care out of our jobs. We just haven't got time to do those extra things that show we care' (UNISON, 2003, p 23).

This consciousness of the adulteration of care was articulated in a more overtly politicised way by some. One convenor for SERCO workers commented: 'for us, the question is how the hell a company can just want to make money out of ill people' (UNISON, 2003, p 23), and a Carlisle cook complained, 'at least with the NHS, even if the wages weren't great you know that nobody is making a fat profit out of you and the morale was a lot better'(UNISON, 2003, p 29).

## Collective forms of resistance

Strike action has been in decline in the UK as well as across the European Union (EU) for several decades (Waddington, 2005). However, under New Labour, there have been several strikes, threats of strikes, overtime bans, walk-outs and unofficial disputes among NHS support workers arising from poor terms and conditions. These have included in-house teams whose terms have been driven down through years of competitive tendering (for example, at South Tyneside Hospital); contracted-out workers in non-PFI settings (for example, at the Glasgow Royal Infirmary against Sodexho and among staff across several hospitals including Whipps Cross in East London, Stockport and Barnsley against the same employer, Rentokil Initial); and staff transferred under PFI. In 2001, workers at the first PFI hospital to be built in Carlisle voted for strikes, overtime bans and a strict work-to-rule over the deterioration in terms and conditions, and staff at Hairmyres have threatened to strike on several occasions against ISS Mediclean.

Best known, however, was the 10-month strike (and longest strike in NHS history) by ancillary workers, mostly women, at the Dudley hospitals in 2000-01. Strikers cited the bulldozing of two existing hospitals and the loss of 70 beds as well as job losses, transfer to the private sector and poorer pay, terms and conditions for future workers (*Socialist Worker*, 2000). The conditions for this strike were created in part by the Department of Health announcement in 1999 that, other than maintenance staff, ancillary workers were not compelled to transfer under PFI but that the outcome should be decided following a value-for-money calculation. The Dudley workers chose to exploit the uncertainty and ambiguity this created. The strike enjoyed considerable local popularity and was backed by UNISON although not by the four local Labour Members of Parliament. It is unlikely that the Department of Health would have been persuaded to agree to the Retention of Employment (RoE) deal (see below) without the sustained action of the Dudley strikers. They voted to end the strike when the NHS trust signed a contract with Summit Healthcare and they were given the option of working for Summit or losing their jobs altogether, and UNISON withdrew support for legal reasons (Deeley and Hudson, 2001).

This action could be sustained for so long only because of the local popular support, and there have been a number of PFI-related community-based (rather than worker-based) campaigns, although the limited character of opposition to PFI has been noted (Ruane, 2000). The most far-reaching of these occurred in Kidderminster where an alliance of trade unions, health professionals, ancillary workers, patients and public organised, protested, lobbied, took legal action, and conducted research to save the local district general hospital whose future status was threatened by the new PFI build in Worcester. Although this failed to save the local hospital, its impact has been felt in the longer term through the local council and parliamentary ballot boxes.

In a context of limited industrial action, most collective resistance to the exploitative and alienating consequences of PFI has been conducted through formal trade union activity. All the large public sector unions – the GMB (General and Municipal Workers Union), TGWU (Transport and General Workers Union), UNISON and

Amicus – have non-clinical members in health settings and provide various forms of support to their members. However, all of UNISON's 1.3 million members work in public services, it is arguably the most hostile to PPPs and it has taken the lead on combating PFI; this is reflected in the discussion that follows. Its goals have been to end PFI; failing this, to end the transfer of staff out of public sector employment in PFI schemes; and failing this, to end the resulting two-tier workforce by securing equivalence of sectoral pay and conditions regardless of employer.

## Ending PFI

UNISON has conducted an explicit 'twin-track strategy' with regard to PFI: opposing the policy in principle but engaging at the level of each scheme to negotiate better terms for members. Its opposition in principle has been executed mainly through the commissioning and dissemination of high-quality empirical research on the distorting and expensive character of the policy, through ministerial lobbying and through formal debate within the institutions of the labour movement. The major public sector unions have collaborated to move motions (for example, in 2002) at the annual conferences of both the Trades Union Congress (TUC) and the Labour Party opposing the policy and/or calling for a moratorium. Nonetheless, such motions, however resoundingly supported at conference, have not altered the Labour government's path.

These unions' efforts to persuade ministers to change direction are not confined to the conference floor; as part of the labour movement and affiliates and donors to the Labour Party, union leaders have some access to ministers. This access is not so frequent nor so effective as that of their counterparts in the 1960s and 1970s and some have suggested that the marginalisation and exclusion of trade unions from policy making is largely the same under Blair as it had been under Thatcher (Lawrence, 2004). The unions also participate in the policy process formally, for instance through written and oral evidence submitted to Select Committee Inquiries.

The unions' websites carry information that goes well beyond the subject matter of narrow material interest to members, and the GMB, Amicus and UNISON currently run pro-public campaigns alongside their more focused bargaining work. To varying extents, they have contributed to the development of a body of literature providing an evolving critique of government policy. For instance, the GMB has commissioned research from the Labour Research Department and the TGWU sponsors the Public Services International Research Unit. UNISON has worked most on PFI, collaborating with academics who have produced detailed analyses of the technical aspects of specific PFI schemes and has disseminated findings through website-available publications and through national and regional conferences organised for this purpose. Examples include Price et al (1999) and Gosling (2004). This approach has succeeded in creating a significant body of knowledge about the shortcomings and risks of the PFI approach to capital investment that is drawn on by many who enter and try to understand this complex area. Dissemination 'downwards' has spread the ability to produce a critique of PFI. Dissemination upwards, however, has not succeeded in its objective of persuading ministers that the policy should be abandoned on the grounds of empirical evidence. The lessons of the failure of this evidence-based approach to politics require serious contemplation.

The other track of the anti-PFI strategy has involved training up and supporting local negotiators in their struggles to secure the best possible terms for the transfer of staff to private employ. The Bargaining Support Unit has contributed substantially to the monitoring of NHS contracts with private companies and evolving pay, terms and conditions.

## Ending the transfer of workers

Perhaps the most significant achievement UNISON has made in relation to PFI is in securing the RoE Agreement in April 2002 for subsequent PFI schemes. This provides for most staff (around 85%) in the main ancillary groups, the 'five trades', to remain in the NHS. Under the RoE, non-supervisory staff in cleaning, catering, portering, laundry and security remain in the NHS. There are exceptions to this in each category: 'risk-bearing' managerial and supervisory staff do transfer; and exceptions may be made where trusts have 'insufficient capacity' to run the service themselves. Moreover, ancillary staff are 'seconded to' and managed by the private 'partner'. However, staff remain on NHS pay and conditions – the full package of terms – and keep their NHS pensions; additionally, contracted-out staff are generally brought back in-house prior to the signing of the deal and regain (unless they prefer their private sector pay) NHS terms and conditions, their NHS pensions and entitlements (although potentially on a 'new starter' basis). Staff working in IT systems and payroll, medical and patient records, central sterile supply services departments, or switchboard and reception services continue to face transfer if their services are included in a PFI deal unless a value-for-money case can be made. It should be noted that in signing up to the deal, UNISON's executive ignored not only the objections of the GMB but also the decision of its own policy-making Health Conference that rejected the RoE as limited and divisive.

## Ending the two-tier workforce

The public sector unions are opposed to what they describe as the 'two-tier workforce' (for example, UNISON, 2004). For instance, UNISON's 'ultimate goal' (UNISON, 2005a) is for a fair wages clause along the lines of the International Labour Organization (ILO) Convention 94 (ILO, 1949). This would replace the Fair Wages Resolution, rescinded by Thatcher in 1983, which had required private companies contracting with public authorities to pay the going rate for the trade or industry based on terms agreed in national collective agreements.

The major affected unions have worked at individual contractor, sectoral and cross-sectoral levels. The Scottish TUC and Scottish Executive Protocol of December 2002 covered all public service sectors and ensured the terms and conditions for any new appointee of the workforce should be no less favourable than for transferred workers. The aim was explicitly to avoid a two-tier workforce in PPPs and to 'exclude changes that would undermine the integrated nature and quality of the workforce'. The unions saw this as a means of making contracting out less attractive to public and private bodies alike. The Protocol has been criticised, however, as 'tinkering at the edge of a disaster' and in practice has not always deterred public authorities from contracting out (Ritchie, 2002; see also Poole and Mooney, 2006, p 571). An additional weakness is that such agreements are limited by their patchiness sectorally and geographically (nothing at all in Northern Ireland, for instance). The unions are keenly aware of this and have been moving towards a sectoral agreement in health in which private contractors are required to pay their own employees the same rates of pay as stipulated by Agenda for Change (AfC), the new pay framework now operating in the NHS. This complements negotiations with individual companies around the terms and conditions of staff in particular schemes. For instance, in 2004, UNISON lodged national claims with 24 contractors, which provide some one third of all NHS ancillary services, asking for parity with AfC (UNISON, 2005b).

In 2005, the GMB, TGWU, UNISON and Amicus struck an agreement with the Department of Health for England, NHS Employers and the private contractor organisations, the Confederation of British Industry and British Services Association (UNISON, nd).

---

The Agreement provided for workers employed on 'soft facilities management' contracts in England to move onto AfC equivalent terms from October 2006 and then any other negotiated changes in the future. Separate negotiations are required for workers in Scotland and Northern Ireland, for 'hard facilities management' workers and for unsocial hours. Even more serious a shortcoming, however, is that the agreement is with umbrella employer organisations but not the individual companies. At the time of writing, not one single private company had agreed to any set of national terms and conditions for staff across different PFI schemes, never mind a national set of terms and conditions comparable with those of AfC.

## Conclusions

The workers' accounts synthesise concerns about onerous workloads, the material context of their work and the services they provide. What they add up to goes beyond recognition of 'acts of distrust'. What these workers describe are acts of aggression, acts of divestment, acts of expropriation as their already meagre levels of pay and benefits are purloined and chipped away, and their modest control over their working environment – and 'their' hospital – and their identity and dignity as part of the 'NHS team' are taken from them. Staff find that they are expected to do more for less; that they are expected to accomplish tasks that are physically impossible to accomplish given the time and resources allocated and, as a result, are compelled to provide poor services; that they are bullied out of their terms and conditions; that they are deprived of their pensions; that they are divided within their own ranks by the poor quality of work, the collapse of a stable workforce and low-trust management practices. They are poorer, more intensively worked, more aggressively managed, more exposed to health hazards, facing a financially riskier old age and deprived of the satisfaction that comes from having pride in their work.

As the union that has invested most in tackling PFI, UNISON's hard-earned but patchy, piecemeal and unsatisfactory achievements must be viewed as a disappointment. The government has not shifted from its pursuit of privatisation and marketisation; it has partially reversed the policy of transferring some ancillary staff only as policy moves on to the transfer of other categories; UNISON has failed to secure comparable terms and conditions for members in private sector employment, to secure a reasonable minimum wage and to prevent some of its poorest members from continuing to pay for 'efficiencies' in the NHS and for the profits of private employers.

The unions' onerous and time-consuming pursuit of company and geographically bound sectoral agreements is unavoidable given the steadfast refusal by government to legislate or regulate for strong and universal protections for workers. By the same token, it is difficult to see how the government could do otherwise once the principle of recommodification of highly labour-intensive services is accepted, despite its protestations that PPPs should not be delivered at the expense of the pay and conditions of staff and that public sector workers are its biggest asset (see Sachdev, 2001).

Given the radical direction of Labour policy and the unions' failure despite ongoing effort to make headway in their agenda, it is reasonable to ask why they remain affiliated to and major funders of the Labour Party: as one Labour conference participant put it in 2001, 'why feed the hand that bites you?'. No doubt union leaders would insist their limited influence over ministers would have been much diminished had they disaffiliated from Labour. However, like the other major unions, UNISON has pulled its punches because of its links with Labour: it has declined to denounce Party policy in the run-up to elections, instead portraying the main threat to public services as emanating from the Conservative Party. It has shrunk from viewing the Labour government as the enemy and this has blunted its sword. Nor has it succeeded in achieving the narrower range of objectives associated with 'business unionism': better pay, terms and conditions for members. Many of UNISON's members continue to live almost a decade into a Labour government on, quite literally, poverty wages that must be supplemented for some by means-tested benefits. This reveals that, in PFI, it is not only these workers, among the poorest paid in society, who subsidise capital but also in this less publicised respect the tax-paying public.

The UNISON leadership first believed that PFI was pursued for pragmatic reasons and that, as empirical evidence of its impact came to light, it would be abandoned as a policy (Ruane, 2000). That conviction, which must surely now have evaporated, has perhaps been replaced by a certain fatalism, a sense that there is no alternative: given the legal obstacles to mounting effective strike action (themselves a product of New Labour's retention of Thatcher's anti-trade union legislation), as well as the public legitimacy obstacles, it is difficult to conceive an alternative to talking with a view to doing deals. The engagement with PFI schemes locally and negotiating for deals nationally, however understandable these approaches are, in fact contradict a policy of opposition to PFI and fatally undermine the associated campaign.

The accounts of workers affected by transfer reflect the interconnectedness of conditions of work, government policy, quality for patients and teamwork. They show how keenly workers 'in the frontline' understand and are able to articulate the multifaceted character of experienced quality and perceive deteriorations in this quality. They show that care rests on relationships with professional colleagues and patients and reveal the contrived nature of the core–periphery divide. This has implications for researching quality in hospital care: methods of investigation that collect data exclusively from senior managers are likely to understate the extent of quality failures (see McMaster, 1995). This holistic grasp needs to be matched by a union strategy to develop better links with professional, patient and public groups.

In 2006, the four big unions joined forces with smaller unions and staff associations and the TUC to create an unprecedented alliance, NHS Together (www.tuc.org.uk/theme/index.cfm?theme=nhstogether). Several of these unions and professional associations are affiliated to the Keep Our NHS Public campaign (www.keepournhspublic. com) and locally some union branches collaborate with other 'save our services' type campaigns. Whether such collaboration represents a genuine attempt to participate in a broad-based popular alliance not dominated by 'producer interest' or whether it is an exercise in 'going through the motions' (Keep Our NHS Public conference delegate, 2006, private communication) remains to be seen. It seems unlikely that effective defence against further privatisation in the NHS can be achieved without genuine partnership.

The broader policy context – the new market in healthcare, competition and diversity – along with the technical small print governing Payment by Results, national tariff setting and funding formulae – are together producing managerial strategies to reduce costs further and to contract out professional staff as well as ancillary. The clarity with which threats to the NHS through privatisation and marketisation may now be perceived as part of a coherent and all-embracing strategy that is seriously destabilising NHS units creates, through recognised common interest, the possibility of alliances in the face of a common enemy. The engagement of the public through rising awareness of cuts in the level and quality of services is critical to such a strategy. The price paid by ancillary workers for recommodification of British healthcare after almost 60 years of socialised medicine looks now to be a price we may all have to pay.

## Further sources

Pollock, A. (2005) *NHS plc* (2nd edn), London: Verso – readable exploration of the processes by which business interests have been advanced in the NHS.

Talbot-Smith, A. and Pollock, A. (2006) *The new NHS: A guide*, London: Routledge – examination of the structure and functions of the many agencies involved in the health services of the devolved countries of the UK.

www.tuc.org.uk/theme/index.cfm?theme=nhstogether and www. keepournhspublic.com – NHS Together and Keep Our NHS Public provide NHS news updates, readable policy analyses and campaigning resources.

www.unison.org.uk/pfi/index.asp – UNISON PFI Campaign provides information, analysis and guides to campaigning.

## References

Crail, M. (1995) 'Danger money', *Health Service Journal*, 1 June, p 9.

Davies, S. (2005) *Hospital contract cleaning and infection control*, London: UNISON.

Deeley, T. and Hudson, J. (2001) 'Hospital strike saga ends with worker climbdown at Summit's approach', *Birmingham Post*, 19 May, p 4.

Foss, N. (1993) 'Theories of the firm: contractual and competence perspectives', *Journal of Evolutionary Economics*, vol 3, pp 127-44.

Frey, B. (1993) 'Does monitoring increase work effort?', *Economic Inquiry*, vol 31, pp 663-70.

Gosling, P. (2004) *PFI – Against the public interest*, London: UNISON.

Hebson, G., Grimshaw, D. and Marchington, M. (2003) 'PPPs and the changing public sector ethos', *Work, Employment and Society*, vol 17, no 3, pp 481-501.

ILO (International Labour Organization) (1949) *C94 Labour Clauses (Public Contracts) Convention 1949*, Geneva: ILO.

Information Centre (2006) *Data table for staff in the NHS*, NHS: Information Centre (www.ic.nhs.uk/pubs/nhsstaff/nhsstaff1995to2005/file).

Lawrence, E. (2004) 'Trade unions', in M. Todd and G. Taylor (eds) *Democracy and participation*, London: Merlin, pp 135-57.

Lister, J. (2003) *Not so great: Voices from the front-line at the Great Western PFI Hospital in Swindon*, London: UNISON.

McMaster, R. (1995) 'Competitive tendering in UK health authorities: what happens to the quality of services?', *Scottish Journal of Political Economy*, vol 42, no 4, pp 409-27.

Monbiot, G. (2000) *Captive state: The corporate take-over of Britain*, London: Macmillan.

Pollock, A., Shaoul, J. and Vickers, N. (2002) 'Private finance and "value for money" in NHS hospitals: a policy in search of a rationale?', *British Medical Journal*, vol 324, pp 1205-9.

Poole, L. and Mooney, G. (2006) 'Privatizing education in Scotland: New Labour, modernization and "public' services", *Critical Social Policy*, vol 26, no 3, pp 562-86.

Price, D., Gaffney, D. and Pollock, A. (1999) *The only game in town: A report on the Cumberland Infirmary Carlisle PFI*, Newcastle: UNISON Northern Region.

Ritchie, M. (2002) 'Kerr strikes PPP deal with unions', *The Herald*, 12 November, p 8.

Ruane, S. (2000) 'Acquiescence and opposition: the private finance initiative in the NHS', *Policy & Politics*, vol 23, no 3, pp 411-22.

Ruane, S. (2002) 'Public–private partnerships: the case of PFI', in C. Glendinning, M. Powell and K. Rummery (eds) *Partnerships, New Labour and the governance of welfare*, Bristol: The Policy Press, pp 199-213.

Sachdev, S. (2001) *Contracting culture: From CCT to PPPs*, London: UNISON.

*Socialist Worker* (2000) 'A fight everyone should get behind', *Socialist Workeronline*, issue 1711, 26 August (www.socialistworker.co.uk/article.php?article_id=1163).

UNISON (2003) *The PFI experience: Voices from the frontline*, London: UNISON.

UNISON (2004) *Fair wages: How to end the two tier workforce in public services and achieve fair wages*, London: UNISON.

UNISON (2005a) *Positively public*, June briefing, London: UNISON.

UNISON (2005b) *Bargaining support*, April factsheet, London: UNISON.

UNISON (nd) *Agenda for change and private contractor staff*, London: UNISON.

Waddington, J. (2005) 'Trade unions and the defence of the European social model', *Industrial Relations Journal*, vol 36, no 6, pp 518-40.

# FIVE

# Control and resistance at the ward-face: contesting the nursing labour process

*Peter Kennedy and Carole A. Kennedy*

## Introduction

The National Health Service (NHS) is the largest employer in Europe, employing in the region of 1.3 million health workers across the primary and secondary care sectors and the community. Nurses are the largest group of health workers, accounting for 440,000, the absolute size of this group alone making them a key component of the healthcare labour process (DH, 2005). This chapter focuses specifically on the nursing labour process. Our overall aim is primarily analytical, to explain and evaluate the various ways in which control is exercised by management over nursing labour, its inherent limits and the possibilities this provides for resistance by nurses to the central dynamics of the nursing labour process. In support of this analysis we call on data from our own 'research'.[1] Clearly, the nursing labour process is shaped intimately by the overall organisational context of the healthcare industry, which, in the UK, has witnessed considerable turbulence and growing instability marked by a shift towards the market. Therefore the chapter begins with a brief overview of these changes since they constitute a primary determinant for managerial controls for healthcare labour. We conclude that the unstable transition to the market is the precondition for understanding the complex, overlapping, management strategies to enforce control over the nursing labour process. These involve an uneven hybrid of managerial controls drawing from Taylorism, new public management (NPM) and the moral management of professional autonomy. Each strategy, whether taken alone or combined, has thus far failed and, in light of the wider contradiction thrown up by the capitalist labour process, will continue to fail in its objective to comprehensively control nursing labour power.

## The NHS and the nursing labour process in context

Up until the end of the 1970s and notwithstanding charges for prescriptions, dentistry and optical services, the market played no fundamental role in the running of the NHS. When it came to decisions over human and physical resource allocation the distribution of care was decided by the 'visible hand' of the state. Gradually, however, the NHS has undergone a series of changes aiming to bring it closer to the market. The attractions of the market for government are clear enough. Unlike the state, the market is thought to have the capacity to generate, through the price mechanism, the means of informing NHS managers (at all levels) of the relative costs of resources and how productively they are deployed towards care. In sum, the market is thought to be the key for management in providing a continuous 'environment of penalties or rewards for inefficient or efficient behaviour' (Donaldson and Gerard, 2005, p 65).

However, although there has been a gradual shift towards the market since 1979, government policy remains contradictory: driven, on the one hand, by the economic case for delivering the NHS closer to the market, and curbed, on the other hand, by popular support and the political necessity to maintain the NHS as a public institution with finance remaining under the central control of the state (Ranade, 1997, p 57). When the New Labour government took office in 1997 the contradiction was such that it was both a willing heir to an NHS that had undergone a shift towards the market in core aspects of its provision and delivery of care *and* a captive of the political pressure to maintain the NHS as a public-funded service.

Consecutive Conservative governments of the 1980s and early 1990s deployed a number of strategies designed to move the NHS closer to the market. They included efficiency drives culled from business sector management that dovetailed with the introduction of internal markets in healthcare, along with tax breaks to encourage the growth of private healthcare, as well as wholesale contracting out to the private sector of non-clinical services such as cleaning, laundry, catering and latterly security (Ranade, 1997; Klein, 2001; Donaldson and Gerard, 2005). The reforms became fundamental in bringing to centre stage issues of accountability, in terms of economic efficiency and value for money within the professional domain of clinical and management decision-making processes. The Labour government has accelerated the transfer of the NHS towards the market (Klein, 2001; Pollock, 2004). In particular, the internal market under New Labour moved beyond general practitioner (GP) fundholding and the purchaser–provider relationship between health authorities and hospital trusts, to one of 'commissioning' packages of care by primary care units from across the public, private and voluntary sector divide (Ranade, 1997).

The shift towards the market has been furthered in England by the conversion of a selection of hospitals into 'foundation hospitals' with the power to borrow capital from the open market and invest surplus capital in ways that provide healthcare with profit. The logic is of course that all hospitals should eventually become foundation hospitals or else wither away in the form of rationalisations in which, in market terms, the more inefficient hospital is eaten up by the more efficient (Pollock, 2004). The same logic is accorded primary care units, which have become central to government strategy to shift the NHS towards the market both in terms of finance and delivery. The private finance initiative (PFI) represents another policy initiative aimed at shifting the NHS from a state-run to a market-driven organisation. PFI allows access to private capital into the building and running of hospitals, the costs and profits to be paid for by taxation in the form of a mortgage. PFI originated with the Conservative government in 1992, but lay dormant until the election of the Labour government who have since pursued this line of marketisation with vigour (Pollock, 1997, 2004).

On the other hand, NHS Scotland has indicated a commitment to keeping the market at arm's length, for example by refraining from interventions such as foundation hospitals. The NHS in Scotland also emphasises its preference for 'devolving responsibility for health to primary care practices and community health partnerships' (NHS Scotland, 2005). Yet devolved responsibility remains under the strict control of the centre through a range of quantitative audits and measurements on processes and outcomes (NHS Scotland, 2005). Moreover, beneath the rhetoric of 'devolved partnerships', the shift towards the market is ongoing, evidenced by, for example, the part-privatisation of blood transfusion services and the almost celebratory mood of the Scottish Executive towards PFI (UNISON, 2006a). Indeed there has been little sign of bottom-up consultation when it came to the decision that a new £300 million hospital in Larbert to replace two existing hospitals in Falkirk and Stirling would be awarded to the private sector. Moreover, the partnership rhetoric is well understood by healthcare workers at NHS Scotland's flagship PFI hospital, Edinburgh Royal Infirmary, where, 'all the decisions are taken by the privately owned Consort group, which is another name for the Balfour Beatty – Haden Building Management organisation' (*The Scotsman*, 2005). Sally Ruane observed in Chapter Four (this volume) how PFI, implemented both north and south of the border, is the thin end of the wedge towards privatisation and the depression of health workers' pay and conditions. Indeed, the different nuances between England and Scotland merely amplify how the shift towards the market has been a long drawn-out process, which has taken, and continues to take, the form of ad hoc and pragmatic changes, poorly thought through and even reversed under political pressure from voters, who by and large continue to reject the market for healthcare (Pollock, 2004).

As in other welfare and public sector organisations, numerous reasons have been cited for the shift towards the market, from lack of management accountability and organisational stasis said to be inherent in state administration, to the power over resource allocation exerted by the medical profession, largely as a result of the political settlement between the medical profession and the state that underpinned the emergence of the NHS, to the inability to meet the demand for healthcare free at the point of need; and, last but not least, to the neoliberal claim that the NHS, as part of an unproductive state sector, crowded out the private sector and needed to be brought back within the market fold (Klein, 2001). However, the shift towards the market has been fundamentally driven by the need to take back control of the healthcare labour process, a control that the growing healthcare worker militancy of the 1970s and 1980s had fundamentally eroded (Harrison and Pollit, 1994).

The period in question was highly politicised. Social democracy, with its belief that one could regulate and intervene in the market to smooth over class inequalities and 'humanise capital', came under serious questioning from both the Left and the Right (Ferguson et al, 2002, p 41). A new militancy spread throughout the public sector workforce, including the healthcare workforce, culminating in increasingly politicised industrial action from ancillary workers, nurses, ambulance crew and professionals allied to medicine that began in the early 1970s and lasted until the early 1980s (Seifert, 1992; Klein, 2001). By the mid 1980s there was a distinct sense in which management was judged to have failed its prerogative to manage and control healthcare workers (Seifert, 1992). As the Griffith Report (1983, p 12) put it, 'if Florence Nightingale were carrying her lamp through the corridors of the NHS today she would almost certainly be searching for the people in charge'. As the next two sections of this chapter demonstrate, since then management has attempted to exact greater control over the healthcare labour process and in particular nursing labour power.

## Direct and indirect forms of control over the nursing labour process

The labour process as an area of analysis is gradually re-establishing itself as a means of explaining the inherent conflicts in the area of the nursing labour process (for example, Lloyd and Seifert, 1995; Ackroyd and Bolton, 1999; Grimshaw, 1999; Allen and Hughes, 2002). Labour process theory in general suggests a number of practices undertaken by management to control its workforce which have been prominent in attempting to control nursing labour power. These include direct control through job redesign, deskilling and individualised effort-reward bargains, known collectively as Taylorism, and more indirect controls involving limited forms of worker control over job design, decision making and the pace of work, defined as *responsible autonomy* (Braverman, 1974; Thompson, 1989; Thompson and McHugh, 1995). With respect to the nursing labour process one argument is that the management function has had some notable success in exercising control by adopting forms of Taylorism. The situation is perhaps more complex, in similar ways to nursery nurses (see Chapter Eight, this volume); nurses have been encouraged to take on multiskills and have also experienced deskilling through the adoption of core–periphery sourcing of elite highly skilled nurses and an army of assistants, in the context of the broader shift towards market principles of economic accountability (Lloyd and Seifert, 1995). If one views neo-Taylorism more broadly to include not only deskilling but also the atomisation of the wage-effort bargain and the rational pursuit of economic efficiency through a core–periphery labour process strategy, then one can say that NHS management has had some success in implementing Taylorism.

In this respect, the introduction of a nurse grading system linking nurses' pay and experience along a continuum between A–I grades has assisted the management function to weaken the collective resolve of nurses and strengthen individualism and personal responsibility, not to mention personal responsibility to remain a 'competent knowledgeable doer'. Moreover, the new grade of 'healthcare assistant' introduced in the 1990s has provided management with the means to link work and pay more closely to local labour market conditions and the performance of standard, low-status, nursing tasks at ward level (Grimshaw, 1999). Taylorism is also facilitated by the hospital context itself. Hospitals are fundamentally bureaucratic in nature and instil standardisation and routine on the nursing labour process to affect the predictable ordering of patients in time and space (Allen and Hughes, 2002, p 26). Moreover, the recent introduction of PFI and the financial squeeze it engenders (see Chapter Four, this volume) adds further grist to the mill of this bureaucratic imperative towards Taylorist regulation of work practice at the core of the NHS confronting and limiting professional aims and objectives (Scambler, 1991). In an interview for our research, nurse 'A' commented:

> 'Most attempts I make to adopt a patient-centred approach to nursing care are stopped in their tracks by management's continued demands for audit controls on the ward. Where I should be sitting by the bedside talking and listening to my patient and introducing their needs into my care plans, more often than not my time is taken up filling in standardised care plans and audit forms issued by hospital management. In university the need for a social model of care is drummed into us yet when we hit the wards the reality is quite different. At university we're taught the importance of communication skills and listening to our patients, not telling them what to do, yet when you become a staff nurse you find yourself slipping into the usual routine of getting the obs done at 10, 2 and 6, doing the medicine rounds at the same time everyday and making sure your patients are up, dressed and washed whether they want it or not. On the wards it became very clear to us as students that "good" nurses were those that always kept busy.'[2]

In addition, it is feasible to argue that, somewhat contradictorily with respect to its longer-term implications, the perennial concern about demographic changes leading to declining numbers of young entrants into nursing has forced the government to consider Taylorist principles of management as a means of raising the efficiency of the existing workforce and so dampen the demand for qualified nursing in the short term.

Yet it is also the case that the impact of Taylorism has remained contradictory. The degradation of work implied can increase job alienation and nurse turnover, making it more difficult to recruit new intakes. As nurse 'B' commented:

> 'At university I was taught the importance of using research to assess, plan, implement and evaluate my care plans for wound dressings. However, every time I attempted to introduce these ideas to the ward they would be criticised

and dismissed by the ward sister. One day I walked in to find her tearing my care plans off the board at the end of the patient's bed and then joking about it to the other staff. The frightening thing was many of the staff were also new to that ward yet they had knuckled down to the usual way of doing things with little attempt at making the changes I wanted to bring in. In the end I knew that ward was so set in its ways it would be impossible to make a difference so I left and joined a nurse bank.'[3]

Moreover, the extent to which a peripheral pool of assistants has been generalised to supplement and dilute the skills of the core nursing workforce has been relatively limited. Ackroyd and Bolton (1999) have pointed out that the emphasis remains on training qualified professional grade nursing. Taylorism may also prove self-defeating because management are also pursuing – in part through the rhetoric of 'holistic nursing' – the vertical expansion of nursing into areas of activity previously the preserve of medicine (Taylor and Field, 1993; Allen and Hughes, 2002). Perhaps, however, the ultimate constraint on pursuing Taylorism is what one King's Fund report refers to as, 'the submerged tension' between 'quality of care' considerations and pressures for cost containment (King's Fund, 1990, p 5). When quality of care is the main consideration there is a need to ensure that nursing staff continue to be intrinsically involved with 'patient-centred' care. Indeed, the imperative to 'involve' increases in the context of rising litigation costs and the necessity to 'manage risk' on the ward (Faugier et al, 1997, p 99; Norman, 1997). As a consequence, management cannot apply Taylorist principles at will as they please. They are compelled to operate under contradictory tendencies: on the one hand, to adopt limited forms of Taylorism wherever feasible and, on the other hand, to cede a modicum of autonomous decision making to the nursing profession (Ackroyd and Bolton, 1999).

Do such forms of indirect control of nursing labour power through methods of responsible autonomy therefore represent a managerialist failure of control? Buroway (1979) has suggested that management may often deploy strategies that attempt to harness worker loyalty to the 'cause' by 'manufacturing consent' with respect to the goals and objectives of the organisation. In our case consent is mobilised through the concession of task autonomy all the better to advance overall control of nursing labour power. One way of management achieving this is through a strategy of 'responsible autonomy'. Management cede limited forms of discretion over how to perform detailed tasks to workers in return for their acquiescence to the organisation in its broader context (Thompson and McHugh, 1995). In the particular confines of public sector professionalism, directing professional autonomy towards the overall aims of management has effectively meant turning professionals into managers, encouraging them to view leadership, budgetary governance and meeting accounting targets as the legitimising ideological premise of good professional caring practice.

Central to the latter is the development of 'responsible autonomy', and central to the transformation of professional ethos into management bottom lines has been the deployment of NPM. The shift towards the market and the general inculcation of a *business ethos* within the NHS, as elsewhere in the public sector, has provided the context for the development of NPM to gain a footing across the professional and management function (Ruane, 2000). NPM is highly variable in practice from one public service to the next. In general terms it defines a cultural shift towards 'performance rather than administrative routines based on conformity with rules and regulations', and towards a situation where 'managerial effort on the most efficient use of resources, a commitment to targets and striving to achieve results which can be demonstrated by output measures' becomes consonant with good professional conduct (Wood, 2000, p 138). Bolton (2005) points to evidence of a concerted effort exerted throughout the NHS management hierarchy to encourage nurses to see their role in terms of entrepreneurs and leaders. Specifically, an ideological battle has been waged in an effort to redefine nursing professionalism in terms of 'commercialised professionalism', in which it is hoped that the language of 'empowerment, energy, innovation and autonomy' becomes intuitively attractive to healthcare professionals, underpinning the delivery of a 'quality service to patients'. In this sense, the inculcation of NPM is an ideological brand of managerial 'newspeak', acting 'as a powerful form of normative control and that health professionals will come to identify with and conceive of themselves in terms of management' (Bolton, 2005, p 6).

Yet, as Bolton also argues, the actual level of influence of NPM is highly variable once one gets beyond senior nursing line managers, who also, by and large, adopt an equivocal standpoint to the ideology, feeling uncomfortable in the management role and viewing themselves as nurses first (Bolton, 2005). As Bolton reflects, at the level of nurse line management the overriding feeling is that 'nurses are firmly attached to their image (however over-idealized) as professionals who possess unstinting compassion and self-sacrifice' (Bolton, 2005, p 16). In fact the realities of NPM may be more to do with old-fashioned work intensification, workforce bullying mixed with the traditional emphasis of 'the good nurse' defined not so much as the 'knowledgeable doer' epitomised by the new era of the super matron, but more as the 'busy doer' of old. In the words of one nurse, modern nursing is 'about a lot of people who work too hard for too little reward and are constantly pressured when they get things wrong and too infrequently rewarded when they get things right' (Cooke, 2006, p 239).

As the issue of NPM demonstrates, attempts to control the nursing labour process through *responsible* autonomy are having limited impact. The daily grind between limited forms of Taylorism and responsible autonomy is a frustrating one, as nurse 'C' indicates:

> 'In my previous job on a day ward dealing with patients with highly sensitive issues nurses were expected to stay at the desk doing paperwork, sitting with patients who were often concerned about procedures was actively discouraged.... I suppose doing so was not getting the job done?'[4]

However, as Dent (1998) pointed out, there were two forms of autonomy, *professional* and *responsible*. The latter referred to discretion and role expansion passed on to professionals by the organisation. The possibility then arises that control over nursing may also be exercised through establishing forms of *professional* autonomy that lead to the *self-discipline* of nurses. Notions of control through self-discipline reflect current managerial attempts to manage the emotional labour of nurses (Allan and Smith, 2005). Personal investment in emotional labour by nurses has echoes of Hochschild's classic study of managing emotional labour to exact greater levels of worker commitment and exploitation (Hochschild, 1983). In particular emotional labour engenders 'the management of feeling to create a publicly observable facial and bodily display as exchange value' (Friedman et al, 1999, p 1).

## The labour process, moral management and professional self-regulation

The moral management of professional autonomy by means of professional self-regulation is another way of attempting to harness control through the management of emotional labour in the nursing labour process. The form of moral management in question – self-regulation through professional autonomy – attempts to weaken the emotional solidarity between nurses and patients and inscribe it in a set of managerial prerogatives. In recent decades, professional autonomy within the nursing process has been ever more narrowly defined in terms of the ethical underpinnings for nursing care and an intensified concern with institutionalising procedures relating to professional codes of conduct and the professional scope of competencies. In what follows we offer evidence that the core of nursing ethics associated with care has been under ideological attack in providing a disciplinary framework with the aim of harnessing nursing ethics towards the requirements of tightening controls over the nursing labour process. We also reflect on the inherent limitations of current management control over the nursing labour process as evidenced by nurses themselves, and relate the limited nature of attempts so far to harness control back to the key contradictions inherent in the capitalist state labour process.

The orthodox understanding of professionalism refers to traits such as specialist knowledge and self-regulation based on duties of service to the community. Professionalism is also a form of moral surveillance and a means of managing emotional labour in ways amenable to organisational goals. Professionalism is not something fixed and eternal but open to interpretation. It can be drawn on by nurses to increase their control over the labour process, as well as be deployed by management against nurses as a form of internal surveillance. In the latter case, abstract roles are established that make visible, reconstruct and render nursing practice docile in relation to organisational aims and objectives. As a profession nursing can use professional autonomy to gain labour market power, set tasks for and monitor the performance of other non-professionals in the labour process and use it as leverage for better pay and conditions of work. By the same token professionalism can be deployed as a negative power against nurses, by regulating ways in which nurses 'know' and conduct themselves. Professionalism, in short, can prove itself effective as an alienating form of the moral management of labour.

In this respect, Fournier's study of the accountancy profession (1999) is instructive. Fournier draws our attention to ways in which 'professionalism' is deployed in accountancy as a moral imperative in the management of employment relations. In particular, he describes how professionalism invokes particular meanings of 'autonomous professional practices' as a means through which the governance of 'professional conduct' and accountability is enacted over an accountant's practice (Fournier, 1999, p 280). Here professional competency is a form of self-regulation that serves to colonise the 'emotional spaces' left open when management concede areas of 'responsible autonomy' to professional accountants. In this way, argues Fournier, professionalism is able to exercise control (governance) over professional employees 'at a distance' (Fournier, 1999, p 282). In short, professionalism 'allows for the reconciliation of control and consent' by establishing the 'responsibilisation of autonomy' through mechanisms that emotionalise work, as the basis for 'instil[ling] professional like norms and work ethics, which govern not simply productive behaviour, but employees' subjectivity' (Fournier, 1999, p 293).

To some extent professionalism in nursing (complete with ethical codes of conduct and the various competencies that underpin the experience of 'professionalism') are deployed as part of the panoply of *intellectual technologies of the self*. Such technologies reconstruct individuals as subjects and objects in such a way as to manage nursing labour power 'at a distance'. In the case of nursing, and healthcare more generally, the contemporary focus on ethical practice acts on professional employees as an intellectual technology of self. Take, for example, the mounting number of specialist health-related journals with ethics as the main focus of deliberation, including, *Nursing Ethics, The Journal of Medical Ethics, Bioethics, Philosophy and Health Care* and *The Cambridge Quarterly Journal of Health Care Ethics*. These are supplemented by nursing educator journals with a wider remit than ethics, which express a growing and sustained interest in nursing ethics around issues pertaining to training and professional practice. Examples here include *Nurse Education Today, Nursing Enquiry, Nursing Times* and *The Journal of Continuing Education in Nursing*.

Scott (1998) attributes this concern with nursing ethics to two divergent objectives. On the one hand, the interest in ethics harbours a genuine concern to promote a more reflexive approach to nursing care. An example of this is the concern to 'de-professionalise' notions of care (Fox, 1999), as well as neo-Aristotelian conceptions of care based on locality and virtuous action. Here, care, and so professional autonomy, is bound up with its fundamental status as a use value/personal and social need in emphasising the empathetic emotional aspects central to the development of professional autonomy that empowers nurses in their labour process. On the other hand, however, there is the more dominant interest in constructing and laying emphasis on the kind of ethics that can serve to underpin an extension of management control within the nursing profession. It is this latter kind of ethical discourse that is finding increasing favour in professional nursing bodies such as the United Kingdom Central Council for Nursing, Midwifery and Health Visiting (UKCC), and it has been instrumental in colonising professional autonomy through discourses associated with the wider management agenda in the NHS. In other words, as elsewhere across public sector professionalism, in the NHS professionalism is becoming a form of management control.

In this respect, since 1979 the UKCC (before its re-emergence as the Nursing and Midwifery Council) has made concerted efforts to prescribe a *code of professional conduct* (UKCC, 1992a). Based around a limited number of fixed and determinate *categorical duties*, the prescribed codes and conducts exhort nurses to act, at all times, in such a manner as to:

- safeguard and promote the interests of individual patients and clients;
- serve the interests of society; justify public trust and confidence;
- uphold and enhance the good standing and reputation of the professions;
- and to be personally responsible at all times for one's practice and, in the exercise of one's professional accountability.

The UKCC's *Scope of professional practice* (1992b) also aims to elaborate, extend and inscribe the values of nursing competencies into everyday nursing practice. At one level this challenges what professional nursing bodies perceive as the task-oriented, handmaiden culture of nursing. However, in the particular context of the NHS it also makes plain to nurses the view that it is their ethical duty to 'go beyond contract' by engaging in flexible working practices on the basis of the 'lifelong learning' of competencies (see Chapter Two, this volume). In this sense, the *Scope of professional practice* bypasses collectivism and promotes individualism. It is one of a number of official professional nursing texts that exhort the principles of individual responsibility and self-regulation designed to place moral imperatives on nursing labour to be at all times accountable and responsible for attaining the prescribed codes and competencies and for individualising risks of judgement as to whether, for example, they are sufficiently competent in any given situation. As nurse 'D' put it,

> 'The pressures of responsibility for patient safety are immense, especially if like me you happened to be a bank nurse on a busy ward, where you're expected to get on with it, muck in and, for example, be competent to take responsibility for dispensing drugs to patients.'[5]

While the *Scope of professional practice* encourages nursing labour to over-stretch the boundaries of nursing practice vertically (into areas of medicine, for example) and horizontally (into areas of line management), justifying this as the individual responsibility of nurses, additional imperatives enshrined in the *Codes of professional conduct* (UKCC, 1992a) support and extend the latter by presenting universal guidelines (universal in the sense of duties unrelated to material constraints such as staffing levels) on what is deemed to be ethically sound conduct. Those nurses who meet the guidelines are consonant with good 'self-regulatory practice'; those who fall short of the guidelines are deemed 'un-regulated' offenders whose '(mis)conduct' (read 'unethical practice') becomes punishable on the basis of clearly prescribed rules. As Heywood reflects, '[t]he object is to encourage nurses to take a closer look at their own performance and, perhaps, to learn – *or be warned* – by other's mistakes' (Heywood Jones, 1990, p xi; emphasis added).

There is also a particular relationship between the professionalising impulse and the expressed interest in defining an ethics of care that we need to consider. It should be noted how the self-regulating powers of the UKCC's codes of conduct are predicated on the acceptance of an ethical accountability that has a firm basis in Kantian-informed, deontological approaches to an ethics of duty to care, with the accent firmly on duty. The latter is particularly well suited to the self-regulation of nurses because of its commitment to a set of universally binding abstract principles of duty (Winstanley and Woodall, 2000). These take little account of either the limitations imposed on the NHS by the wider social context or the many institutional constraints nurses experience on the ward. In addition, such an ethics of duty is premised on a conception of society as an aggregation of atomic individuals. This facilitates the potential for individualising responsibility on the job and, therefore, deepening a nurse's sense of individual compliance to the institutional authority of the NHS as well as their own professional bodies. It is this definition of ethics that provides a particularly potent form of professional self-regulation. The extent to which the latter succeeds in controlling nursing labour power is, however, doubtful, in part due to the inherent limits of control.

## Limits of control

We now return to the central question posed by this chapter: how effective is the moral management of nursing labour power, and how far down the nursing hierarchy does its ideological and moral influence stretch? It may seem obvious that the moral management works most completely on senior nursing management rather than the bulk of nurses who are invariably over-worked at the 'ward-face'. Certainly, in our own study of nursing attitudes to professionalism, we found a general vague awareness of UKCC professional guidelines on competencies and duties of practice. Despite the fact that ethics is a principal part of nursing education, no nurse that we interviewed could recall what the specific duties and competencies set by the UKCC were. What was said repeatedly is that ethics is a central concern for nurses. Here, where it seeps most imperceptibly into the culture of practice, it has its most profound effects. Our study, for example, found that, on the one hand, that UKCC notions of abstract and individualised duty to care were detectable in the strong sense of individual responsibility in day-to-day care. The two quotes below from nurses 'E' and 'F' respectively reflect this internalisation of the moral duty to care:

> 'If you didn't pick up on something, you know which you really should have....You really get to know them [the patient] if they are in, for a good few days. I just feel as if you miss something you would feel terrible and you wouldn't be looking for other people to blame, well I certainly wouldn't, if I knew the person and something happened to them and I didn't notice then I would take it really personal.... I wouldn't be saying like, that someone else should have been watching them.' (nurse 'E')

> 'I think you know there comes a certain sense of responsibility because at the end of the day you are looking after their care, you're not looking after their treatment you are looking after their care ... it's just natural, I think it's instinctive and everyone should have that in them. It's not a job you would do for the money.... It's something that you should care deeply about.' (nurse 'F')[6]

However, as the following quote from nurse 'G' also indicates, sentiments of the above kind were no less or more frequent than sentiments indicating clear resistance to and disdain for the kind of abstract and formalised duties expressed in professional guidelines:

> 'I was pulled up...the other day for being *unprofessional* lacking diplomacy and tact and that's coming from by the way, a *good* staff nurse, she's good at her job, but I've watched how she behaved on the ward and she does have this professionalism, you know, she's got very limited amount

> of contact talking with the patients, if she's got a task to do, if she's got to care for them, but it's kept to a minimum, do you know what I mean?'[7]

Ultimately, one must consider the combined effect of all attempts by management to control the nursing labour process. In this respect, it can be said that the limited forms of Taylorism, work flexibility and the exhortations of NPM, along with attempts to instil professional self-surveillance, have had tangible success in increasing the intensification of the use of nursing labour at ward level (Cooke, 2006). The imperative to extract the maximum possible from nursing labour power has been fundamental to the Labour government's policy towards the NHS. As Cooke (2006, p 225) reflects,

> Since the 1980s the NHS has been subject to successive waves of cutbacks and this search for cost savings has continued under New Labour: targets for 2003-2006 include a 2 percent improvement in 'value for money'. Generally this has increased throughput of patients while reducing capacity; NHS inpatient capacity has halved since the 1980s. At the same time acute activity has increased; 'finished consultant episodes' rising by 38 percent between 1990 and 1998. The effect on nurses of faster throughput combined with higher rates of bed occupancy has been heavier workloads as nurses care for larger numbers of more dependent patients.

Moreover, other indications of work intensification, and so the partial success of management strategies, are also suggested by the fact that '55% of all staff worked unpaid additional hours, while 43% of all staff worked between one and five additional unpaid hours per week, 9% worked between six and 10 additional unpaid hours, and 3% said they worked more than 10 hours unpaid overtime in an average week' (UNISON, 2006b, p 2).

Having said this, attempts to harness control over the nursing labour process through the moral exhortations of professional duties of care can only go so far before such ideological pretensions are weakened considerably by the material limits and contradictions facing the NHS, not least the haphazard shift towards the market under the stewardship of Labour government health policy. The relatively high rate of employees leaving nursing suggests that the moral pressures surrounding professional imperatives such as the duty to care are indeed powerful, but unattainable given the current state of the NHS, leading in many cases to nurses giving up their careers. Morals are governed by the material boundaries within which they are established. A survey conducted by UNISON revealed that a majority of nurses were experiencing staff shortages, over-work, poor pay, being under-valued and falling quality of work, leading as many as eight out of ten nurses to consider leaving nursing altogether (BBC, 2000). Not surprisingly, given the above, the NHS has been plagued by high rates of nursing 'wastage' (number of nurses leaving nursing altogether). Moreover, a recent Royal College of Nursing (RCN) survey of the nursing labour market reported a high percentage of nursing 'wastage', with approximately just under one in every ten registered nurses leaving the NHS in England year-on-year since 2001 (RCN, 2005, p 23). One consequence is an ageing workforce unable to attract younger workers to nursing (only 7.5% of midwives are under 30 years old, 60% of nurses are over 40 and one out of four nurses are over 50: UNISON, 2006b, p 3), and compelled to draw on a reserve army of nursing through bank nursing and the importation of nurses from abroad (see Chapter Two, this volume). Forty per cent of UK recruitment of nurses comes from overseas, while in England there has been a 61% increase in the use of bank nursing since 1997 (RCN, 2005, p 18). 'Without the doubling of the rate of overseas recruitment the NHS would have barely maintained the numbers of nurses it employs despite the expansion of nurse training places and better recruitment and retention' (UNISON, 2006b, p 6). In such a climate moral exhortations towards a duty to care quickly become transformed into management by stress or a growing sense of estrangement by nurses.

Furthermore, the apparent systematic nature of the increase in management bullying of nursing staff is suggestive of a NPM function that is losing the battle to control the nursing labour process. In this respect, the most recent NHS staff survey conducted by the Health Commission (2006, p 3) found that 16% and 15% of staff surveyed in 2004 and 2005 respectively reported being bullied by 'colleagues'. Another report by the RCN puts the rate of bullying higher at 23% and as high as 45% for some minority ethnic groups, indicating that racism is also a feature of the bullying culture of the NHS. The RCN reports in particular that nursing colleagues are the source of bullying/harassment in nearly a third (30%) of cases with management often perceived as the main source. 'Senior managers are the problem in one in five cases (21%), and the immediate supervisor/manager is the source for one in four (24%) respondents' (RCN, 2005, p 48).

## Conclusions

What the above account demonstrates is that Taylorism, NPM and professional self-regulation have failed to fully control nursing labour, either separately or collectively. One other measure of this failure is the discrepancy between the recent amount of money poured into the NHS and the actual increase in measurable effort or outcomes (Appleby and Harrison, 2006). From the vantage point of Labour government health policy and the imperative of NHS management to control healthcare labour power, the attachment to care without due recognition of audits, targets and economic measurements as authentic constituents of professional practice, pose serious limits to management's ability to wrest control of the nursing labour process. Such limits force one to consider the central contradiction at the heart of the nursing labour process: whether nursing should be defined in terms of care and need or redefined in terms of value for money and profitability. This of course refers to the central contradiction of labour processes such as nursing that are in transition between the state and the market.

We began this chapter by situating the NHS and the nursing labour process within the wider NHS transition towards the market. We also noted the very welcome recent re-emphasis on the labour process as a means of grasping the underlying dynamics and contradictions of this transition. However, it is also the case that the re-emphasis on the labour process is without due reference to the antagonisms of the specifically capitalist nature of the labour process that underpin the shift towards the market. Once we begin to broaden the context to include the contradictions and antagonisms thrown up by the capitalist labour process, we also begin to shed more light on both the apparent incapacity of NHS management to control nursing labour power and the deeply ingrained nature of nursing resistance to the attentions of management. We therefore conclude this chapter with a discussion of the main contours of these contradictions and antagonisms.

The inherent limits to management control over nursing labour remind us that the NHS labour process is one in which the objective basis of commodity fetishism is at best weak and at worst non-existent as a means of internal control over labour. In the capitalist labour process workers produce both use values and value; and the 'labour' one speaks of is both at the same time concrete and abstract (Marx, 1954). We forget this distinction at the cost of losing the central dynamic of the labour process and thus an understanding of why 'labour' is ultimately beyond the control of management. Abstract labour, the substance of value, is the primary aim of the capitalist labour process and takes precedence over labour to produce use values. The primary aim of capitalist production is the profitable expansion of capital and it is this that value, not use value, is the repository for. The emphasis on value creation is the basis of capital's domination over labour power within the capitalist labour process. This is because the overarching emphasis on value and profitability is of prime importance both to capitalist profitability and for the workers' continued livelihood, consumption patterns and career prospects. That value, not use value, is the arbiter of production, provides the basis for, if not acceptance of, the disciplinary effects on labour power of a reserve army of labour. Marx refers to the latter as the *relation of commodity fetishism*, which is the systemic form of control over labour inherent to the capitalist labour process (Marx, 1954). Commodity fetishism exerts a powerful force over how we view capitalist production and the quest for value over use value as natural and inevitable within society. Commodity fetishism tends to restrict conflict within boundaries for higher wages and better conditions and perhaps to ensure the quality of services one produces. However, one is far less likely to resist value production or the profit motive itself. In relations of commodity fetishism, the capitalist labour process has its own inbuilt control over the labour process, with management strategies offering ways of *endorsing, supplementing* or *adjusting* this essential form of control, wherever it is breached or is weakest, and in accordance with any particular organisation's location within a market and the balance of class forces internal and external to the organisation in question.

However, the same degree of objective control is not established in state public sector organisations and in our case the nursing labour process. One can speak of state or public sector labour processes that are not *directly* regulated by commodity fetishism. As a consequence management control strategies are both more necessary (because they must impose control over services as use values, and therefore the politics of need), but are, for the same reasons, that much more complex and difficult to impose over the labour of state sector professionals (Carter, 1997). State labour processes, despite imperatives towards 'cost-efficiency', 'economic accountability' and 'value for money', are still defined in terms of service provision as use values and/or direct personal/social needs and not the expansion of value (Carter, 1997). The nursing labour process is left in a situation where value production, and so the inner control mechanisms of commodity fetishism, remain absent or at least marginal as systemic forms of control over nursing labour power. It is a situation that makes managerial controls all the more necessary yet all the more precarious and fallible. As we have seen with respect to the failure of Taylorism, NPM and professional self-regulation as means of effecting control over nursing, although necessary, are never sufficient to deal with the limits inherent to the nursing labour process.

This failure comes out in a number of ways. The inability to retain staff coupled with an increasing concern with growing levels of absenteeism and sickness (*Nursing Times*, 2006, p 16) are classic instances of individualised forms of industrial conflict that display something much more fundamental. As isolated individual acts taken by individuals they have a complex causality. However, taken overall they are more systemic in nature; they are indicative of the relative powerlessness of *both* management and nurses to exert control over the labour process in any decisive fashion. This relative powerlessness creates the situation we witness today in the NHS, where the resources pumped in become absorbed less productively by the system (see Chapter Two, this volume). However, the stasis facing the NHS also expresses the broader contradictions of the NHS and the position the organisation now finds itself in as it lingers unstably between the public and private sector, the state and the market, between services expressed as use values and needs and services defined more narrowly as 'products' of economic value. It reflects an NHS where neither democratic accountability nor the law of the marketplace govern. In this respect, nurses and all healthcare workers are involved in a struggle on two fronts: against the controls inherent to the market and against the controls imposed on it by the state through the various mechanisms of managerial governance discussed in this chapter. As things stand, with the NHS in transition between market and state, nursing labour will continue to be defined by failures of control in the context of ongoing attempts to impose hybrid forms of market and state controls. And the controls currently manifested as various targets, indicators and efficiency measures and audit cycles, conjoined by Taylorism and the moral discourses of NPM and professionalism, will continue to meet formal and informal resistance from nurses and healthcare workers in general (see Chapter Four, this volume).

The past teaches us that public ownership may save healthcare from becoming just another marketable commodity, made to profitable order and based on ability to pay. However, the past also teaches us that public ownership is a sop: it does little to facilitate meaningful control over the course, direction and nature of healthcare and of how it should be practised. The past also reveals that not only did public ownership of healthcare arise on the basis of the gross inequalities in health generated and sustained by the market, but also that the market could not provide healthcare *for all* as a profitable enterprise. Prior to the NHS the market could not be trusted to reproduce labour power for capital and there is no evidence it can do so today. In this context, the New Labour government are happy to endorse decentralisation and partnership as a method of containing a problem rather than advancing a solution; and only this so long as power and money remain centralised within the state. Perhaps a much more realistic 'Third Way' would be that time when the powers of democratic control and accountability lay firmly in the hands of health carers and the people they care for.

## Notes

[1] Since 2000 the authors have conducted a series of focus groups and then interviews with nurses, which have been concerned to document experiences of professionalisation and labour process change.

[2] Nurse 'A' was a registered general nurse working in a general medical ward in Glasgow who was interviewed by one of the authors (a nurse) in December 2001.

[3] Nurse 'B' was a newly qualified registered general nurse working in a 'care of the elderly' unit in Glasgow who was interviewed by one of the authors in January 2004.

[4] Nurse 'C' worked as a bank nurse on a day ward unit at an infirmary in central Scotland and was interviewed by one of the authors in May 2006.

[5] Nurse 'D' worked as a bank nurse in a general ward unit at an infirmary in central Scotland and was interviewed by one of the authors in January 2006.

[6] Nurses 'E' and 'F' were nursing diploma students who spoke to the authors during a larger focus group discussion with nursing diploma students in Glasgow during August 2000.

[7] Nurse 'G' was a nursing diploma student who took part in the August 2000 focus group discussion.

## Further sources

Allen, D. and Hughes, D. (2002) *Nursing and the division of labour in healthcare*, Basingstoke: Palgrave Macmillan. This book offers sociologically informed insights into the contemporary division of nursing labour and the implications this has for the profession's orientation to healthcare.

Pollock, A. (2004) *NHS Plc: The privatisation of our health care*, London: Verso. This book offers a timely and trenchant critique of Labour government policy and the negative implications that transferring the NHS towards the market has for healthcare.

Thompson, P. and McHugh, D. (1995) *Work organisation. A critical introduction* (2nd edn), Basingstoke: Macmillan Educational. Unfortunately there are no textbooks related specifically to nursing and labour process theory; however, this book provides an excellent introduction to labour process theory and debates, which can be usefully applied to healthcare labour processes.

www.healthmatters.org.uk/issue50/withoutcommandments – *healthmatters,* an independent quarterly magazine covering current issues in healthcare and public health policy.

www.unison.org.uk/healthcare/index.asp – UNISON is the major union representing healthcare workers and provides a wealth of information about current changes to the NHS and how these affect workers and patients.

www.rcn.org.uk/ – The Royal College of Nursing represents the professional interests of nurses.

## References

Ackroyd, S. and Bolton, S. (1999) 'It's not Taylorism: mechanisms of work intensification in the provision of gynaecological services in an NHS hospital', *Work, Employment and Society*, vol 13, no 2, June, pp 367-85.

Allan, T.H. and Smith, P. (2005) 'The introduction of modern matrons and the relevance of emotional labour to understanding their roles: developing personal authority in clinical leadership', *International Journal of Work Organisation and Emotions*, vol 1, no 1, pp 20-34.

Allen, D. and Hughes, D. (2002) *Nursing and the division of labour in healthcare*, Basingstoke: Palgrave Macmillan.

Appleby, J. and Harrison, A. (2006) *Spending in the NHS. How much is enough?*, London: King's Fund.

BBC (2000) *Most NHS nurses 'consider quitting'*, 4 October (http://news.bbc.co.uk/1/hi/health/956001.stm, 3/07/06).

Bolton, S. (2005) 'Making up managers: the case of the NHS nurses', *Work, Employment and Society*, vol 19, no 1, pp 5-23.

Braverman, H. (1974) *Labor and monopoly capitalism: The degradation of work in the twentieth century*, London: Monthly Review Press.

Buroway, M. (1979) *Manufacturing consent: Changes in the labour process under monopoly capitalism*, Chicago, IL: University of Chicago Press.

Carter, B. (1997) 'Restructuring state employment: labour and non-labour in the capitalist state', *Capital and Class*, Autumn, vol 63, pp 65-84.

Cooke, H. (2006) 'Seagull management and the control of nursing labour power', *Work, Employment and Society*, vol 20, no 2, pp 220-47.

Dent, M. (1998) 'Hospitals and new ways of organising medical work in Europe: standardisation of medicine in the public sector and the future of medical autonomy', in P. Thompson and C. Warhurst (eds) *Workplaces of the future: Critical perspectives on work and organisations*, London: Macmillan.

DH (Department of Health) (2005) 'Doctors and nurses on the up', Press release (www.dh.gov.uk/PublicationsAndStatistics/ PressReleases/ID_4106795).

Donaldson, C. and Gerard, K. (2005) *Economics of health care financing*, Basingstoke: Palgrave.

Faugier, J., Ashworth, G., Lancaster, J. and Ward, D. (1997) 'An exploration of clinical risk from a nursing perspective', *Nursing Times Research*, vol 2, no 2, pp 97-107.

Ferguson, I., Lavalette, M. and Mooney, G. (2002) *Rethinking welfare: A critical perspective*, London: Sage Publications.

Fournier, V. (1999) 'The appeal to professionalism as a disciplinary mechanism', *Sociological Review*, vol 47, no 2, May, pp 280-307.

Fox, N. (1999) 'Beyond health: post modernism and embodiment', London: Free Association Books.

Friedman, A., Lindgren, A. and Sederblad, P. (1999) 'Post-Fordist regulation in the service sector: emotional labour in Sweden and England', 17th Annual International Labour Process Conference, 29-31 March.

Griffith Report (1983) *NHS management inquiry*, London: HMSO.

Grimshaw, D. (1999) 'Changes in skills-mix and pay determination among the nursing workforce in the UK', *Work, Employment & Society*, vol 3, no 2, pp 295-328.

Harrison, S. and Pollit, C. (1994) *Controlling health professionals*, Buckingham: Open University Press.

Health Commission (2006) *National survey of NHS staff, 2005 summary of key findings*, London: Commission for Healthcare Audit and Inspection.

Heywood Jones, I. (1990) *The nurses code: A practical approach to the code of professional conduct of nurses, midwives and health visitors*, Basingstoke: Macmillan.

Hochschild, A.R. (1983) *The managed heart: Commercialisation of human feeling*, Berkeley, CA: University of California Press.

King's Fund (1990) *Prospects for nursing in the 1990s*, London: King's Fund.

Klein, R. (2001) *The new politics of the NHS* (4th edn), Essex: Prentice Hall.

Lloyd, C. and Seifert, R. (1995) 'Restructuring in the NHS: the impact of the 1990 reforms on the management of labour', *Work, Employment & Society*, vol 9, no 2, June, pp 359-78.

Marx, K. (1954) *Capital, Volume One*, London: Lawrence and Wishart.

NHS Scotland (2005) *Delivering for health* (www.scotland.gov.uk/ Publications/2005/11/02102635/26382, 07/2006).

Norman, S. (1997) 'Minimising risk while maintaining standards', *Nursing Times Research*, vol 2, no 2, pp 86-7.

*Nursing Times* (2006) 'Avoiding long term sickness', *Nursing Times*, vol 102, no 27, 4-10 July, p 16.

Pollock, A. (1997) 'What happens when the private sector plans hospital services for the NHS?: 3 case studies under PFI', *British Medical Journal*, no 314, pp 1266-71.

Pollock, A. (2004) *NHS Plc: The privatisation of our health care*, London: Verso.

Poole, L. (2000) 'Health care: New Labour's NHS', in J. Clarke, S. Gewirtz and E. McLaughlin (eds) *New managerialism, new welfare?*, London: Sage Publications, pp 102-22.

Ranade, W. (1997) *A future for the NHS? Health care in the millennium* (2nd edn), London: Longman.

RCN (Royal College of Nursing) (2005) *At breaking point? A survey of the wellbeing and working lives of nurses in 2005*, Hove: Employment Research Limited.

Ruane, S. (2000) 'Acquiescence and Opposition: the private finance initiative and the National Health Service', *Policy & Politics*, vol 22, no 3, July, pp 411-24.

Scambler, G. (ed) (1991) *Sociology as applied to medicine* (3rd edn), London, Bailliere Tindall.

Scott, P.A. (1998) 'Professional ethics: are we on the wrong track?', *Nursing Ethics*, vol 5, no 6, pp 477-85.

Seifert, R. (1992) *Industrial relations in the NHS*, London: Chapman Hall.

Taylor, S. and Field, D. (1993) *Sociology of health and health care*, Abingdon: Blackwell.

*The Scotsman* (2005) Reader response to 'Public "frozen out" of NHS policy-making' (http://news.scotsman.com/topics.cfm?tid=57&id= 1611232006, 11/2006).

Thompson, P. (1989) *The nature of work: An introduction to debates on the labour process* (2nd edn), London: Macmillan.

Thompson, P. and McHugh, D. (1995) *Work organisation: A critical introduction* (2nd edn), Basingstoke: Macmillan Educational.

UKCC (United Kingdom Central Council) (1992a) *Codes of professional conduct*, London: UKCC.

UKCC (1992b) *Scope of professional practice*, London: UKCC.

UNISON (2006a) *Private finance illusion: A briefing on the private finance initiative* (www.unison-scotland.org.uk/briefings/pfijuly06.pdf, 11/2006).

UNISON (2006b) *UNISON response to the Health Select Committee inquiry: Workforce needs and planning for the health service – March 2006* (www.unison.org.uk/acrobat/B2493.pdf, 07/2006).

Winstanley, D. and Woodall, J. (eds) (2000) *Ethical issues in contemporary human resource management*, London: Macmillan.

Wood, R. (2000) 'Social housing: managing multiple pressures', in J. Clarke, S. Gewirtz and E. McLaughlin (eds) *New managerialism, new welfare*, London: Sage Publications.

# SIX

# 'I didn't come into teaching for this!': the impact of the market on teacher professionalism

*Henry Maitles*

## Introduction

New Labour started in 1997 full of hope with the positive slogan of 'Education, Education, Education' as its mantra. And, indeed, in terms of policy papers, Acts and statements, there has been much activity; for example, in the legislative field there have been eight major education Acts in England and another going through Parliament as I write (2007). In general, these policies have impacted on education in ways that have both highlighted the failings in the whole educational philosophy of New Labour and the strength and depth of feeling that people have towards local schools and the comprehensive education system in general. This chapter examines how various initiatives – the continued introduction of the market in education and the related issue of academies, exam-orientated pressures, work intensification and growing inequality – are impacting on teachers' work and workload. While the impact of neoliberalism and the market is pervasive throughout the UK, where there are differences in approach, either through devolved government policy or teacher opposition in the different countries of the UK, these are highlighted. The chapter also examines teachers who oppose these trends, both individually in the classroom and collectively through campaigns and industrial action.

## 'Market, Market, Market'

In common with other areas of policy, the New Labour governments have pushed forward with their neoliberal agenda in education, sold as the 'Third Way'. Of all the market reforms enthusiastically introduced by the Conservative governments and taken on board by New Labour, testing and league tables were to be the most divisive. The 1988 Education Reform Act introduced compulsory testing at ages

7, 11, 14 and 16. Because of the obvious and increasing stress levels on children (Davies and Brember, 1999; Birkett, 2001), teachers (who took concerted industrial action over this) and many parents (who organised widespread lobbying and support for teachers) opposed this kind of testing both in Scotland and England/Wales, but piecemeal introduction was achieved. It is noticeable, although not taken on board by policy makers, that major surveys over many years of pupil opinion identify exams and testing as being part of the problem of 'bad' schooling (Blishen, 1967; Burke and Grosvenor, 2003).

Linked to the testing were league tables, introduced in 1993 as an 'aid' to parental choice. For most families, of course, it is no such thing; the higher ranked schools are usually private, specialist, grammar or comprehensives (usually oversubscribed) in middle-class areas. Some commentators go as far as to maintain that this is a new form of segregation, as 'race', ethnicity and class become ever more the factors in determining the school one attends (Gewirtz et al, 1995; Whitty et al, 1998; Gale and Densmore, 2003). Besides, the league tables are themselves so flawed that even New Labour use them with some trepidation and their use was discontinued in Wales and Scotland from 2003. The nature of raw data tables can hide much more than they show[1], particularly if the evidence of the links between social inequality and educational attainment is valid. Quite simply, the effort by government to measure a person's ability by exam performance is quite meaningless. As suggested above, getting good 'A' levels, GCSEs or 'Highers'[2] is generally less a sign of outstanding excellence and achievement and more the good luck of being born to parents who are relatively well off. This whole trend is further exacerbated by international league tables, such as TIMSS (Trends in International Mathematics and Science Study) and PISA (Programme for International Student Assessment), which have sent educational managers all over the world into a panic; the language is constantly one of worry about competitiveness and being left behind.

Yet, the unfortunate consequence is that money follows the 'successful' schools in the league tables as parents are keen to get their children, where feasible, into these schools. This leads to the development of over-subscribed schools close to 'sink' schools. This was worsened by New Labour plans to introduce performance-related pay that has the potential to pit teacher against teacher, as well as school against school. As New Labour sets this agenda, the Conservatives see a green light to press ahead with even more extreme policies. At the 2005 and 2006 Conservative conference, they recycled their educational voucher scheme, now called a passport, which will exacerbate and weaken cooperation between schools as they are forced to compete for these vouchers. Not only is it a boost to the private sector as parents will be able to 'spend' their vouchers in the independent schools, but a transfer of resources (effectively a bribe) towards those middle-class parents who switched allegiance to New Labour from 1997. Paradoxically, it is a return to policies outlined by the Conservative extreme Right fringe in the 1970s (Boyson, 1975), now given credence by New Labour.

And there is another twist. Effective teaching and the government's own citizenship strategy suggests that school students should have the wherewithal to discuss, analyse and become involved in activity around issues. In school, when asked, pupils talk about active learning strategies as being the way they like to learn and that in this way they learn best (Save the Children, 2001; Burke and Grosvenor, 2003; Rudduck and Flutter, 2004; Maitles and Gilchrist, 2006). This is not something new. John Dewey argued some 90 years ago that 'give the pupils something to do, not something to learn; and the doing is of such a nature as to demand thinking; learning naturally results' (Dewey, 1915). The children interviewed in the sources above claimed that they enjoyed learning most when they were learning by doing; this could be practical or creative activities, talking and learning activities, school trips, speakers and contacting pupils in other countries through the internet. For example, an S2 pupil (the equivalent of Key Stage 3, usually about 12/13 years of age) cut right through the obsession with worksheets so common in schools and explained in his own way the need for deeper learning, by saying that 'Less writing and more talking would be better. Teachers just say "get on with this worksheet" or "read through this worksheet" – but see if you had more discussion – everyone gets all the points – you'd understand it more if you went over it' (Save the Children, 2001). The word used most often to describe good lessons was 'fun'. Similarly, in her study of Swedish 11-year-olds, Alerby (2003) found that the word 'fun' was used to describe positive experiences. However, the concentration on league standings leads to exactly the opposite kind of learning. Out goes deep learning and in comes shallow rote learning as this regurgitation in exams is the key measurement of a 'good' school. Indeed, it reaches the level of farce when Ofsted on their website, after years of urging teachers to get more pupils through exams, are now complaining that teachers are 'teaching to the test'. Of course they are; Ofsted has demanded it for years. It reached its nadir in July 2006, as a teacher was struck off the General Teaching Council (GTC) in England for 'cheating' by submitting aspects of his own work as evidence of pupil work; his excuse was that he wanted his pupils to achieve better exam results and he felt under pressure to deliver this (TES, 2006). The Qualifications and Curriculum Authority (QCA) has announced, in response to supposed cheating in course work, that the whole range of activities under the heading of course work will no longer count. It will exacerbate for many teachers the rote learning nature of exams and will discriminate against pupils from poor backgrounds, who often find exams particularly difficult.

This is not to say that there are no differences between schools in similar areas; often schools in similar areas can have moderately different results. The differences between schools in similar areas are minute yet pondered over, whereas the real difference is not between schools in similar areas but between schools in affluent areas and those in areas of poverty. Nonetheless, research in the 1980s (Mortimore et al, 1988) outlined a number of reasons why some schools did better than others in similar areas. Mortimer et al assumed that social class accounted for more than 90% of achievement and outlined a number of factors that explained the other 10%: first, a collaborative way of working between staff (including senior staff) and pupils; second, a commitment to equality of opportunity; and third, first-class teachers who turned down the chance of an 'easier' life in an 'easier' school because they were politically committed to improving the chances of working–class children. Most of this research was deliberately ignored and 'effective' schools were said to be those that had a hierarchy among staff, greater discipline, streaming and selection. Indeed, as Gale and Densmore (2003) point out, the hierarchical and market-orientated approach leads to disaffection, deskilling and alienation by staff, leading to attitudes that amount to 'I don't want to know about the politics, just tell me what to do'. In a damning critique of the school effectiveness research and school improvement industries, Slee et al (1998, p 5) maintain that:

> ... while purporting to be inclusive and comprehensive, school effectiveness research is riddled with errors: it is excluding (of children with special needs, black boys, so called clever girls), it is normative and regulatory ... it is bureaucratic and disempowering. It focuses exclusively on the processes and internal constraints of schooling, apparently disconnected from education's social end – adulthood.

Unfortunately, it is on this school effectiveness anvil that our educational policy is now being forged. And, there are further unfortunate effects of this culture of league tables, target setting and school effectiveness. Research from Nick Davies (2001) and Gillborn and Youdell (2000) suggests that, although unconsciously in many cases, educational rationing is in use in schools. The agenda set out by the league tables leads to Gillborn and Youdell describing a 'triage' system operating in schools. Triage is a system used in hospital casualty departments to prioritise those patients who need urgent or immediate attention, as opposed to those whose case is not urgent or, indeed, those who are beyond meaningful help. In schools, it can lead to a situation of concentrating on those under-achievers at the margin of the 'good' grades, with whom some effort could lead to improved grades. The other groups, the 'safe' and those 'without hope' can be left with little attention – effectively their education is being rationed as schools become desperate to get pupils into the 'good' grades.

The concentration on exam targets also affects virtually any attempt to develop better rounded people. Thus, initiatives (however limited), such as education for citizenship, are always couched in terms of their impact on school targets and, indeed, often arguments are heard that these initiatives are a waste of time as they do not help the school, or the teachers, make their targets. Gillborn and Youdell (2000, p 199) comment that '... our case study schools have responded by interrogating virtually every aspect of school life for the possible contribution to the all consuming need to improve the proportion of pupils reaching the benchmark level of five or more higher grade passes'. One observer (Seddon, 2004, p 24) nicely summed it up: 'contemporary education policy, practice and politics has become primarily framed within a dominant economic discourse which marginalizes and obscures the political purposes of education necessary to the formation and sustainability of a democratic citizenry'. There is thus a distinct effect on schools and teachers; rather than embedding the citizenship agenda, it is in many cases marginalised – the boxes are ticked – but the experiences for the pupils are often tokenistic (Maitles, 2005). The dominant neoliberal policy effectively obscures the other stated functions of education.

The major overall impact of these kinds of policies has been to further the hierarchical structures in schools. To ensure the success of these policies, there has been an increased importance given to headteachers and senior management teams (SMTs); an average 1,000-pupil secondary school will have an SMT of about six and a strong pyramid structure. Most teachers feel that they have limited involvement in any aspect of decision making and even the (relatively) well-paid SMT is seen as being in place to implement decisions rather than being involved in policy. For the teachers in the schools, this process has had a pervasive impact on aspects of professionalism. As everything is geared to the assessment agenda, teachers themselves are under pressure to deliver exam results. For many, the best way to do this is to slavishly follow the syllabus, and not to allow anything to divert from this. As one exasperated head of department put it at an HMI (Her Majesty's Inspectorate, Scotland) conference, '... give us the tests and we'll ensure that the pupils pass!'. The experience has perhaps three aspects to it. First, teachers are encouraged to be isolated from each other, at least in terms of decision making; second, as Gale and Densmore (2003) pointed out, the concentration on outcome rather than process leads to a closing down of debate; and third (and as a consequence of the first two points), there is a reduction in the kind of meaningful work, which is replaced by a mechanical fake professionalism of implementation of decisions taken elsewhere and grudgingly implemented with a 'we don't like it and are only obeying orders' mentality. Harvie (2006) analysed this in terms of the alienation that it engendered; indeed, he argued that this 'alienated labour in the classroom' led to worsening relationships between teacher and student. While it is not necessary to agree with every aspect of his views on teachers as 'productive labourers', this is an important insight into the central area of concern over 'discipline' (or rather 'indiscipline') in the classroom. It enables us to move beyond the moral panic view of out-of-control youth and to examine classroom behaviour in terms of alienated labour and relationships, and thus begin to understand it.

Linked to this has been an attack (or at very least a re-assessment) on professionalism. Michael Barber, former Head of the No 10 Delivery Unit, developed his models of teacher professionalism; according to him teachers were at 'uninformed professionalism' in the 1970s, at 'uninformed prescription' in the 1980s, at 'informed prescription' in the 1990s, and now (thanks to New Labour) at 'informed professionalism'. Many teachers (Dainton, 2005) and educational commentators (as we discuss below) would challenge this simple interpretation. Indeed, Gale and Densmore argued that the New Labour policies have led to a situation where teachers feel isolated, professionalism is delineated as doing an efficient job irrespective of what it is, debate is consequently closed down and meaningful work is reduced. Webb et al (2004, p 185) described it thus: 'The negative aspect of curriculum reform in England that was cited most frequently as having adversely affected primary teachers' professionalism was the loss of opportunities to be creative, to design programmes of work and so generate ideas to motivate and interest children'.

What makes this important is that surveys suggest that one third of all teachers are considering leaving the profession over the next five years; the reasons given by the teachers are workload, initiative overload and the target-driven culture (Gillard, 2005). The study by Webb et al (2004) found that the crucial factors discouraging teachers from remaining in teaching were work intensification, low pay, deteriorating pupil behaviour and a decline in public respect. Positive influences on teacher retention were commitment to children, professional freedom and supportive colleagues. They found in England that 'all the English teachers were in agreement that what was needed to make teaching a more attractive profession was not additional income but a cut in workload' (p 186). This intensification of work has certain characteristics and impacts directly onto professionalism and scholarship (see Apple, 1986; Hall, 2004; Ballet et al, 2006). These are described as:

- Less 'down time' during the working day, resulting in less time to keep up with developments in subject areas and less time to reflect on and refine teaching skills.
- A chronic and persistent sense of work overload.
- Negative effects on the quality of results as only that which is essential and immediately accomplishable is done and isolation from colleagues increases as there is no time for feedback, collaboration or sharing of ideas.
- Diversification of expertise makes teachers become more dependent on external specialists, creating doubts about one's own competence.

Smyth et al summarised the six types of control over teachers (2000, pp 39-46), which have a devastating impact on professionalism:

- *Regulated market control:* metaphors of the market and consumer demand are imposed on schools; success and profits go to those who best meet consumer demand. Teachers' work is evaluated in terms of measured outputs set against cost. Competition is the key element in relations between schools (Hatcher, 1994).
- *Technical control:* this is embodied in structures rather than people – in, for example, notionally 'teacher-proof' teaching materials and textbooks, and in specified competences (Apple, 1986, 1996).
- *Bureaucratic control:* hierarchical power is embedded in the social and organisational structure of institutions – jobs are differently divided and defined, have different salaries, and supervision, evaluation and promotion arrangements. The potential for establishing a career operates as a control mechanism.

- *Corporate control:* the focus of the institution is on economic rather than social good. A competitive ethos prevails. Managers focus on economic goals. The headteacher is perceived more as a line manager than as a first among professional equals.
- *Ideological control:* hegemonic beliefs – for example, that a good teacher has certain characteristics – become part of the dominant ideology within schools. These ideas and beliefs are reinforced in pre-service and in-service training. Certain conceptions of teachers' work become naturalised – for example, a move away from child-centred to market-based discourse.
- *Disciplinary power:* minor procedures and routines are specified (times, dress, expected responses) in ways that become anonymous and functional within a school; teachers and others within the school regulate their own behaviours to meet these expectations. Smyth described this as a 'triumph of technique over questions of purpose' (Smyth et al, 2000, p 46).

The degree of control exerted over teachers' work, and the mechanisms of imposing that control vary at different times and in different political and economic circumstances. Sometimes control is overt, sometimes consensual, but the effects of this control over teachers' work are shown in terms of notions of intensification, deskilling and proletarianisation. The intensification of their work – expressed most commonly in the lament that 'there's no time for this any more' – leaves teachers feeling harassed, stressed and demoralised. Work eats into leisure time, undermines opportunities for sociability and contributes to a sense of isolation. Teachers lack time for keeping up with developments in their field of knowledge; this can lead to a form of intellectual deskilling, lower morale and confidence about work and a greater reliance on pre-packaged curriculum materials. Partly to deal with the increasing stress levels, the inclusion of pupils with special educational needs into the mainstream and as a cheaper option, New Labour turned to teaching assistants in the classroom (particularly following the workload agreement in England and Wales and the McCrone settlement in Scotland). In theory, the 'best' teachers were to see themselves as hospital consultants, overseeing the work of junior colleagues and classroom assistants, in this analogy, as nurses (Morris, 2001). Research into their role has been limited, although there is some evidence (Hancock and Collins, 2005; Bach et al, 2006) that classroom teachers welcome and value the teaching assistant role, there is increasing concern from the teaching unions about teaching assistants being a substitute rather than additional support.

Of course, this is not just a British phenomenon. There is widespread agreement among educational commentators about current trends in teachers' work in developed countries (for example, Apple, 1986, 1996; Smyth et al, 2000; Troman, 2000; Hall, 2004). These international trends can be summarised as:

- teachers' diminishing power to determine the curriculum they teach and how they teach it;
- a new emphasis on teachers' managerial and administrative role with pupils and with other adults working in school;
- changing pay structures, and a dismantling of union-won agreements;
- changing conditions of service and new regulatory controls over competence and behaviour.

The overall policy has been called 'new managerialism' or 'corporate managerialism' (Clarke et al, 1994; Deem et al, 1995). Blackmore (2001) and Moller (2004), for example, argued that this led in schools to an ever-increasing regulation of performance at the expense of genuine school improvement. It is a focus on outcomes rather than process and this slots in nicely with an assessment-driven, league table system. These management techniques have imported the language of business – consumer choice, corporate culture, customer demand – and impacted on the collectivist culture in schools (Whitty et al, 1998; Danaher et al, 2000). It has been well argued (Jamieson and Wikeley, 2001; Gale and Densmore, 2003; Wrigley, 2006), following path-breaking work earlier in the 20th century from Baran and Sweezey (1966) and Braverman (1974), that these models of management come from the world of mass production in the car industry and are dangerous to educational environments. Sachs (2001) and Apple (2000) argued that the model dominated at the expense of a 'democratic professionalism', which included collaboration, consultation and a participatory ethos. There is a pervasive nature to this corporate managerialism; as in the very nature of competitive, capitalist managerialism, the model makes it difficult for opponents as 'once a group of school leaders begins to operate upon market principles in their locality, it becomes difficult for other adjacent schools to opt out of competitive marketing relationships' (Grace, 1995, p 212). As Gale and Densmore (2003, p 27) put it, 'social, economic and political problems are converted into technical ones, with technical solutions'. The nature of the competition forces those who do not wish to compete either out of business or to adopt the very work practices of the most aggressive. The Conservatives called it 'there is no alternative'; New Labour repackaged it as 'the only show in town'. Interestingly, Gray (2006) identified the move away from four-year BEd (Bachelor of Education) degrees to one-year PGDE (Professional Graduate Diploma in Education) qualifications as central to this, as it suggested a move from education to training.

Lest we become too depressed with the pervasive impact of the corporate culture and new managerialism, as workers have constantly fought back against the ravages of the assembly line and industrial capitalism, so many education workers are now trying to develop alternatives that are collectivist, consultative, collaborationist and democratic. They have been pitted against the new managers who are either forced to or want to measure everything through the raw data. Nonetheless, there are inspiring examples from around the world. For example, Apple and Beane (1999) gave examples of democratic schools from across the US, and Macbeath and Moos (2004) and Wrigley (2006) showed similar examples from across the world. Rudduck and Flutter (2004), Flutter and Rudduck (2004) and Maitles and Gilchrist (2006) explained that it was beneficial to the teachers, pupils, schools and parents to have a consultative, democratic approach in the classroom. And, indeed, following on from the Rethinking Schools movement in the US, Rethinking Education in England has developed from NUT (National Union of Teachers) branches and the anti-SATS (Standard Attainment Tests) alliance (www.rethinkinged.org.uk). Its agenda is to organise opposition and intervention against the ravages of the neoliberal model.

However, in terms of alternatives to the new managerialism, there is one serious caveat. As yet, the teacher unions tend to be reactive to the corporate model, concentrating on pay, facility time and other workload issues. Not that this is unimportant, but it tends to concede the ground to the managers. And, any gains in terms of time can be quickly eroded by management. For example, teachers in Scotland won a 35-hour week as part of their McCrone settlement, but a recent report from a major respected study found that teachers were working nearer a 45-hour week (TESS, 2006) and, indeed, it was now higher than before the agreement came in. The McCrone settlement also introduced continuing professional development (CPD) for teachers (most to be done in teachers' own time) and a charter teacher scheme, which is beginning to unravel as unpopular with management (it gives money without managerial responsibilities and thus undermines the rigid promotion structure in schools) and with teachers (it has to be done in one's own time at evenings, weekends or holidays and costs £7,000, effectively discriminating against single parents and female teachers with young children). Paradoxically, teachers seem to accept the longer working hours and intensification of their work, for in order 'to do a "good job" you need to be as "rational" as possible' (Apple, 1986, p 46). Thus, 'the ideology of professionalism for teachers legitimates and reinforces features of proletarianization' (Densmore, 1987, p 149; Harvie, 2006). In reality, the degradation of the teaching role has led many to reinterpret their work in terms of a 'misrecognised professionalism', by assuming that the technical and effective execution of prescriptions by others is the ultimate proof of their expertise and competence (Apple, 1986; Densmore, 1987; Hargreaves, 1994; Apple and Jungck, 1996). Gray (2006) suggested that the most worrying aspect of this might be that the lack of professional identity could lead to a demise in professional commitment as vocation was no longer seen as important.

Interestingly, in the next section on trust and academy schools, the unions have been much more active in opposing the initiative; it seems to be a step too far, even for the conservative NUT and NAS/UWT teaching unions. A key task for activists is to marry the opposition to the new managerialism into the opposition to its logical outcome, the academies.

## Academy and trust schools

A further development in the New Labour strategy has been the attempt to further establish academy and trust schools. This goes completely against the grain of comprehensive education and gives individual rich business interests (or groups of wealthy or religious interests) a major say over education policy, at the same time as it cuts out as much public control as possible. Parents will no longer be able to appeal to local councillors if things are problematic; these schools are effectively beyond democratic control. The government claims that it will not lead to further class segregation but the evidence of those trust schools already established is that they have lower levels of free school meals and pupils from areas of deprivation than the schools they replaced and that backdoor selection does take place. Indeed, some commentators (Walford, 2001; Chitty, 2004; Taylor et al, 2005) have argued that these very policies increase the inequalities in education that the government claims it wants to narrow. As I write this, the House of Commons inquiry into loans/donations/school sponsorship for honours scandal has started (although some of the evidence is sub judice as it is potential criminal fraud), following the taped conversation of key Blair education consultant Des Smith, 'promising' honours for huge donations to the project. What a legacy for Blair's education policy. And, as a final irony, the whole academy process is now under investigation by the Audit Commission as it has been argued that the whole process gives no value for money!

And it doesn't end there. The government has outlined its 'Five-year Strategy' for education (DfES, 2004) (a series of policy documents on which legislation was framed). There is to be a restriction in timetabling options for lower ability students aged 14-16, in effect a return to junior comprehensives, which failed generations of pupils. These pupils will get vocational courses and 'functional literacy and numeracy'. Their education will be reduced to training for work; no history, literature, poetry, art, music, drama, politics, sociology for them, but rather a dumbed-down curriculum that will train them for work. And in this we spy the real impact of the marketisation of education; the idea of schools as labour-producing entities, as opposed to education for life, is obvious. The distortion of the curriculum is thus designed to fit the neoliberal agenda.

There is no surprise that these proposals, and in particular the trust schools, have led to widespread condemnation and activity. We had the spectacle in Parliament of David Cameron's Conservatives giving support to New Labour to get the proposals through in the teeth of opposition from over 70 Labour backbenchers, for whom this was a step too far and, indeed, the government offering some minor concessions to win over waverers. Outside Parliament, the opposition has had much more backbone as groups of parents and teachers and local activists have campaigned to stop their schools being taken over by trusts, sometimes successfully, others not. Every time there is a proposal to turn a local school into an academy, there is a campaign to attempt to overturn the decision, the most recent being in Oldham where the local NUT branch is opposing turning the four local schools into academies and is organising parents, pupils, teachers and school governors in the campaign. There is a need to spread and share successes, such as that at Northcliffe School in Doncaster (Bailey, 2005); in this case the school, community, unions and pupils organised under the slogan of 'Our Pits, Our Jobs But Not Our Schools' against an attempt to develop an academy school under the Christian fundamentalist Emmanuel School Foundation (Harry Potter books banned). The campaign was so popular and so wide that the Department for Education and Skills withdrew the proposal due to 'opposition from parents and teachers' in February 2005 (*The Guardian*, 2005). Opponents have further organised a series of conferences for parents, pupils, teachers and educationists where opposition has been articulated and strategies developed. It is not yet a done deal; the level of opposition is large (the first conference to organise this opposition in April 2006 had over 250 delegates), and there is much evidence that what parents want is a good local comprehensive school. And, if the 2006 local government elections in England show anything, it is that disillusion with the New Labour government's policies is widespread and education strategy has been a major impactor on that.

In Scotland, where education policy is controlled by the Scottish Parliament and where prior to May 2007 New Labour was constrained by a coalition partner, these policies have not as yet been taken to the same level, although it should be noted that the Labour/Liberal Democrat coalition had in their policy outlines proposals for highly funded specialist science academies; while it is stressed that there will be no selection, many fear that there will be informal selection by aptitude. It may be tempting to suggest that the policies implemented in England do not affect Scotland, but the reality is that the neoliberal agenda in England does have an impact. For example, the recent salaries campaign in the higher education (HE) sector had the university principals in Scotland concerned that Scottish universities were being left behind; the logic of their statements was that Scottish universities needed the fee income to compete and the Executive needed to increase funding or allow fees. What there has been in Scotland in the school sector is the spread of private finance initiatives (PFIs) in the rebuilding of schools; however, their impact on policy is not nearly as clear and schools remain under public control, although there are widespread complaints from headteachers that the 'internal market' in schools means that they have to hire their own schools for extra-curricular activities or homework clubs from the developers. Indeed, some local authorities have turned their backs on the public–private partnerships (PPPs) and are raising money to refurbish schools in other ways.

## Reducing inequality: size matters

In theory, micro school level factors and macro poverty reducing factors were to work together to reduce inequalities, and one major area of improvement would be smaller class sizes. Yet the governments in Westminster and Edinburgh, in contrast to most of those involved in education, continue to argue that smaller classes in upper primary and secondary schools are not important to academic success and that 'scarce' resources must be pumped only into nursery, primary 1 and 2 and the first two years of secondary education in English and Maths. However, even within this priority area, the government's own figures between 1995 and 2005 make grim reading (*Social Trends*, 2004), and, in terms of other countries in Europe, the most recent figures show Britain poor in terms of pupil:teacher ratios (Guinness, 2004; OECD, 2005; *Sunday Herald*, 2006).

Yet, research from the US, and in particular New York and California, suggests that reducing class sizes in secondary schools can have a major impact in terms of the quality of learning and teaching, heightened classroom participation and communication skills, enthusiasm for increased reading, a noticeable decline in the number of disciplinary referrals, a rise in teacher morale, improvements in both student absenteeism rates and teacher health absence rates and much improved parental involvement. And, at least for the teachers, this is one of the areas that teachers feel would make their jobs more rewarding. Interestingly in these pilot projects in the US, the major improvements were where significant reduction in class sizes was introduced, where classes were reduced from over 30 to under 20 (American Federation of Teachers, 2000; Educational Priorities Panel, 2000; HEROS, 2000; California, 2001). It is not that the evidence is uncontested; some believe that the issue of size is secondary to the teaching strategies used (Cherian and Mau, 2003; Pedder, 2006). While they correctly suggest that there is more to good teaching than small class sizes, 'poor' teachers tend to sink without trace in the big classes and, crucially, in smaller classes 'good' teachers can spend more time with individual pupils and can introduce even better active learning experiences.

## Conclusions

New Labour is so wedded to its neoliberal agenda that, as in health policy, no matter what it does in education terms it does not challenge the underlying poverty that is the cause of most of the problem. Without this, there is the plethora of policies – increasing the market in education, continuing to allow selection at age 11 (almost Orwellian in that David Blunkett managed to phrase 'Watch my lips – no selection' into meaning 'Watch my lips – we will allow selection'), 'Fresh Start' initiatives for 'failing' schools, continuation of league tables in England, under-funding (especially in comparison to the private sector), large class sizes, especially from the third year of primary school onwards, various other area-based initiatives, specialist and trust schools and so on. The impact on schools comes through the drive for more managerial control, together with diverse policy initiatives. Will these reforms help or worsen educational inequalities caused by disadvantage and poverty and will they help teachers in the classroom? The experience of the first two-and-a-half terms of the Labour government suggests that unfortunately we are seeing a worsening of both. Yet, opposition is widespread from educationists, teachers, parents and students. The neoliberal agenda for education is uppermost in the minds of government, their advisers and the civil servants but welfarism doggedly holds on, particularly in the minds of teachers and parents. That is why every neoliberal change is implemented grudgingly, without enthusiasm and with resistance in the classroom and communities. In that sense, there is strong similarity between education policy and practice and that in the other areas of policy described in this book.

## Notes

[1] For example, a weak teacher in a high-achieving independent school might have a class of high achievers who should get an A at GCSE but achieve a B; this will still be within the A–C category and the teacher and school deemed 'good'. An excellent teacher at a school where pupils are low achievers may work particularly hard and enthuse pupils, who, instead of achieving an E, get a D; this is outwith the A–C success band and the school and the teacher can be deemed as failing.

[2] 'Highers' are the Scottish school (taken by students in secondary years 5/6) and further education (FE) qualifications that are the common currency for university entrance.

## Further sources

Anti Academies Alliance, www.antiacademies.org.uk.

Ballet, K., Kelchtermansa, G. and Loughranb, J. (2006) 'Beyond intensification towards a scholarship of practice: analysing changes in teachers' work lives', *Teachers and Teaching: Theory and Practice*, vol 12, no 2, April, pp 209-29.

Gale, T. and Densmore, K. (2003) *Engaging teachers*, Maidenhead: Open University Press.

Gillborn, D. and Youdell, D. (2000) *Rationing education*, Buckingham: Open University Press.

Hill, D., McLaren, P., Cole, M. and Rikowski, G. (eds) (1999) *Postmodernism in educational theory: Education and the politics of human resistance*, London: Tufnell Press.

# References

Alerby, E. (2003) '"During the break we have fun": a study concerning pupils' experience of school', *Educational Research*, vol 45, no 1, pp 17-28.

American Federation of Teachers (2000) *Small class size: Education reform that works*, Washington: AFT.

Apple, M. (1986) *Teachers and texts. A political economy of class and gender relations in education*, London: Routledge.

Apple, M. (1996). *Cultural politics and education*, Milton Keynes: Open University Press.

Apple, M. (2000) *Official knowledge: Democratic education in a conservative age*, New York, NY: Routledge.

Apple, M. And Beane, J. (1999) *Democratic schools*, Buckingham: Open University Press.

Apple, M. and Jungck, S. (1996) '"You don't have to be a teacher to teach this unit": teaching, technology and control in the classroom', in A. Hargreaves and M.G. Fullan (eds) *Understanding teacher development*, Teacher Development Series, London: Cassell, pp 20-42.

Bach, S., Kessler, I. and Heron, P. (2006) 'Changing job boundaries and workforce reform: the case of teaching assistants', *Industrial Relations Journal*, vol 37, no 1, pp 2-21.

Bailey, M. (2005) 'Academies and how to beat them: "our pits, our jobs, but not our schools"', *Forum*, vol 47, no 1.

Ballet, K., Kelchtermansa, G. and Loughranb, J. (2006) 'Beyond intensification towards a scholarship of practice: analysing changes in teachers' work lives', *Teachers and Teaching: Theory and Practice*, vol 12, no 2, April, pp 209-29.

Baran, P. and Sweezey, P. (1966) *Monopoly capital: An essay on the American economic and social order*, New York, NY: Monthly Review Press.

Birkett, D. (2001) 'The school I'd like', *Education Guardian*, 16 January.

Blackmore, J. (2001) 'The implications of school governance and the new educational accountability for student learning and teacher professional identity', Unpublished PhD thesis, quoted in J. Moller (2004) 'Democratic leadership in an age of managerial accountability', in J. Macbeath and L. Moos (eds) *Democratic learning*, London: RoutledgeFalmer.

Blishen, E. (1967) *The school that I'd like*, Harmondsworth: Penguin.

Boyson, R. (1975) *The crisis in education*, London: Woburn Press.

Braverman, H. (1974) *Labor and monopoly capital: The degradation of work in the twentieth century*, New York, NY: Monthly Review Press.

Burke, C. and Grosvenor, I. (2003) *The school I'd like*, London: RoutledgeFalmer.

California (2001) *Class size reduction*, California: California Department of Education.

Cherian, M. and Mau, R. (eds) (2003) *Teaching large classes: Usable practices from around the world*, Singapore: McGraw-Hill.

Chitty, C. (2004) *Education policy in Britain*, Basingstoke: Palgrave Macmillan.

Clarke, J., Cochrane, A. and McLaughlin, E. (eds) (1994) *Managing social policy*, London: Sage Publications.

Dainton, S. (2005) 'Reclaiming teachers' voices', *Forum*, vol 47, nos 2 & 3.

Danaher, P.A., Gale, T. and Erben, T. (2000) 'The teacher educator as (re)negotiated professional: critical incidents in steering between state and market', *International Journal of Education for Teaching*, vol 26, no 1, pp 55-71.

Davies, J. and Brember, I. (1999) 'Reading and mathematics attainments and self-esteem in years 2 and 6 – an 8 year cross-sectional study', *Educational Studies*, vol 25, no 2, pp 145-58.

Davies, N. (2001) *The school report*, London: Vintage.

Deem, R., Brehony, K. and Heath, S. (1995) *Active citizenship and the governing of schools*, Buckingham: Open University Press.

Densmore, K. (1987) 'Professionalism, proletarianization and teacher work', in T. Popkewitz (ed) *Critical studies in teacher education*, London: Falmer Press, pp 130-60.

Dewey, J. (1915), *The school and society*, Chicago, IL: University of Chicago Press.

DfES (Department for Education and Science) (2004) *Five year strategy for children and learners*, London: DfES.

Educational Priorities Panel (2000) *Smaller is better: First-hand reports of early grade class size reduction in New York City public schools*, New York, NY: Educational Priorities Panel.

Flutter, J. and Rudduck, J. (2004) *Consulting pupils*, London: RoutledgeFalmer.

Gale, T. and Densmore, K. (2003) *Engaging teachers*, Maidenhead: Open University Press.

Gewirtz, S., Ball, S. and Bowe, R. (1995) *Markets, choice and equity in education*, Buckingham: Open University Press.

Gillard, D. (2005) 'Rescuing teacher professionalism', *Forum*, vol 47, nos 2 & 3.

Gillborn, D. and Youdell, D. (2000) *Rationing education*, Buckingham: Open University Press.

Grace, G. (1995) *School leadership: Beyond education management*, London: Falmer.

Gray, S. (2006) *Teachers under siege*, Stoke on Trent: Trentham.

*Guardian, The* (2005) 'Local schools for local people', 19 February.

Guinness (2004) *The European data book*, Middlesex: Guinness.

Hall, C. (2004) 'Theorising changes in teachers' work', *Canadian Journal of Educational Administration and Policy*, vol 32.

Hancock, R. and Collins, J. (eds) (2005) *Primary teaching assistants*, London: David Fulton.

Hargreaves, A. (1994) *Changing teachers, changing times: Teachers' work and culture in the postmodern age*, London: Cassell.

Harvie, D. (2006) 'Value production and struggle in the classroom', *Capital and Class*, vol 88, pp 1-32.

Hatcher, R. (1994) 'Market relationships and the management of teachers', *British Journal of Sociology of Education*, vol 15, no 1, pp 41-62.

HEROS (2000) *Class size research*, Lebanon, TN: HEROS.

Jamieson, I. and Wikeley, F. (2001) 'A contextual perspective: fitting round the school needs of students', in A. Harris and N. Bennett (eds) *School effectiveness and school improvement – Alternative perspectives*, London: Continuum.

Macbeath, J. and Moos, L. (2004) *Democratic learning*, London: RoutledgeFalmer.

Maitles, H. (2005) *Values in education: We're citizens now*, Edinburgh: Dunedin.

Maitles, H. and Gilchrist, I. (2006) 'Never too young to learn democracy!: a case study of a democratic approach to learning in a religious and moral education secondary class in the West of Scotland', *Educational Review*, vol 58, no 1, pp 67-86.

Moller, J. (2004) 'Democratic leadership in an age of managerial accountability', in J. Macbeath and L. Moos (eds) *Democratic learning*, London: RoutledgeFalmer.

Morris, E. (2001) *Professionalism and trust: The future of teachers and teaching*, London: Social Market Foundation.

Mortimore, P., Sammons, P., Stoll, L., Lewis, D. and Ecob, R. (1988) *School matters*, London: Open Books.

OECD (Organisation for Economic Co-operation and Development) (2005) *Education at a glance*, Paris: Centre for Educational Research and Innovation.

Pedder, D. (2006) 'Are small classes better? Understanding relationships between class size, classroom processes and pupils' learning', *Oxford Review of Education*, vol 32, no 2, pp 213-34.

Rudduck, J. and Flutter, J. (2004) *How to improve your school*, London: Continuum.

Sachs, J. (2001) 'Teacher professional identity: competing discourses, competing outcomes', *Journal of Educational Policy*, vol 16, no 2, pp 149-62.

Save the Children (2001) *Education for citizenship in Scotland: Perspectives of young people*, Edinburgh, Save the Children Scotland.

Seddon, T. (2004) 'Remaking civic formations: towards a learning citizen?', *London Review of Education*, vol 2, no 3, pp 171-86.

Slee, R., Weiner, G. and Tomlinson, S. (eds) (1998) *School effectiveness for whom?*, London: Falmer.

Smyth, J., Dow, A., Hattam, R., Reid, A. and Shacklock, G. (2000) *Teachers' work in a globalizing economy*, London: Falmer Press.

*Social Trends* (2005) *Social Trends 35*, London: The Stationery Office.

*Sunday Herald* (2006) 'Union to hold ballot on class sizes', 11 June.

Taylor, C., Fitz, J. and Gorand, S. (2005) 'Diversity, specialization and equity in education', *Oxford Review of Education*, vol 31, no 1, pp 47-70.

TES (*Times Educational Supplement*) (2006) 'Top set told to copy work', *TES*, 21 July.

TESS (*Times Educational Supplement Scotland*) (2006) 'Empowered or smothered?', *TESS*, 6 October.

Troman, G. (2000) 'Teacher stress in the low-trust society', *British Journal of Sociology of Education*, vol 21, no 3, pp 331-53.

Walford, G. (2001) 'From common schooling to selection? Affirming and contesting the comprehensive ideal 1976-2001', in R. Phillips and J. Furlong, *Education, reform and the state: Politics, policy and practice 1976-2001*, London: RoutledgeFalmer.

Webb, R., Vulliamy, G., Hämäläinen, S., Sarja, A., Kimonen, E. and Nevalainen, R. (2004) 'Pressures, rewards and teacher retention: a comparative study of primary teaching in England and Finland', *Scandinavian Journal of Educational Research*, vol 48, no 2, April, pp 169-88.

Whitty, G., Power, S. and Halpin, D. (1998) *Devolution and choice in education: The school, the state and the market*, Buckingham: Open University Press.

Wrigley, T. (2006) *Another school is possible*, London: Bookmarks.

# SEVEN

# Ambiguities and resistance: academic labour and the commodification of higher education

*Alex Law and Hazel Work*

Academic workers today are far removed from their ivory tower image. Once eulogised as an other-worldly haven of disinterested intellectual pursuit, free-thought, imagination and scientific breakthroughs, academic labour is becoming increasingly defined by market relations and the managerial conditions under which it operates as paid wage labour. In one sense this is nothing new. Ninety years ago Thorstein Veblen (1918) lamented an earlier commercialisation of universities while in the late 1960s E.P. Thompson (1970), and the New Left more generally, protested against the rise of the 'industrial university'. It also reflects a tendency in the development of capitalism to de-professionalise and proletarianise high-status forms of work, or, as Marx and Engels (1998, p 38) put it, to tear the halo from once venerated occupations.

This chapter charts the changing landscape of higher education (HE) in Britain from the point of view of academic labour. It first establishes the deepening of neoliberal priorities and managerial prerogatives throughout the sector. It then considers how this has intensified and proletarianised the academic labour process. Crucially, we argue, the indeterminate nature of academic labour and the active resistance of academic workers themselves limit the extent of their subordination to managerial prerogatives. Finally, we consider the growing militancy of lecturers, illustrated by the industrial action in 2006 over pay.

## Higher education under New Labour

With the introduction of tuition fees and the abolition of maintenance grants[1] New Labour signalled their commitment to the socio–ideological preferences of the New Right. In HE New Labour has maintained the regulatory and management regimes introduced under Conservative rule (Deem and Brehony, 2005; Ryan, 2005). New Labour embraced the utilitarian agenda of the New Right that reduces educational value to economic ends and deployed the discourse of globalisation to help naturalise and legitimate neoliberal policies within HE (Cole, 2005). Policies that bear the stamp of New Labour propose a vision of society that has a greater resonance with the political preferences of the New Right than old Labour (Callinicos, 2006). As Brehony and Deem (2005, p 409) suggest, 'The New Right have gone but the policies that its adherents promoted are alive and well in the guise of new Labour'. Tony Blair's modernisation discourse attempted to ideologically dismantle the social democratic welfare state, advocating instead a 'new market state under the dominance of private monopoly capital' (Ainley, 2004, p 508; Cole, 2005, p 4). This alignment of HE to the global free market is especially evident in New Labour's approach to the development of 'lifelong learning' and 'the Learning Society' in the so-called 'knowledge economy'. Such concepts emerged in the 1960s and early 1970s to promote a socially aware and liberal humanist idea of HE (Faure, 1972; Husen, 1974). By the 2000s they were wrapped in discourses about the free market and the forces of globalisation. New Labour produced 23 initiatives on lifelong learning and the Learning Society in their first two years in office (Coffield, 2000, p 6). *The learning age: A renaissance for a new Britain* (DfEE, 1998) set out New Labour's vision of HE in a 'Learning Society' and built on the earlier Dearing Report (1997) and the Fryer Report (1997). The restructuring of HE was linked in all reports to 'global competition' and the 'liberalisation of markets' (Fryer, 1997, p 11). Even in Scotland, with its different educational traditions and devolved institutions, universities have felt the pressure to submit to the neoliberal archetype of HE.

This neoliberal orientation was reinforced in *The learning age* (DfEE, 1998, p 9): 'We are in a new age – the age of information and of global competition. Familiar certainties and old ways of doing things are disappearing'. In this 'new' age, HE has been given a primary role in coping with and facilitating the appropriate responses to the global economy. In New Labour's marketised utopia 'competitive economic success' depends on 'universities and colleges sharing their expertise with industry and services in a pioneering way' (DfEE, 1998, p 25). Promotion of the global market ensures that HE commodifies knowledge more completely and, in the process, transforms universities 'into a pliant service industry for the late capitalist market system' (Bertelsen, 1998, p 130). The 2004 Higher Education Act further constructed an economistic ideology for HE. As a result, a fundamental tension exists between the funding of and access to HE. The symbolic and material impact of the introduction of variable top-up fees in England and Wales has the potential to negate the government's stated aim to raise participation levels in HE by the end of the decade. The introduction of top-up fees has raised the level of student debt and, as many commentators have noted, has discouraged those from 'non-traditional' groups, especially low-skilled working-class families, from entering HE (Archer et al, 2003). In response an Office of Fair Access was invented to regulate the implementation of top-up fees and to keep an eye on universities' plans for wider access. Yet this mechanism has failed to counter the main problem with participation levels in HE: the deepening middle-class colonisation of HE (Archer et al, 2003; Galindo-Rueda et al, 2004). New Labour's commitment to the idea of a social meritocracy has ensured that pervasive inequalities within the HE system have been reproduced intergenerationally.

In *The future of higher education* (DfES, 2003), the expansion of HE has been legitimated by 'national economic imperatives'. Third Way ideas about social justice and equality have taken a back seat behind the duties of individuals who 'have the responsibility to maintain themselves as marketable commodities in a flexible labour market (viz insecure and uncertain) and to bear the risks of that insecurity themselves' (Levitas, 2004, p 48). Entrepreneurial individualism pervades New Labour HE policy statements. For example, 'Individuals should invest in their *own* learning to improve their *own* employability, professional competence, and earning potential' (DfEE, 1998, p 26; emphasis added). Here New Labour recuperates two themes from the New Right: a utilitarian view of education and a focus on individual rather than social responsibility. This instrumental approach subscribes to a vision of HE where 'there is scant trace of the notion that education and learning can be ends in themselves' (Jones and Thomas, 2005, p 623). Such narrow utilitarianism mirrors the earlier reform process of successive Conservative governments. Then the critique of HE was that it had failed the British economy. Numerous policy documents, from *Improving research links between higher education and industry* (Advisory Council on Applied Research and Development, 1983) to the 1992 Further and Higher Education Act, promoted reform of the system largely on the basis of economic needs and requirements. Economic imperatives, not social egalitarianism, provided the main rationale for the transition from an elite to a mass system of HE. The 1988 Education Reform Act and the 1992 Further and Higher Education Act gave further expression to the utilitarian vision of HE. The 1988 Act proposed a deepening of the competitive and entrepreneurial emphasis within the system and made provision for the abolition of tenure within universities. The 1992 Act created new funding councils for Scotland, England and Wales, separated the funding allocated for teaching and research and abolished the binary divide in HE.

All of the aforementioned measures were instituted with the aim of creating a 'purer' form of market competition between universities. HE has been made to respond to the whimsy of market and 'consumer' demand. In so doing, any notion of the speculative and experimental pursuit of knowledge has been devalued in favour of applied and commercially oriented knowledge. Evidence-based policy (although perhaps that should read 'policy-based evidence'), as Hodkinson (2001, p 386) noted, reflects New Labour's penchant for 'a strong positivism and crude realism'. This instrumental and commercial emphasis continues in the discussion of research and 'knowledge transfer' in the 2003 White Paper (Jones and Thomas, 2005) and in the assumptions of the Lambert Review (2003). Lambert took it as axiomatic that business–university collaboration could be improved through 'best practice' managerialism in university governance. Such commercialising mania has led the Funding Council in England to argue in what Callinicos (2006, p 23) called 'semi-literate' terms for universities to 'play a greater role in fostering productivity and economic growth through making third stream activity their second mission, after teaching'. New Labour's enthusiasm for the tenets of new managerialism (now, surely, old managerialism) demonstrates the extent to which the neoliberal agenda has been ensconced as its deepest assumption.

## Managerialism in higher education

Managerialism played a crucial part in the New Right's initial assault on HE. The funding cuts made by Margaret Thatcher's government in 1979 and 1981 were accompanied by demands for greater accountability and efficiency within HE. Such demands may have been couched in Margaret Thatcher's homily of 'good housekeeping', but the emphasis placed on greater public accountability, efficiency gains, quality inspection, audits and the pursuit of 'sound management practices' led to a range of initiatives that enabled the government to institute new forms of control over the system. The setting up of the National Advisory Board in 1982 and the Jarratt Report of 1985 stimulated a need for new managerial practices. Jarratt recommended the use of performance indicators to direct funding allocations to institutions, the University Grant Committee's first 'research selectivity' exercise, the introduction of quality assessment procedures and the general emphasis on 'value for money' established a competitive framework for the allocation of funds and resources within HE.

The new managerialism challenged the liberal ideal of HE. As Pollitt (1990, p 49) recognised at the time, 'private-sector disciplines can be introduced to the public services, political control can be introduced, budgets trimmed, professional autonomy reduced, public service unions weakened and a quasi-competitive framework erected to flush out the "natural" inefficiencies of bureaucracy'. These took the form of quality audits, performance indicators, league tables, devolved budgets and cost centres, higher staff:student ratios, increased workloads, deteriorating levels of pay and increased levels of surveillance and control. Barnett (2003, p 96) argued that the quality mechanisms installed pernicious forms of instrumental reason that 'classify and constrain academics'. In common with the degradation of welfare professionalism discussed elsewhere in this book, audit culture aims to 'reconstitute the cultural and cognitive practices of education professionals at the very point where words issue from their mouths or their fingertips' (MacLure, 2005, p 398). Indeed, audit culture has become 'the unifying principle of the modern university', where questions about intellectual and ethical value are substituted for 'measurement' and 'accounting solutions' (Peters, 2005, p 73).

In response to business demands for lighter regulation and accountability (see the Lambert Review, 2003), in 2006 Gordon Brown announced that future research funding would move to a metric system with less expensive overheads than panel review. Whatever system is adopted will merely reinforce existing patterns of funding inequalities and the pressure will be on academics to conform to whatever paradigm is dominant at that time, especially in social sciences and the humanities (Lipsett, 2006). Quantitative measurements like these do not measure the objective reality of research activity but actively shape and distort research to suit the form of metrics deployed. Similarly, the burden of the periodic teaching reviews of quality and standards has been reduced so that institutions have largely undertaken the monitoring of their procedures themselves. Internal monitoring regimes have shifted the administrative burden on to staff in addition to their core activities, while centralised administrative functions have expanded.

New Labour constantly seeks to deepen and extend managerial prerogatives throughout HE. *Higher education: Easing the burden* (BRTF, 2002) and the *Review of research assessment* (Roberts, 2003) did not, for example, question the legitimacy of the 'evaluative state' or the 'contractual state'. Instead they sought to ease the 'accountability burden' to raise efficiency in teaching and research. Such measures have been bolstered by the 'full economic costing of research', first mooted by the Treasury in 1999 and implemented in 2004. These reflect the depth of New Labour support for contractual and accounting mechanisms to control and manage labour in HE. Academics feel that HE is increasingly permeated by bureaucratic managerialism and suffused by an ideology of efficient work performance through monitoring, target setting and private sector organisational models. New managerialism is seen as a mechanism through which manager-academics maintain relationships of power and domination over members of staff through 'divide and rule' techniques that stratify academic workers into productive researchers and excellent teachers and the less competent or industrious (Brehony and Deem, 2005). Audit culture and marketisation have challenged the professional autonomy of academics (Beck and Young, 2005). This is felt in departments across the sector, with some facing highly authoritarian styles of interpersonal supervision of their duties and demands that academics blithely obey centrally derived decrees. At the apex of the managerial hierarchy, where vice-chancellors centralise power a highly autocratic, personalised system of decision making further alienates academic workers.

The simulated market has had a profound impact on academic work (Barnett, 2003). The abolition of the binary divide did *not* create, to use a cliché, a 'level-playing field' within HE. New universities simply cannot compete with the resource base of the old institutions (Ryan, 2005). As a result, both the audit culture and the realities of unequal competition for funding and resources have reinforced the class bias of elite institutions and their students (Callinicos, 2006, p 19). While the massification of HE has affected every corner of the sector, it is the post-1992 institutions that have borne the brunt of teaching more students with less human and economic resources (Salter and Tapper, 1994). Those institutions and academics on the lower rungs of the ladder are less able to mitigate the debilitating impact of the managed market. New Labour's proposals for creating a 'more diversified' system of HE where institutions would specialise in either teaching or research will further entrench existing class biases. Functional specialisation conflicts with the belief that academics are distinguished from other educationalists because they combine primary research with their teaching practice. Specialisation also deepens class distinctions. As Archer et al (2003, p 193) argued, the maintenance of a two-tier system ensured that 'middle class privilege and dominance in higher education and employment is sustained'. Individuals from poorer neighbourhoods are not only less likely to go into HE in the first place but also end up studying in quite different institutions (Galindo-Rueda et al, 2004, p 81). Class distinctions are thereby reinforced between the elite institutions, so-called red-brick universities and post-1992, 'new' universities. Nonetheless, the baleful effects of marketisation impacts on all the dark recesses of HE. As Barnett (2003, p 89) argued, once the ideology of the market and competition entered the university sector it 'brooks no half measures' and reshapes all the 'contours of academic life'. New Labour's embrace of the tenets of neoliberalism in HE ensures that the market will continue to reorient and reorder the lives of both the academic community and the students entering HE, ensconcing class privileges that are such a hallmark of UK HE.

## Restructuring the academic labour process

University management is undoubtedly a complex task, made increasingly difficult by the competing and often contradictory demands in the immediate process of academic production. First, senior management must manage in line with the general demands of the state for public probity and accountability for large sums of money and large-scale built capital in the form of estates and plant. Second, they need to satisfy external auditors, who act as surrogate customers, and, ultimately, the government of the day about the standards and value of their chief product: the reproduction of a skilled, versatile labour force. Third, they need to attract actual 'customers', students, and therefore the income that they have come to represent. Fourth, many universities are embedded in specific localities and play a sometimes decisive role in the local economy, particularly in economically disadvantaged urban areas. Finally, and at the heart of the whole managerial complex, is their need to manage and organise diverse groups of workers, 'from professors to porters'.

Inside the academic labour process itself, managerialism inhibits self-directed autonomy and independent thinking. However, academic managerialism is a self-contradictory project. Traditionally the academic labour process was conceived in artisanal terms as combining small-scale teaching with leading-edge research conducted by self-directed intellectual workers (Wilson, 1991; Dearlove, 1997). This was made dependent on the application of craft-based discretion, diligence and proficiency acquired through a lengthy apprenticeship of independent study for higher research degrees. A confident sense of intellectual self-determination was generated by the notion that academics work at the frontier of knowledge and understanding (Bourdieu, 1988; Halsey, 1992). Academic competence was therefore felt to be a collegiate function of the horizontal relationships of peer groups from the intellectual community, not of vertical controls of bureaucratic or managerial hierarchies found in industrial workplaces. Thus the academic labour process had the trace of Habermas' ideal-speech community of autonomous and equal participants striving towards professional consensus. Legal rights were enshrined in the 1988 Education Reform Act for academics to freely 'question and test received wisdom and to put forward new ideas and controversial or unpopular opinions without placing themselves in jeopardy of losing their jobs or the privileges they may have' (Shepherd, 2006, p 1). Yet academic self-censorship appears to be rife. A growing culture of bureaucratic conformism stifles critique and innovation as academics fear managerial reprisals for stepping out of line. Far from the other-worldly image of dons unconcerned about the crude material things, academics are under continual pressure to contribute 'added value' to the educational product and enhance the competitive standing of their institutions with students and employers. A growing polarisation of academic labour divides into a small elite of global academic 'stars' and a much larger group of nationally recognised academics.

Converting the indeterminate labour power of academics into concrete labour performed is the central problem of senior management. Unless the work performance of academics can somehow be regulated, calibrated, canalised or controlled, their subordination to managerial imperatives will remain at the purely formal level. Their problem becomes how best to commodify academic labour (Willmott, 1995). As one study into senior university staff conceded:

> Many of our respondents' comments can be read as a confirmation that universities are being reconstituted as knowledge factories organized by managers, whose aim is to intensify and commodify the production and distribution of knowledge and skills to whomsoever has the wherewithal to purchase them. (Prichard and Willmott, 1997, p 300)

Here a key problem is that of transforming the tacit knowledge embedded in particular disciplines and organisational settings into the kind of codified knowledge that could be made subject to generic managerial orders and controls. Examples of standardisation under the watchwords of 'transparency' and 'accountability' abound, including 'criterion-referenced marking', 'learning outcomes' and the modular system of teaching. Modularisation is an example of how the principles of an industrial process based on cellular production, flexible working practices, batch production and team work that were once viewed as solutions to failing Fordist techniques of flow line production have been imported into academia.

Time is fragmented into semesters and modules and only counted as productive when it can be measured and recorded by reporting systems like the Transparent Approach to Costing (TRAC), which measures the 'full economic cost' of each unit of academic working time. In the face of large student numbers, centralised timetabling administrators allocate space and teaching hours, removing any vestiges that time allocation or work space remains under the control of academics. This is part of a managerialist drive to save on space and time economies at the same time as dramatically increasing student numbers. In some universities staff have been moved out of traditional rooms to open-plan accommodation (Thomson, 2006, p 5). In such spaces it has proved impossible to carry out scholarly work that demands private, concentrated study. Neither have claims been borne out that open-plan spaces necessarily produce stimulating collaborative and innovative research environments. Instead, staff and unions compare them to the panoptican work spaces more familiar to call centres, and the Health and Safety Executive (HSE) cite offices with more than 10 work stations as a potential 'risk factor' in sick building syndrome. Issues of employee privacy and confidentiality are also at risk when open-plan offices become hothouse environments. For instance, at Sussex University's £10 million Freeman Centre, which houses the university's world-renowned Science and Technology Policy Research Unit (SPRU), staff collegiality and mutual trust broke down in an incident where it was claimed that confidential documents may have been read by colleagues competing for the same 'potentially lucrative consultancy work' (Baty, 2007a, p 2). The amount of non-residential space in British universities per full-time equivalent student has been estimated to have fallen by 42% between 1992 and 2001 (Tysome, 2006a, p 40). This has given rise to overcrowding and anonymised classes, which has had profound implications for the standardisation of teaching and assessment.

Moreover, as universities respond to the wider audit culture of public sector accountability, management face the contradiction of enforcing internal bureaucratic regimes at the same time as demanding increased entrepreneurial efforts from academics. Audits reflect the move from the idea of a high-trust, autonomous community to a low-trust managerial culture of surveillance and transparency. This shift is mediated by a combination of worker flexibilities with an increasing burden of administrative rigidities. While all this activity may give the appearance of recording productivity and thereby stimulate further 'efficiencies', it may also belie a reality of falling 'productivity', as energies are consumed wastefully in administrative activities. It may also become a self-fulfilling prophecy, simply creating activities that merely satisfy arbitrary metric constructions while the intellectually taxing business of critical thinking and pedagogy goes on elsewhere, unrecognised and unrecorded. Such metrics are artificially massaged to put the best face on departmental performances. Callinicos (2006, p 17) compared this to the wilful mis-planning in the command economies: 'The exercise in many ways resembles the absurdities of the old bureaucratic, command economy in the Soviet Union: since such a big chunk of universities' money depends on RAE [Research Assessment Exercise] ratings, they have an incentive to massage their submissions, just as Stalinist enterprise managers used to try to deceive the central planners'. Moreover, subject specialisation as expressed in departments, divisions, schools, faculties and RAE clusters stands in contradiction with efforts to centralise managerial functions. University managers thus face a perpetual dilemma of legitimate authority:

> Managers cannot actually do the teaching and research
> they might see as desirable; bureaucratic authority is weak
> in universities, and so top down approaches to changing
> teaching and research and university organisation are bound
> to be problematic and resisted. (Dearlove, 1997, p 66)

Yet precisely because of managerial limitations the temptation is always present for senior administrative staff to become more directive and interventionist by micro-managing the direction and resourcing of teaching and research.

As well as the fragmentation of activities, massification is creating pressures towards standardisation, interchangeability and rationalisation as universities strive for economies of scale and 'value for money' from cost centres. Some argue that this has led to the 'McDonaldisation' of HE and the 'McUniversity' (Parker and Jary, 1995). However, such ideal types neglect the more ambiguous and uneven mixing of instrumental controls and self-directed autonomy in the academic labour process. Moreover, the various forms of resistance to external controls over the academic labour process tend to be neglected in accounts of the inexorable rationalisation of the academic labour process. Academics are a heterogeneous group, whose specific shade, balance and extent of activities differs between, and even within, institutions, departments and subject areas.

> These differences extend to the conception of the discipline,
> the varying practices of teaching and research and, at a
> fairly fundamental level, the different market situations of
> academics as lecturers, consultants and researchers, as well
> as the different career prospects of the students they teach.
> (Miller, 1991, p 122)

At its core the academic labour process has not been fundamentally
transformed by managerialism. In terms of teaching, academics continue
to perform core activities of lectures and seminars, take responsibility
for the pastoral care of students, and set and grade assessments of various
types. Increasingly, however, they also participate in university reporting
and committee structures. New teachers are being forced to undertake
as part of their probation externally accredited generic training in
teaching techniques and principles as a measure of their competence
as educators, another loss of academic control over subject-specific
socialisation into the teaching craft.

Both students and academics face mutual entrapment in managerialist
discourses. Students who find themselves struggling with the level or
the amount of work may be able to exercise their consumer rights and
project their difficulties onto their teachers in the manner of the 'failing
teachers' discourse circulating in the school sector. In self-defence,
lecturers protect themselves from the claims of the sovereign consumer
by the very measurements and criteria of work proficiency that are
symptomatic of external control over their own labour process. Many
academics also take responsibility for and direct the work of others, for
instance, low-paid hourly tutors on a course or supervising contract
researchers on a research project. As such, academics have become part
of a chain of managerial command that needs to be supplied with
periodic reports about performance or 'staff development'. Increasingly,
academics carry out a range of administrative duties such as producing
reports on students, modules and programmes or sharing the work
of university and departmental committees. Employers' own research
found that academics leave their employer for another because they
are dissatisfied with their career prospects, workload, managers and pay
levels (UCEA, 2005).

Academic labour therefore retains much of the character of an artisanal
labour process but one that is formally subordinated to managerial
controls. However, aspects of a more substantive subordination of
academic to managerialist imperatives are beginning to make themselves
felt (see Chapter Two, this volume). With the growth of their working
day academics produce additional output for their employer by simply

extending the length of the surplus working time beyond the value they are paid for their labour power. In some cases universities have been able to extend the average working week by nearly one-and-a-half days, with lectures timetabled from 8.30am and finishing at 6.30pm (Tysome, 2006a, p 40). Academics are also working longer throughout the year, at weekends and evenings, taking fewer holidays and carrying out research in their own time. On average academics take only 24 annual days leave out of an average entitlement of 31 days (Swain, 2006, p 1), with more demands on time during the working day, fewer holidays to recuperate and less time to reflect, prepare teaching or undertake personal study. In the process, levels of job satisfaction have fallen dramatically and worker health has suffered. Among the symptoms reported are depression, sleeplessness, anxiety, tiredness, headaches and poor concentration, symptoms of the managerial attempt to objectify, extend and intensify intellectual labour from the embodied person of the academic worker.

Academic proletarianisation and managerialism in universities over the past 20 years has represented an attempt to intensify the effort bargain of academic workers, as well as absolutely extending working time, while holding constant or reducing the relative value of wage levels (Miller, 1991). Managerialism is not therefore some ideological aberration or whimsy on the part of neoliberal educational institutions (although it has its fair share of counterproductive management fads, just as private capital also does). Rather, it is a more or less thoroughgoing attempt to control, direct and regulate academic labour by quantitative abstractions in order to commensurate the relative value of diverse labour power. In the case of one British university (Leeds Metropolitan), for example, a management discussion paper entitled 'Developing a culture of high performance at Leeds Metropolitan' said: 'By ensuring that staff are recruited, developed, assessed and rewarded in relation to a set of core behaviours, we can align individual performance and organisational culture' (Baty, 2007b, p 6). Talk of 'aligning' the 'core behaviour' of individual workers to the organisational goal of 'high performance' smacks of the crudest forms of discredited behaviourism. The overriding objective of managerialism is to simplify traditionally high levels of complex labour. 'The costs of education vary according to the degree of complexity of the labour power required' (Marx, 1976, p 276). Higher levels of training and education raise the socially necessary time, and thus the value, of skilled labour power, both of academics and graduates. 'All labour of a higher or more complicated character than average labour is expenditure of labour power of a more costly kind, labour power whose production has cost more time and labour, and which therefore has a higher value, than unskilled or simple labour power' (Marx, 1976, p 305). If these costs can be cheapened below average levels an initial competitive advantage ensues in the reduced socially necessary labour times for individual capitals and capital-in-general (see Chapter Two, this volume). The problem of neoliberal education is that of simplifying education on a national basis in order to cheapen it by making intellectual labour more determinate.

In so doing, neoliberal managerialism risks killing the goose that lays the golden egg. Indeed, the effort to cheapen the value of academic labour has proven unable to decisively shift it from the formal subsumption of discretionary labour to real subsumption of labour (Marx, 1976). Certainly, there has been a greater capital intensity and use of information technology (IT) in the academic labour process.[2] There is a growing concentration of academic capital, with mergers and alliances between departments and institutions beginning to rationalise subject areas and functions that were previously scattered and duplicated piecemeal across the sector. Managerialism is also re-organising the technical and social divisions of labour, with administrative specialisation usurping academic autonomy and sharper cleavages between 'research-led' institutions and 'teaching-led' institutions.

Efficiency drives have extended not only to research and teaching 'outputs' but even to the 'efficient' social interaction between academics and the 'efficient' use of time and space. Far from any ideal-speech situation, communication between academic workers is often conducted according to the reality principle of economy and opportunity cost calculations. Hence, more effort has been expanded on 'networking' with someone 'useful' rather than with someone in a dependent and vulnerable position in the hierarchy. This also reflects the incipient self-alienation that lurks behind barely concealed academic instrumental behaviour.

> Matter-of-factness between people, doing away with all ideological ornamentation between them, has already itself become an ideology for treating people as things. (Adorno, 2005, p 42)

In the shape of email swamping, information and communication technologies (ICT) have also helped to ratchet up demands on intellectual labour (Eagleton, 2006). Emails are composed in haste, as remote commands or curt queries, without much regard for the renewal of social bonds between intellectual workers. If dialogical exchange suffers from such conceits, so much the worse for all inessential communication. No time is lost with irrelevant formalities. Indeed, in many cases the name of the addressee can be reduced to a stark initial. In these ways a brisk manner between co-workers is adopted and even approved of as a no-nonsense mark of busy-ness.

## Market competition for academic labour power

By such routes, academics are proving themselves self-entrepreneurs, some more willingly, some more reluctantly. Individual and departmental research agendas are governed less by the self-guided autonomy of knowledge of academic lore than by the themes and priorities determined by government, research councils, industry and charitable trusts. Competition for individual promotion has been staked out on the terrain of income generation for the corporate university. While this has helped establish research teams in elite institutions to retain their market advantage, funding applications and projects have been routinised, elevating research technique and 'useful' knowledge over the speculative, critical and marginal intellectual endeavour. Academics have to market themselves and find a taker for their labour in the form of competitive bidding for funding from the funding councils and chalking up 'prestige' publications for the cyclical RAE competition (Willmott, 2003). Teaching across the sector has been made subject to multiple forms of surveillance and 'transparency' while research has been increasingly confined to 'centres of excellence'. In maintaining the social distinction of the scholastic university from the vocational institution research has therefore assumed higher status than teaching within many institutions, while nationally resource allocation has followed internationally competitive research (DfES, 2003, chapter 2).

Within the academic labour process, therefore, things are uneven, segmented and contradictory. On the one hand, the relative indeterminacy of *academic* labour has created a significant problem for imposing centralised control over it. On the other hand, the idea that academic labour is self-determining has ignored the limits imposed by the waged *labour* side of the equation. Most academics, most of the time, labour as inventively and as autonomously as possible under the directly encountered conditions of managerial authority. In this process, academics have found themselves labouring to labour, struggling to create the conditions that allow them to perform intellectual and educational work. Academic proletarianisation refers then not only to the deteriorating salaries of academic workers compared to other 'professional' groups but, crucially, to the passing of control over the labour process to managerial disciplinary techniques, increased fragmentation and the flexible expansion of work, especially bureaucratic duties, in order to increase worker 'productivity' and organisational competitiveness (Miller, 1991; Harvie, 2006). Access to academic employment has been increasingly determined by managerial selection panels and human resource departments rather than by a self-organising profession. Moreover, although routinely couched in talk about collegiality and professionalism, academic work has become more competitive, fragmented, individualistic and isolating. But this alienating process is far from complete or uncontested. For academics, reputation and prestige, and the self-image of professional autonomy conflict with the new battery of external controls, some direct, some arm's-length, demanded by university managerialism. Centralised decrees tend to fall faster and reporting, above all on resource usage, is bounced back upwards more rapidly through the flatter management command structure of modern universities. Lacking the modulating friction of complex intermediary levels of university administration and senior academics, directives issued directly from centralised management are only mitigated by a continuing sense of academic commitment to subject areas rather than particular institutions or departments. Success in the academic labour market has always been marked by strong individualising tendencies around the distinctive market capacities and resources that individual sellers of intellectual labour power can realise at the point of the wage contract exchange. This limits the extent to which academic labour can be fully subsumed as a productive force by managerialism.

Things, however, appear quite different at the bottom of the university hierarchy. An increased reliance has been placed on part-time and hourly-paid under-labourers, whose exploitation helps keep afloat the vestiges of professional autonomy for the 'core' workforce (Crace, 2005). A peripheral reserve army of educational labour, often female, is maintained as hourly-paid contract staff or part-time teaching and research workers (Bryson, 2004a). They suffer the most precarious employment conditions, the worst pay and the worst conditions but are expected to carry the burden of under-labouring for more secure 'core' staff. They are too often treated as an after-thought for trade union representation and collective bargaining. Many universities depend on fixed-term contract workers to carry out research and teaching. European Union (EU) regulations introduced in July 2006 give staff with more than four years' continuous employment the right to a 'permanent' contract. Around 70,000 short-term academic workers are employed in British universities, with some like Edinburgh

University agreeing to a deal to make their 1,000 fixed contract workers 'permanent' employees (Sanders, 2006a; Wojtas, 2006).

At The Open University alone, almost 8,000 part-time associate lecturers provide a stark example of the increasing exploitation of peripheral under-labourers. Widely seen as an egalitarian university since it was founded by the socialist, Jennie Lee, The Open University intensively sweats the resources of its part-time workers. It makes huge capital savings by displacing the cost of office space and equipment onto thousands of individual associate lecturers who use their own homes as work space and provide all their own equipment, including telephones, computing equipment and stationery. Students submit their work directly to the private addresses of the associate lecturers, increasingly in electronic format, whose homes in effect become a front office for the university. While displacing these costs onto the lecturers, The Open University has managed to keep wages to a bare minimum. One way this was done was by moving from a piecework system of paying associate lecturers by numbers of students and course work marked to an academically related pay scale that pays a salary of less than a tenth of the lowest salary of full-time staff, even though the actual student workload can vary considerably. Pay levels have fallen in the past 25 years, from around half way up the lecturer scale to the level of junior administrative roles (Forman, 2005). Despite the job requirement to be a subject specialist, associate lecturers were placed at an inferior point in the new academic scale as a result of the national Framework Agreement. Unfortunately, the trade union accepted the further downgrading of associate lecturers, with the branch president arguing that 'associate lecturers are not academic staff'. Rank and file activists campaigned to remove branch officials and to install academic parity between full-time and part-time workers. Currently, The Open University is engaged in a wide-ranging three-year review of its student support system, which is likely to result in further sweating of the associate lecturer resource.

Despite the idea of a 'permanent' employment contract, academic life is being made less secure in other ways. Across the sector redundancies have followed 'market' restructuring. Departments have been closed or scaled down in response to falling student numbers or low RAE scoring. For instance, in June 2006 lecturers threatened industrial action over 35 redundancies at Liverpool John Moores as part of 'restructuring' plans to axe courses (Tysome, 2006b). Computing lecturers, including a long-standing union activist, were issued with compulsory redundancy notices at London South Bank. In early 2007, in Scotland alone redundancies and departmental closures were being fought at Strathclyde University, Dundee University and Glasgow University's Dumfries campus. At Sussex University, the Vice-Chancellor Professor Alasdair Smith notoriously attempted to axe the highly rated chemistry department in March 2006 because it struggled to recruit students. Soon after it was reprieved student numbers doubled. Months later staff and students united to demand the resignation of Professor Smith after 45 redundancies were announced. One academic made the comparison of Professor Smith's management style to that of New Labour: 'Smith is a bit of a Tony Blair. He seems personable, but at the same time he has presided over this incredibly autocratic management team. They simply impose their will' (Fazackerley, 2006a, p 4). After these problems at Sussex, Professor Smith was due to take over as chair of the Universities and Colleges Employers Association (UCEA), the body responsible for carrying out collective bargaining with the university trade unions. Such authoritarian management also carries with it a hostility to organised labour, as was made evident in recent spates of industrial action in the sector.

## Academic trade unionism and resistance

Because of the relative indeterminacy of their labour power, academics can also elect to engage in informal go-slows, non-cooperation, and pure obstruction. They can shift work demands onto others, above all, students. On the one hand, they can strike a derisive posture for students by being wilfully unhelpful, obstructive and offhand, and provide tedious and standardised teaching and assessment. On the other hand, they can adopt a populist rapport with students that indulges, panders and flatters them. This may serve to reinforce students' own work-refusal strategies by reducing demanding learning tasks and artificially inflating their grades. All the while positive student feedback is ensured while minimising the effort bargain. A positive impression is created for the benefit of their equally distracted line managers. As Harvie (2006, p 24) argued:

> Teachers may therefore adopt this tactic as a means of freeing-up class time in order to pursue their own and/or their students' interests. But since managers perceive such work-reduction tactic as 'efficiency gains' – using them as a way to drive down (socially necessary) labour times – there is a strong incentive for individual teachers to conceal their full effects.

But where Harvie and others can see this as a romantic refusal of work that pushes the costs of surveillance and monitoring of work performance back onto capital, it has debilitating effects for any critical pedagogy, especially for students from working-class backgrounds. Academics appear to be caught on the horns of a dilemma between the hidden stresses of excessive and contradictory workloads and the pragmatic instrumentalism of work avoidance. As employment, personal and educational grievances continue to pile up, a recognition of the dual character of academic labour – proletarian and artisanal – is necessary to counter the alienating and atomising effects of neoliberal managerialism.

Academic discontent is fuelled not only by the degradation and expansion of workloads but also by pay levels. New Labour is determined to move towards a more flexible human resource strategy in universities. This will install pay differentials around an arbitrary idea of 'the best' teachers and researchers, to be determined by how close academics conform to bureaucratic measures. Hence extra funding will be made available to institutions through the block teaching grant 'once individual institutions have human resource strategies that demonstrate to the national funding councils that they will take steps to move towards market supplements or other differentiated means of recruiting and retaining staff, and commit themselves to rewarding good performance' (DfES, 2003, p 52). Relative to other 'professions' like the police, the civil service and medicine, academic pay fell by some 40%. Between 1980 and 1998 it lagged 39% behind average wage rises (Bryson, 2004b, p 47; Stothart, 2006). Pay for female academics is typically some 15% behind that of the average male salary (Bryson, 2004a; Curtis, 2004). Meanwhile, with the dramatic increase in student numbers 'productivity' rose by an estimated 150% in 30 years (Baty and Thomson, 2006, pp 16-17).

For two decades universities claimed financial austerity to explain away the declining value of academic salaries. Meanwhile, top management, citing commercial comparators, continue to be rewarded handsomely with large salary hikes. By 2006 the average salary for a vice-chancellor was over £150,000, a 25% average rise over just three years (Taylor, 2006). This led to sporadic episodes of industrial militancy among a group that has traditionally shunned such means of protest in the past. 'Symbolic' strikes in 2004 and 2006 were followed by further industrial action including a refusal to assess student course work. The employers nationally took an uncompromising stance on pay settlements and have been willing to test the determination of HE unions, especially the Association of University Teachers (AUT), to fight to restore parity with other professions. A national Framework Agreement was agreed in 2004 that employers claimed at the time was worth between 3% and 5% when implemented in August 2006. This followed a spate of strikes to limit the unilateral power of local institutions. At both the University of Nottingham and London Metropolitan University in 2004 local managers attempted to impose new terms and conditions on workers, leading to strikes and calls for boycotts (or 'greylisting') of the respective institutions (Harvie, 2006). Under the Framework Agreement, all university workers were to be transferred to a single pay spine, the details of which were to be agreed locally. An 'academic role profile' of routine duties undertaken was meant to determine where academics would be pegged in the new pay scale. Academics who fell short of minimum roles associated with their current position would be 'red-circled' and given three years to reach the standard of routine work functions.

Although the finances of some institutions are in a poor state and the UK spends proportionately less on HE than its main economic competitors, the past decade has been a boom time for university revenues. Amidst government rhetoric that universities must become more entrepreneurial, 'dynamic and self-determining' marketised institutions, the state remains, of necessity, the financial underwriter of HE, funding it to the tune of around £10 billion in 2006. For this investment universities claim that they contributed £45 billion to the UK economy in 2004, a rise of £10 billion over five years. Universities are therefore one of the UK's major industrial sectors (Fazackerley, 2006b). Universities supplement state funding with income from the global market in students, which generated £1.4 billion for British universities in 2005 (Tysome, 2006c). The combined income of English universities rose by 35% in real terms between 1995 and 2004. According to the employers' own research revenue is predicted to grow by a further 39% by 2011 (Sanders, 2006b).

This buoyant financial situation nationally fuels academic resentment over pay, productivity and deteriorating conditions at work. It also gave a serious pay claim from the academic unions a real chance of success. In January 2006 the unions submitted a claim for 23% over three years, which the employers immediately rejected as costing more than half of the top-up fee income. Employers countered that lecturers could already expect an additional rise of 3% to 5% due to the Framework deal done in 2004. Unconvinced by the employers' position, more than 80% of union members voted in a ballot for industrial action short of strike. A one-day strike in March 2006 was widely supported. A boycott of exams and assessments began the next day. The employers hardened their position, refusing even to meet striking unions for talks unless they suspended the action. Their initial offer of 6% over two years was rejected instantly and the dispute carried into the exam period of April to June.

In the face of barely concealed employer divisions, academic unions could have made the breakthrough in pay that had been promised for years. Despite the fact that the academic unions were divided – by academic and non-academic staff, full-time and part-time, fixed-contract staff, senior grades and lecturers, and three different academic unions, AUT, the National Association of Teachers in Further and Higher Education (NATFHE) and the Educational Institute of Scotland (EIS) – the industrial action was well supported, although more vigorously and resolutely in some places than others. Throughout, the National Union of Students (NUS) nationally supported the lecturers' action but around 20 student unions circulated a petition criticising the action while offering 'moral support' for their case for better pay. In the face of threats to effectively lock out academics at Northumbria and Oxford Brookes, mass meetings voted for indefinite strike action forcing management to retreat. At Leeds, Bristol and Liverpool large demonstrations were held against management intimidation. University exams were in disarray in many places, with management contingency plans proving costly and ineffectual. External bodies like the Law Society, the British Psychological Society and the Royal College of Physicians cast doubt that such managerial contingencies could guarantee academic standards. The Quality Assurance Agency (QAA) accused universities that attempted to award qualifications without full exam results of compromising standards.

Throughout the dispute new members joined the union in greater numbers than ever before, with 1,300 joining the AUT, giving its largest ever membership roll of 49,000, while another 1,000 joined NATFHE in March alone (AUT, 2006). But by June a three-year pay deal of 13.1% was agreed that fell well short of the original claim. All industrial action was suspended by the union leaders with immediate effect, even before a ballot had been conducted. Even the union general secretaries were forced to concede that 'we are acutely aware that this will still not make up the ground lost over past decades' (UCU, 2006). Demobilised (and demoralised) union members voted to accept the deal, with a substantial minority rejecting it, indicating that they were prepared to 'resume serious industrial action'. Some lecturers were persuaded by the moral argument that they were harming students more than management.[3] Other, more militant members held a large meeting to establish a national network of rank and file activists, the

UCU Left (Universities and Colleges Union). It was just as the action was being called off in June 2006 that the main unions, AUT and NATFHE, merged into a single union for further education (FE) and HE (although in Scotland the EIS continues to represent most post-1992 institutions) to become UCU. Member demoralisation in the aftermath of the action meant that turnout to elect Sally Hunt as the UCU General Secretary in March 2007 was as low as 14%, with around 100,000 members failing to vote. Despite leading the 2006 pay campaign fiasco, Hunt faced divided opposition and benefited from the desire among many members to vote for a female union leader.

## Conclusions

Academics have been assailed on all sides by competing demands on their work time and have been increasingly required to adopt generic administrative and managerial skills. An endless striving has been set in train in HE for managerial regimes in terms of efficiencies, 'value for money', transparent costing, output measures, performance appraisals and so on. This has had, and is having, thoroughgoing effects on academic workers, their health and pay, their sense of vocation and service, the declining value placed on critical education and research, and their propensity to adopt traditional methods of industrial militancy. A steady, although uneven and contradictory growth in the intensification of academic work has seen 'productivity' output rise in absolute and relative student numbers, pass grades, and publication and citation measurements. Alongside the individualising tendencies of the RAE, the importation of managerial discourses and practices mean that for many of Britain's university lecturers, the academic department of today is a world largely transformed from the romantic mythical world of 'donnish dominion'. The consequence of all this has been a shift from a self-directed 'artisanal' labour process to an uneven process of bureaucratisation of much academic work, typically controlled from a distance by numerous productivity indicators. As such, major challenges face academic trade unionism in this environment of work degradation, worsening personal health problems, relative low pay and deepening managerialism. In her 2007 election campaign, UCU General Secretary Sally Hunt re-stated her commitment to wage a trenchant campaign against privatisation, excessive workloads, fixed-term contracts and low pay. Yet, the semi-bureaucratisation of academic labour, the continuing hold of the ideology of professionalism and the competitive career structure will make effective union organisation and action a challenging prospect whether New Labour retains its hold on office or not.

## Notes

[1] Reinstated in the 2004 Higher Education Act for students from poor backgrounds.

[2] See Noble (2003) for technological deskilling in the US and resistance to it. See also Levidow (2002) for a global survey.

[3] See, for instance, the comments of a dozen lecturers at the end of the dispute, many, tellingly, speaking anonymously, in 'Dispute leaves a bitter taste', *The Times Higher Education Supplement*, 28 July 2006, p 14.

## Further sources

New Labour's vision for HE is spelt out in Cm 5735 (2003) *The future of higher education*. This can be usefully cross-referenced to the analysis by Ainley (2004) of the function and extent of the 'new market state' education, including higher education and Ryan (2005). Beck and Young (2005) analyse some of the key points of tension in the redefinition of professionalism in higher education. Colin Bryson (2004a, 2004b) has produced a number of empirical studies of workers in higher education. These can be placed in the context of the neoliberal policies for 'the knowledge economy' by Willmott (2003), Callinicos (2006) and Harvie (2006). See the UCU website, www.ucu.org.uk, for union perspectives on higher education and the union activists website, www.uculeft.devisland.net. *The Times Higher Education Supplement* is a weekly newspaper that carries regular reports on working conditions and industrial relations in the sector.

## References

Adorno, T. (2005) *Minima moralia: Reflections of a damaged life*, London: Verso.

Advisory Council on Applied Research and Development (1983) *Improving research links. between higher education and industry*, London: HMSO.

Ainley, P. (2004) 'The new "market-state" and education', *Journal of Education Policy*, vol 19, no 4, pp 497-513.

Archer, L., Hutchings, M. and Ross, A. (2003) *Higher education and social class. Issues of exclusion and inclusion*, London: RoutledgeFalmer.

AUT (2006) 'Membership hardens as dispute lines harden' (www.aut. org.uk/index.cfm?articleid=1601#).

Barnett, R. (2003) *Beyond all reason: Living with ideology in the university*, Buckingham: SRHE and Open University Press.

Baty, P. (2007a) 'Open-plan risk to collegiality', *The Times Higher Education Supplement*, 16 March, p 2.

Baty, P. (2007b) 'Autonomy falls prey to performance cultures', *The Times Higher Education Supplement*, 23 March, p 6.

Baty, P. and Thomson, A. (2006) 'Who will break first in the battle of the giants?', *The Times Higher Education Supplement*, 14 April, pp 16-17.

Beck, J. and Young, F.D. (2005) 'The assault on the professions and the restructuring of academic and professional identities: A Bernsteinian analysis', *British Journal of Sociology of Education*, vol 26, no 2, pp 183-97.

Bertelsen, E. (1998) 'The real transformation: the marketization of higher education', *Social Dynamics*, vol 24, no 2, pp 130-58.

Bourdieu, P. (1988) *Homo academicus*, Cambridge: Polity Press.

Brehony, K.J. and Deem, R. (2005) 'Challenging the post-Fordist/flexible organisation thesis: the case of reformed educational organisations', *British Journal of Sociology of Education*, vol 26, no 3, pp 395-414.

BRTF (Better Regulation Task Force) (2002) *Higher education: Easing the burden*, London: BRTF.

Bryson, C. (2004a) 'The consequences for women in the academic profession of the widespread use of fixed contracts', *Gender, Work and Organisation*, vol 11, no 2, pp 187-206.

Bryson, C. (2004b) 'What about the workers? The expansion of higher education and the transformation of academic work', *Industrial Relations Journal*, vol 35, no 1, pp 38-57.

Callinicos, A. (2006) *Universities in a neoliberal world*, London: Bookmarks.

Coffield, F. (2000) *Differing visions of a Learning Society*, Bristol: The Policy Press.

Cole, M. (2005) 'New Labour, globalization and social justice: the role of education', in G. Fischman, P. Mclaren, H. Sunker and C. Lankshear (eds) *Critical theories, radical pedagogies and global conflicts*, Lanham: Rowan and Littlefield.

Crace, J. (2005, 'Punch the clock', *The Guardian*, 24 May.

Curtis, P. (2004) 'Women paid less at every university', *The Guardian*, 2 September.

Dearing Report (1997) *Higher education in the Learning Society*, London: The Stationery Office.

Dearlove, J. (1997) 'The academic labour process: from collegiality and professionalism to managerialism and proletarianisation?', *Higher Education Review*, vol 30, no 1, pp 56-75.

Deem, R. and Brehony, K.J. (2005) 'Management as ideology: the case of "new managerialism" in higher education', *Oxford Review of Education*, vol 31, no 2, pp 217-35.

DfEE (Department for Education and Employment) (1998) *The learning age: A renaissance for a new Britain*, London: DfEE.

DfES (Department for Education and Skills) (2003) *The future of higher education*, Cm 5735, Norwich: The Stationery Office.

Eagleton, T. (2006) 'Your thoughts are no longer worth a penny', *The Times Higher Education Supplement*, 10 March, pp 18-19.

Faure, E (1972) *Learning to be: The world of education today and tomorrow*, Paris: UNESCO.

Fazackerley, A. (2006a) 'Sussex rebels pray for coup', *The Times Higher Education Supplement*, June, p 4.

Fazackerley, A. (2006b) 'Sector brings in 45bn to UK', *The Times Higher Education Supplement*, p 5.

Forman, S. (2005) 'Rebel ALs rock boat over HERA deal', *Open House*, vol 401, pp 1, 7.

Fryer, R.H. (1997) *Learning for the twenty first century. First report of the National Advisory Group for continuing education and lifelong learning*, London: DfEE.

Galindo-Rueda, F., Marcenaro-Guiterrez, O. and Vignoles, A. (2004) 'The widening socio-economic gap in UK higher education', *National Institute Economic Review*, vol 190, pp 75-88.

Halsey, A.H. (1992) *Decline of donnish dominion*, Oxford: Clarendon Press.

Harvie, D. (2006) 'Value production and struggle in the classroom: teachers within, against and beyond capital', *Capital & Class*, vol 88, pp 1-32.

Hodkinson, P. (2001) 'Researching the Learning Society', *Work, Employment and Society*, vol 15, no 2, pp 385-93.

Husen, T. (1974) *The Learning Society*, London: Methuen.

Jarratt, Sir A. (1985) *Report of the Steering Committee for Efficiency Studies in Universities*, London: CVCP/UGC.

Jones, R. and Thomas, L. (2005) 'The 2003 UK government higher education White Paper: a critical assessment of its implications for the access and widening participation agenda', *Journal of Education Policy*, vol 20, no 5, pp 615-30.

Lambert, R. (2003) *Lambert Review of business–university collaboration*, London: The Stationery Office.

Levidow, L. (2002) 'Marketizing higher education: neoliberal strategies and counter-strategies', in K. Robins and F. Webster (eds) *The virtual university: Information, markets and management*, Oxford: Oxford University Press.

Levitas, R. (2004) 'Let's hear it for humpty: social exclusion, the Third Way and cultural capital', *Cultural Trends*, vol 13, no 2, pp 41-56.

Lipsett, A. (2006) 'Arts academic slate metrics', *The Times Higher Education Supplement* 28 July, p 4.

MacLure, M. (2005) 'Clarity bordering on stupidity. Where's the quality in systematic review?', *Journal of Education Policy*, vol 20, no 4, pp 393-416.

Marx, K. (1976) *Capital: A critique of political economy, Volume One*, Harmondsworth: Penguin.

Marx, K. and Engels, F. (1998) *The Communist manifesto: A modern edition*, London: Verso.

Miller, H. (1991) 'Academics and their labour process', in C. Smith, D. Knights and H. Willmott (eds) *White collar work*, London: Macmillan.

Noble, D. (2003) 'Digital diploma mills', in B. Johnson, P. Kavanagh and K. Mattson (eds) *Steal this university: The rise of the corporate university and the academic labor movement*, New York, NY: Routledge.

Parker, M. and Jary, D. (1995) 'The McUniversity: organisations, management and academic subjectivities', *Organization*, vol 2, no 2, pp 319-38.

Peters, M.A. (2005) 'The posthistorical university? Prospects for alternative globalizations', in G. Fischman, P. Mclaren, H. Sunker and C. Lankshear (eds) *Critical theories, radical pedagogies and global conflicts*, Lanham, MD: Rowman Littlefield.

Pollitt, C (1990) *Managerialism and the public services*, Oxford: Basil Blackwell.

Prichard, C. and Willmott, H. (1997) 'Just how managed is the McUniversity?', *Organization Studies*, vol 18, no 2, pp 287-316.

Roberts, Sir G. (2003) *Review of research assessment*, Bristol: HEFC.

Ryan, A. (2005) 'New Labour and higher education', *Oxford Review of Education*, vol 31, no 1, pp 87-100.

Salter, B. and Tapper, T. (1994) *The state and higher education*, Essex: The Woburn Press.

Sanders, C. (2006a) 'Sort out casual problem, says UCU', *The Times Higher Education Supplement*, 14 July, p 52.

Sanders, C. (2006b) 'Soaring revenues stoke pay debate', *The Times Higher Education Supplement*, 30 June, pp 1, 6.

Shepherd, J. (2006) 'Staff are silenced by fear of reprisals', *The Times Higher Education Supplement*, 4 August, p 1.

Stothart, C. (2006) 'Top cop gets £20k more than professor', *The Times Higher Education Supplement*, 12 May, pp 6-7.

Swain, H. (2006) 'No, life is not just one long holiday', *The Times Higher Education Supplement*, 14 July, p 1.

Taylor, M. (2006) 'AUT calls for inquiry into vice-chancellor's pay', *The Guardian*, 9 March.

Thompson, E.P. (1970) *Warwick University Ltd: Industry, management and the universities*, Harmondsworth: Penguin.

Thomson, A. (2006) 'Door slams shut on a room of one's own', *The Times Higher Education Supplement*, 5 May, p 5.

Tysome, T. (2006a) 'Lecturers hours rise', *The Times Higher Education Supplement*, 4 August, p 40.

Tysome, T. (2006b) 'Union blames "miscalculation" as axe hangs over 35 jobs', *The Times Higher Education Supplement*, 30 June, p 5.

Tysome, T. (2006c) 'Overseas cash injection rises', *The Times Higher Education Supplement*, 11 August, p 2.

UCEA (2005) *Recruitment and retention in higher education: Full report*, Brighton: Institute for Employment Studies.

UCU (2006) 'Deal reached in HE pay talks', *UC*, June, p 3.

Veblen, T. (1918) *Higher learning in America: A memorandum on the conduct of universities by businessmen*, New York, NY: Hill and Wang (1957 edn).

Willmott, H. (1995) 'Managing the academics: commodification and control in the development of university education in the UK', *Human Relations*, vol 48, no 9, pp 993-1027.

Willmott, H. (2003) 'Commercialising higher education in the UK: the state, industry and peer review', *Studies in Higher Education*, vol 28, no 2, pp 129-41.

Wilson, T. (1991) 'The proletarianisation of academic labour', *Human Relations Journal*, vol 22, pp 250-62.

Wojtas, O. (2006) 'Edinburgh management and union forge unique alliance to address fixed-term contracts', *The Times Higher Education Supplement*, 4 August, pp 4-5.

# EIGHT

# The paradox of 'professionalisation' and 'degradation' in welfare work: the case of nursery nurses

*Gerry Mooney and Tricia McCafferty*

## Introduction

The focus of this chapter is on a particular group of employees who have long been central to the welfare state in the UK, childcare workers. Childcare, at least as organised in and across the public sector, is a highly visible element of welfare provision (even if childcare labour itself has for a long time been largely invisible). In part this chapter, and the research that has driven it, is concerned to illuminate an area of welfare work that has tended to be neglected across much of the literature in social policy, industrial relations and the sociology of work more generally. There are, of course, significant exceptions to this and we will call on some of the insightful work that has been undertaken in this field as the chapter unfolds.

There are other important reasons for choosing to focus on nursery nurses. One of the key arguments that will be developed is that while the welfare labour of childcare workers, now termed by government the 'early years workforce', has frequently been overlooked, it has come increasingly to be regarded as an important factor enabling the 'modernisation' of the UK welfare state (Kessler et al, 2006, p 673). This has occurred primarily as a result of the government's re-focus on childcare across a range of welfare policies, for instance the New Deal for employment and Sure Start, among others. It is also, as with workers in some other welfare sectors (see Davies, 2003, on health workers, for example), a labour force that the government is determined to remake in its own mould.

While many childcare workers, and in particular nursery nurses, have long struggled to combat the widely held view that they 'simply look after children' – performing a 'natural'/private role in the public sphere

– many of them are now discovering that they are increasingly centre-stage in relation to a range of important social policy objectives and in recent legislation such as the 2006 Childcare Act for England and Wales (see, in addition, the National Childcare Strategy, 1998: DfEE, 1998; the Scottish Childcare Strategy, 1998: Scottish Office, 1998; see also Wincott, 2005). This new legislation and other childcare policies bear the hallmarks of New Labour policy making, in particular in the emphasis that is given to the issue of parental choice and the provision of 'high-quality' services (which, for the government, requires a more highly skilled and 'professional' workforce). In turn childcare workers are being called on to undertake a range of additional responsibilities. Early Years policies have become a major priority for government. As the Prime Minister commented in 1999, 'we have made children our top priority because, as the Chancellor memorably said in his Budget, "they are 20% of the population but they are 100% of the future"' (Blair, 1999, p 16). For Pearce and Paxton the government's commitment to childcare provision has far-reaching implications for the new welfare settlement that New Labour is attempting to forge:

> Embedding entitlements to childcare and early years education in a high-quality publicly regulated and comprehensive service should form the centrepiece of progressive institution-building in the early 21st century, just as the NHS did in the immediate post-war period. (Pearce and Paxton, 2005, p xxi)

Pearce and Paxton's sympathetic New Labour-influenced rhetoric aside, this serves to highlight the central role that is being accorded to childcare provision in UK social and employment policy today. Perhaps not surprisingly, however, less is said about the ways in which such policies will impact on the childcare workforce, or that these workers are among the lowest paid in the entire public sector/welfare industry, with nursery nurses generally

> ... less well rewarded than those in other non-degree posts in local authorities, despite appearing to carry out 'like' work similar to better paid degree-level occupational groups. They also earn considerably less than average earnings. (Findlay et al, 2005, pp 62-3)

Using data from the 2005 Annual Survey of Hours and Earnings (ASHE), Findlay et al compared salaries for non-degree-related posts in Scottish local government (2005, p 55). In January 2005, the median maximum salary for a nursery nurse was £17,340 compared with £19,029 for housing officers, £21,732 for administrative officers and £24,396 for finance officers. As public sector UNISON highlights, pay across the childcare sector is 'notoriously low' (UNISON, 2006a, p 10).

While the conditions and pay of local authority-employed nursery nurses are often better than in the private and informal sectors, they remain relatively low paid with limited career and promotion prospects (see Scott et al, 2000; UNISON, 2003, 2006a, 2006b; Findlay et al, 2005; Colley, 2006). Given that pre-school education and other services have historically been viewed as a preserve of female labour, not surprisingly there are few sectors where gender segregation is greater, with women comprising around 99% of the nursery nurse labour force (Cameron, 2001; Colley, 2006). Focusing on the conditions and experiences of marginalised, low-paid and an overwhelmingly female labour force provides new insights into the ways in which welfare work is being increasingly subjected to a range of different and often contradictory pressures, and how they impact on the working conditions of those in the frontline of service delivery.

It is worth re-stating here that the post-1945 Beveridgean welfare state was developed and expanded on the back of the labour of a large number of low-paid workers. The labour of underpaid and undervalued female workers was absolutely central to this. As has been highlighted elsewhere in this book, female labour is also central to the restructured and 'modernised' welfare state that is being developed by New Labour. Clearly, what Blair has declared as a welfare state 'designed not for yesterday, but for today' (quoted in Ferguson et al, 2002, p 164) continues to be predicated on traditional concerns for low-cost/high-'output' labour. To fully grasp what this means for childcare workers, such as nursery nurses, requires us to consider the voices of workers themselves, as we do in this chapter.

Drawing on the 2004 Scottish nursery nurses strike, and its unfolding outcomes, we seek to illuminate the ways in which this group of workers, like others across the welfare sectors, are, in the words of one nursery nurse interviewed during our research, increasingly required to do 'more and more for less and less'. In particular we argue that nursery nurses are being subjected to the multiple and contradictory processes of a renewed 'professionalisation' – or arguably and more correctly the rhetoric of professionalism – and 'upskilling', and of increasing work intensification and degradation.

Local authority pre-school education provision in Scotland has yet to be fully exposed to the marketisation and privatisation impulses that are underpinning the reform of childcare provision in England or elsewhere across the public sector. In England under the badge 'Every Child Matters', the 2006 Childcare Act forced local authorities to hand over children's centres to the private and voluntary sector, local authorities identified for 'last resort' provision only (UNISON, 2006b, p 24). In some local authorities in England (for instance, Greenwich in London) nursery nurses have been expected to provide cover for teachers (UNISON, 6 June 2006: www.unison.org.uk). However, in other ways New Labour's economic and social agendas are increasingly bearing down on pre-school workers such as nursery nurses across the UK. There is greater emphasis on performance, inspection and regulation, additional duties and increasing tensions between employee-led approaches, management and employer demands and organisational structures. There is also a greater emphasis on costs and budgets and on accounting procedures, all of which increase the feeling of bureaucratic overload. These are combining to reshape the social and employment relations of workers in these fields as well as contributing to problems of morale. Often dismissed as less important than other forms of work, a sense of being undervalued pervades care work in the UK (see also Wills, 2003).

Taking Scottish local authority nurses as an example serves to illustrate just how far New Labour's reform programmes are attempting to reshape work across large swathes of the public services – including those that remain, for now at any rate, under the control of local authorities. Further, given the different histories of childcare provision between Scotland and the rest of the UK, particularly England, with local authority provision playing a more significant role north of the border, an examination of developments in Scotland can illuminate how care work in local authorities is being subjected to many of the same pressures being experienced by workers elsewhere in welfare services. Since 2004 the provision of nursery places for three-year-olds has been compulsory and local authorities are now legally bound to offer 2.5 hours per day, 33 weeks per year from the term following a child's third birthday. In Scotland in 2006 approximately 97.5% of children who were eligible for free ante-pre-school and pre-school education were registered with local authority or partnership providers (93,042 children). Of all registered childcare and pre-school education centres 41.8% were in the public sector, 22.3% were in the private sector and 34% were in the voluntary sector (Scottish Executive, 2006a). In the third most deprived areas, 49% of childcare and pre-school education centres were local authority-managed, compared to 35% in the third least deprived areas.

The growing tensions generated around childcare provision as a result of government policies have been illustrated in sharp terms in Scotland in recent years. We return to this later in the chapter.

## Labouring for the 'social investment state'

The notion of a 'social investment state' derives from the arguments of Giddens (1994, 1998) that the central objective of New Labour's Third Way approach is to facilitate 'investment in *human capital* wherever possible, rather than direct provision of economic maintenance' (1998, p 117; original emphasis). This focus on 'supply-side' issues is reflected in, for example, the recurring emphasis on education and training. Following the work of Ruth Lister (2003), among others, it is argued here that investment in children (including childcare) – the 'citizen-workers' of the future – has been central to New Labour's social policy agenda. As Lister noted, the child is identified as a key 'cipher for future economic prosperity and forward-looking modernisation' (2003, p 433). Child tax credits, the National Childcare Strategy and Sure Start represent some of the most visible dimensions of this approach. Moreover, as we explore below, building the human capital of children is an endeavour that cannot begin too soon for the government.

As might be anticipated the government's policies in this area have been widely reviewed and critiqued (see, for instance, Prout, 2000; Ridge, 2002). While childcare has expanded and taken on new responsibilities, there is a gulf between the rhetoric of affordable childcare for all and the reality on the ground. In such a context 'informal' types of child caring are often the only types available for many parents. Thus, alongside the renewed emphasis on public childcare, both state and private, the increasing shift towards the familialisation of caring, using family members for instance, or informalisation (paying neighbours and/or teenage children for childcare and so on), works to undermine the assumption that the state has a responsibility to provide childcare (and indeed other care) services. The growing familialisation and informalisation of childcare *alongside* the seemingly paradoxical shift towards professionalisation are key dimensions of the changing milieu in which local authority-employed nursery nurses work. This also works to reinforce women's position in public labour in the so-called '5Cs' – that is, caring, clerical, cleaning, catering and cashiering work – work that is reflective of women's general position in the private/domestic sphere.

Further, as Prout observed, policy is centred on the expectation of 'the better adult lives that will ... emerge from reducing poverty. It is not on the better lives that children will lead as children' (2000, p 305). For example:

> For pre-school children there is strong evidence that pre-school ... results in higher educational attainment, both at primary and long-term ... [it] produces wider benefits eg a reduction in crime rates, improved health outcomes and attitudinal outcomes, such as self-esteem and aptitude for learning.... Learning at home with parents combined with high quality pre-school education, makes a positive difference to children's social and intellectual development. (House of Commons Work and Pensions Committee, 2003, para 13)

> In their adulthood, today's children will form the nation's workforce for years to come: they will become the parents of future generations of children, the community leaders, the volunteers, the entrepreneurs and business leaders, the politicians, artists and sporting heroes of the future. If they are to be properly equipped with the skills, knowledge and dispositions to play these roles, they must have the best possible support at the very start of their lives. (Scottish Parliament, 2006, para 3)

The explicit recognition that the determination of life chances may well occur in the early years is accompanied by a strong belief that the development of human capital in the ultimate service of the economy is a process that begins almost from birth. However, investment in children – and in particular for our purposes in this chapter, in childcare – have other rationales for New Labour. The provision of childcare is also related to the promotion of social inclusion (as entry to paid work) for another one of New Labour's key 'problem' groups – 'workless' lone parents, especially women. In January 2007 Work and Pensions Minister John Hutton announced plans to introduce more stringent requirements for lone parents on benefit to look for paid employment, supported by proposals to increase the availability of childcare provision (source: *The Guardian*, 30 January 2007). Along with a range of other strategies, childcare is crucial for New Labour's goal of promoting employability and increasing women's participation in the labour market. The provision of childcare, then, is important for labour market 'activation' and 'active welfare'. 'Work' as paid employment is seen as delivering a range of cross-generational advantages:

> Lone mothers say that work is about more than money, although that is important. Work for them means that they do not have to depend on benefits. They can show their children that income is about work rather than benefits.... They want to work so that they can set an example to their children, and can bring them up to understand that life is about work and not just claiming benefits. (Harman, 1997, p 7)

There is a 'double edge' to New Labour's strategy here. In childcare and Early Years education, New Labour's goals for both 'customers' (parents) and 'service providers' (in this case, nursery nurses) amounts to the same: 'upskilling' and the development of 'human capital' as *the* route out of poverty (especially for lone parents as customers) and the key to professionalisation and social value enhancement (for nursery nurses as providers). However, while there is considerable emphasis on 'formal' 'upskilling' there is a generalised process of de facto 'downskilling'. In other words, an emphasis on what we would term 'credentialism' but not work autonomy, at least as this has traditionally been understood in welfare professionalism.

This 'upskilling' represents one of the most obvious dimensions of New Labour's competitiveness and social inclusion synergy but is additionally indicative of a drive to tackle what it perceives as the 'drain' of unproductive labour implicitly, in this context, female single parents. The development of childcare policies across the devolved UK is therefore matched to both economic and social objectives (see Prime Minister's Strategy Unit, 2002; WAG, 2002; Brown, 2004; HM Treasury, 2004; Scottish Executive, 2004, 2006b, 2006c; Scottish Parliament, 2006).

Women, when employed as childcare workers, facilitate the entrance or return of other women to the labour market (often to childcare itself). National competitiveness and social inclusion are therefore enhanced. In all of this women are identified as both a target and a vehicle for social policy interventions. However, while child carers and Early Years educators live out their day-to-day lives in what we could term 'worker improvement factories', as we have seen, many remain in the 'prison' of general low-paid and undervalued work.

Local authority nursery nurses are working with some of the most vulnerable groups in society. As is evident from our research below and from other work in this field, childcare workers struggle on a daily basis to help meet the needs of some of the most disadvantaged children and families, and all too frequently in a context where resources are very limited, where there are often reductions in public services and, increasingly, where a more punitive social policy ethos is developing (see Jones and Novak, 1999; Cook, 2006). Public sector childcare has often played a crucial (although not always successful) role in the task of helping children from disadvantaged backgrounds by both providing a 'place of safety', particularly for 'children in need' and by assisting their transition to school.

Therefore, taking all these roles and responsibilities together, childcare workers do much more than 'look after children' (see Kelso, 2002; Mooney and McCafferty 2005). They are a key group of workers in a central area of New Labour's social inclusion strategy, fundamental to the production and reproduction of the worker-citizen. Following this we argue that the childcare and the Early Years education labour process parallel the intensification of work that is occurring elsewhere across the public and welfare sectors on the one hand, and a growing pressure to engage, both manually and mentally, in a complex and varied set of tasks on the other. There are then, combined and contradictory pressures playing out here, the tensions of work intensification, routinisation and upskilling.

In relation to upskilling there is a specific burden placed on workers such as nursery nurses regarding the accumulation of human capital. New Labour's wider 'responsibilisation' strategy means that they are the key agents through which their own marketability can be enhanced, through gaining compulsory qualifications, which is now a requirement of obligatory registration; and, as we have argued above, they are also pivotal actors in enabling some women to re-enter the labour market. They are at the frontline of Early Years development when children, as the government perceives it, will be taking their first tentative steps in their development of human capital. It is, therefore, key groups of women workers that are all too often at the heart of skills investment under New Labour, rather than men as human capital theory presents it (see Becker, 1975).

The prevalence of women in the public sector means that the brunt of New Labour policy is disproportionately borne by female workers. Figures differ but women comprise somewhere between two thirds and four fifths of the total public sector labour force (Thornley, 2006, p 345). Those women workers who comprise 81% of the wider social services workforce in Scotland (Scottish Executive, 2006b, 2006c), for example, increasingly need to negotiate the exigencies of a marketised version of caring that has been steadily (although unevenly) emerging in recent times. In addition, with the childcare and pre-school education sector almost entirely populated by female workers, the impact, both positive and negative, of governmental policies such as welfare-to-work and Sure Start will have particularly direct effects on them.

There is a growing demand for childcare workers across the UK. Such demand reflects familial, demographic and economic trends as well as government initiatives. In the general retreat of the welfare state, which has frequently involved an erosion in the working conditions and career opportunities that often characterised the professional jobs that were open to female workers in the 1960s and 1970s, childcare is arguably one of the few areas that has undergone much expansion and that has been targeted for further development. There are around 350,000 childcare workers in England (Simon et al, 2003, p 1) and just over 34,000 workers in the entire Early Years and childcare workforce in Scotland (Annual Labour Force Survey Scotland, 2004/05: www. scotland.gov.uk). The main growth in employment has taken place largely in the private sector and informal forms of provision (including after-school clubs, holiday clubs and care undertaken by nannies and childminders), and as such serves to reproduce class and gender divisions, reflecting as it does the '*relationship of many women to New Labour's welfare state as (low paid) employees, mothers and "citizens"*' (Wakefield, 2004, p 45; emphasis added). The fundamental contradiction of this is that unemployed single mothers are being pressured to put their own children into childcare, much of it familial or informal, in order to facilitate their own engagement in paid childcare labour.

There is also evidence that demand for childcare is growing at the very time when there are increasing problems with the recruitment and retention of childcare workers (see Simon et al, 2003; UNISON, 2003), and reports from some parts of the UK of cuts in the numbers of nursery teacher posts, for example in Glasgow between 2004 and 2006 (*The Herald*, 29 December 2006). In certain parts of the country labour is being increasingly supplied by migrant workers, as part of existing and emerging 'global care chains' of labour (see Hochschild, 2001; see also Kofman and Sales, 1998; Ehrenreich and Hochschild, 2003; Wills, 2003; May et al, 2006).

New Labour has made much of its commitment to addressing issues of equality and social justice. The multiple impacts of government policy and the additional work that this is often creating, however, is undermining any sense that equality and social justice at work is being protected, even less enhanced.

## Uncovering the nursery nursing labour process

Thus far we have been concerned to provide a picture of the general social context within which nursery nurses are operating. In particular we have highlighted the wider policy environment, noting the renewed emphasis on childcare provision to support other New Labour social policy objectives. In this section we now consider the ways in which the labour process of nursery nursing in the local authority sector in Scotland is, through public sector modernisation, working to condition and shape the experience of an important group of welfare workers, and how such workers, in taking industrial action, effectively drew attention to the contradictions of some of the central premises of the New Labour project.

The example of the proposed modernisation of childcare and, especially, the issues that emerged around the 2004 Scottish nursery nurses strike help to demonstrate how much of New Labour's social policy agenda is dependent on the labour of an overwhelmingly female, poorly paid and increasingly angry workforce. Importantly, it acts as a useful illustration of how experience of working 'for' New Labour in the public sector often involves a contradictory mix of additional responsibilities, pressure to 'upskill' and invest (mainly in their own time) in career and personal development and the dilution of former autonomies (however limited). As Fairbrother and Poynter point out:

> This dilution has facilitated the re-shaping of hierarchies within the public service labour process and has accorded individuals working within it new social responsibilities that aim at their ideological co-option into programmes of social engineering initiated by the Labour Government. (Fairbrother and Poynter, 2001, p 320)

In the case of the Scottish nursery nurses strike, and the subsequent publication in 2006 of the Scottish Executive's Early Years education and childcare workforce review that it triggered (Scottish Executive, 2006b, 2006c), this is best summed up as an uneasy compromise between 'old-fashioned' 'practical' work, emotional labour and the added 'knowledge' dimension that, in New Labour's terms, characterises 'modern' work experience.

A number of the comments made to us during our research at the time of the 2004 Scottish nursery nurses dispute made clear that the labour process of nursery nursing is being actively reshaped as a result of the mix of new social policy priorities and welfare reform as well as demographic trends and in the general market for childcare labour:

'Since I moved to work for the council there are new initiatives every year; key workers; new ratios; profiling.... We've got planning; evaluation; observation; recording – all weekly, sometimes daily.... I blame the government – it's them that brings it all out and they don't give you extra money for it. [People] don't realise they don't pay the staff extra for it.' (Striking nursery nurse 1, Fife)

'Everyday it seems that there are new responsibilities being given to us – from all sorts of directions. And of course the core work that we always did is still there – but the employers are wanting us to be more involved with activities that were not in our remit in the past.' (Striking nursery nurse 4, Renfrewshire)

There are different dimensions to these added responsibilities as we noted earlier in this chapter. In part there is – as in other areas of social policy – a concern to 'join up' or 'integrate' the work of different sectors and providers in an effort to deliver a 'better' service to 'consumers', here, the parents of pre-school-age children. We have also observed the new emphasis on childcare workers supporting policies aimed at promoting employability and in addition, in Scotland at least, a renewed emphasis on the development of 'cognitive' abilities of pre-school children. The Scottish Parliament's Education Committee, reflecting on proposed changes in pre-school education in 2006, noted that:

... in general early years services in Scotland are broadly play-based, but are less adult directed than, for example, those in England, where there tends to be a more structured emphasis on building towards learning 'emerging' literacy and numeracy skills ... child care should begin to focus not only on care but on the stimulation of young people and how their early experiences help their education. (Scottish Parliament, 2006, paras 68, 69)

While it is not within the scope of this chapter, nonetheless we cannot ignore that such trends may have counterproductive effects. A narrow utilitarian view is evident here with evidence of a growing emphasis on cognitive skills, learning outcomes and transferable skills. Let us not forget that we are talking about pre-school-age children here. If the important formative years of human development, from two to four years of age, are subjected to competing and perhaps contradictory demands, this may have adverse repercussions for both the children, their parents, schoolteachers and for society as a whole. There are also contradictory demands at work: play-centred activities are seen as important to a child's development but these depend *exactly* on the porosity of the working day that characterises nursery nursing labour. The adding on of more and more tasks, taking on younger children, increasing concerns with 'behaviour management' and so on work to fill (or over-fill) the working day in an indeterminate although often highly structured way:

> 'When I first started 10 years ago there was more scope for us to shape the day in ways that we knew worked for our particular children. There are too many different demands on us now. Do this, do that, do the next thing. There is little time to do the proper planning and spend enough time with each child.' (Striking nursery nurse 2, Glasgow)

The development of Early Years curriculum across the devolved UK reflects a desire on the part of the government to transform nursery nursing into a form of 'educare' (see www.literacytrust.org.uk; www.everychildmatters.gov.uk). Educare (and 'edubusiness') and the concern to develop pre-school curricula and other changes in pre-school objectives has direct consequences for frontline staff. In the Scottish Parliament report mentioned above, in relation to the higher staff to child ratios that prevail in pre-school establishments in England compared with Scotland, the Committee further comments that an increase in the ratios in Scotland is to be expected:

> It does not seem unreasonable to suppose that a workforce trained and skilled to a higher level than at present, as the Scottish Executive has committed itself to working towards, might be able to look after slightly higher numbers of children per adult than the current, less skilled workforce. (Scottish Parliament, 2006, paras 84, 85)

The desire to increase the number of children in pre-school education is then accompanied by a concern to ensure that cost control is maintained. However, higher ratios and additional responsibilities will operate – and are operating now – to both expand the responsibilities of Scottish local authority nursery nurses and other pre-school workers, thereby increasing their overall workload. This is a classic example of work intensification. But alongside this we note the emphasis on retraining, the pursuit of new and additional qualifications and upskilling. How does this sit with the central claims of labour process theory following Braverman (1974) that the 'degradation' and deskilling of labour is central to the capitalist labour process?

In areas such as pre-school education, what is emerging is a combination of continuing (and increased) worker responsibility, a renewed emphasis on professionalism/professionalisation and the intensification of work. Following Harvey (1995, p 765) we argue here that 'up-skilling (as opposed to deskilling) may also represent an intensification of work, since the terms and conditions under which skill is enhanced are centrally relevant'. Harvey's study focused on the 'extended role' in intensive care nursing and midwifery in the early 1990s, with specific groups of nurses expected to undertake tasks normally performed by doctors and consultants. The idea of an 'extended role' can be useful in helping to understand some of the increasing pressures on nursery nurses, while acknowledging the different contexts. Harvey (1995, p 767) further argues:

> It will be suggested that in terms of up-skilling the ideological constraints and material conditions under which skill is enhanced is centrally relevant. It follows, therefore, that upskilling may not in practice necessarily be linked to job-satisfaction, greater autonomy or increased economic remuneration.

This can also work to undermine any sense of open-ended, play-based relationships with infants. Harvey's argument is directly relevant for our understanding of the position that an increasing number of nursery nurses find themselves in today. Additional responsibilities do not deliver to the worker the 'empowerment' that government and employers are all too keen to highlight, but increasing levels of stress, pressure to meet increasingly diverse goals and greater regulation of work activities. In this sense job degradation can and does take place alongside a drive to upskill.

Taking the arguments of Hochschild (1983) and Colley (2006), we argue that emotional labour is central to the labour process of nursery nursing. Much of women's work in the public sphere is highly 'emotional', public service labour, not least because 'the display of emotion is an integral expectation of gender-stereotyped "women's work" in caring and personal social service occupations (and) partly because of women's difficulty in escaping the socially constructed gendered role of nurturing others established early on in family life ...' (Colley, 2006, p 16). For Hochschild such emotional labour is highly exploitative, subject to domination and managerial control (although rarely without struggle nor always complete). In relation to nursery nurse education, 'learning to labour with feeling', as Colley puts it, is central. Such emotional work is performed in the ways in which nursery nurses are expected to 'give of themselves' in the work setting. Among the qualities that are considered central here are patience, warmth, empathy, caring, kindness, gentleness and understanding, among others. Caring is often seen as a relationship between frontline staff and the children and their parents with workers expected to demonstrate commitment to developing such relationships. Colley (2006, p 25) further argues:

> In occupations like childcare and care of the elderly, the management of one's own and others' feelings is not a private adjunct to work, not a sub category of caring. It is a key feature of the workplace, a form of paid labour, or to be more accurate, of labour *power* – the capacity to labour.

Importantly, then, this rejects any idea that emotional work is less exploitative in some ways than other forms of labour. However, such 'soft skills' are typically undervalued across care work (see Innes et al, 2006).

Nursery nurses, as we have observed, often find themselves working with some of the most disadvantaged children, parents and families. As we will see below, they frequently take on a parental role, providing essential care for those in their charge. And to reinforce a point made above, there is an often hidden dimension to this and one that New Labour is pushing to develop. In working with 'socially excluded' parents, nursery nurses find themselves increasingly engaged in the responsibilisation and personalisation agendas being engineered by government (see Armstrong, 2006). 'Poor' or 'inadequate' parenting is a particular target of government policy here, seen by New Labour as a primary cause of 'anti-social' behaviour. In this nursery nurses are being pinpointed as among those who can take responsibility for, in New Labour terms, the moral welfare of others, for re-educating parents, and who will under-see the 'proper' socialisation of children at a very young age – a 'moral economy of caring'.

Nursery nurses then are frontline workers at the leading edge of a diverse range of social policy initiatives. Hence, crucially, they work at the very heart of the New Labour 'project' both in terms of policy practice, in relation to welfare governance and in implementing reform and modernisation strategies. It comes as little surprise that this has resulted in increasing workloads and a range of additional pressures. It is arguably more of a surprise that some nursery nurses have found themselves on the frontline of resistance to key aspects of government policies.

## Resisting New Labour: the 2004 Scottish nursery nurses strike

We claimed at the outset that an examination of the issues surrounding the Scottish nursery nurses strike in 2004 helps to illuminate key aspects of New Labour's policy initiatives and how these are impacting on those workers at the frontline of service delivery. The nursery nurses strike lasted for approximately 14 weeks and was the longest all-out national strike in Scotland since the 1984 miners strike. It is also one of the most notable episodes of strike activity among female workers in UK labour history. This was no local dispute but a national strike over the pay and conditions of around 5,000 low-paid, public sector childcare workers in an overwhelmingly female workforce, the vast majority of whom were members of the main public sector union, UNISON.

During the strike open-ended interviews were held with 20 nursery nurses from several different local authority areas in Scotland (including Fife, Glasgow, Inverclyde and Renfrewshire). All were women of varying age and experience. Among those interviewed were several who were employed in local authority-run nurseries, some in pre-school centres and one who worked in a primary school. These workers undertook a range of different roles in 'nursery nursing' work, illustrating the complex division of labour that exists within the pre-school education and care sector. Each was asked similar questions relating to the background to the strike, how they viewed changes in government childcare policies and their opinion on UNISON's national pay demand.

Nursery nurses have rarely been viewed as a group of militant workers. However, as their counterparts elsewhere in the public sector have discovered, over the past decade or so, former reputations increasingly count for little in the context of government policies towards the public sector and welfare delivery. In February 2004, following a pay and re-grading dispute that first emerged in 2001/02, in a ballot of nearly 5,000 UNISON members across Scotland, nursery nurses voted by 81% to

19% for indefinite strike action in pursuit of a significant increase in pay and a new career structure replacing the national payment agreement and conditions of service scheme established in 1988. Without a pay increase for 15 years, a key argument made by the strikers was that their pay and conditions were increasingly out of step with their enhanced role as *the* key workers in the provision of Early Years education. They found themselves at the forefront in the delivery of flagship government strategies without any improvements in their working lives. This latter point alludes to further complexity behind this dispute that played a major role in strengthening the nursery nurses' resolve. As with many of the other public sector strikes that have occurred in recent years, this dispute involved a challenge to central New Labour assumptions and confronting public sector reforms head on. This dispute was, therefore, one in which a complex interplay of grievances over pay combined with increasing demands from government led to a generalised sense among the pre-school workforce that they were being asked to do, in the words of a number of our interviewees, 'more and more for less and less', even as they were in the middle of the strike.

Both the Scottish and National Childcare Strategies highlighted additional responsibilities for childcare workers but completely failed to address pay and working conditions:

> 'Without us HMI [Her Majesty's Inspectorate] inspections would be a disaster. It's ordinary nursery nurses that get these things through but again there is no recognition of that in our wages.' (Striking nursery nurse 6, Renfrewshire)

> 'All we have heard from management is that we need to get more qualifications, more training, go on more courses and the like, but when we ask will we get more pay for this there is silence.' (Striking nursery nurse 7, Renfrewshire)

Further, it is notable that progress through the pay scales took a significant length of time for nursery nurses (between five and fifteen years to reach the top of the pay scales on average), with a relatively high proportion remaining on the top grade for more than 10 years (see Findlay et al, 2005). Given the enhanced role that they were expected to perform in pre-school education and how their pay lags even further behind other public sector groups, notably teachers, it is not difficult to uncover the roots of grievances among nursery nurses:

'We do a professional job with the kids and are important to their education. I know that with all the paperwork there are people taking work home. So we are just like teachers. Alright, we don't mark but taking work home is one of their main things and that's just the same as us.' (Striking nursery nurse 3, Paisley)

The issues highlighted here relate in very direct ways to the social inclusion strategy and 'modernisation' reforms of New Labour, in particular to ideas of 'integrated' and 'joined-up' services. The following comments support the fact that there are often tensions between these policy objectives (which often become most visible on the frontline):

'One policy that's made things more difficult is with nursery places for three- and four-year-olds. One group are ready for school and one are just out of nappies. My council's policy is to mix them because they say the four-year-olds bring the wee ones on. But nobody's thought about how hard it is to tell a story when at the back they are all quiet and at the front they are kicking each other or just standing up.' (Striking nursery nurse 1, Fife)

'I don't see why they can't make a special case. They seem to for teachers. They are treated like royalty. Ok you don't need a degree for this but you need qualifications and it's much harder than it used to be. The law's coming in to say you need top qualifications.' (Striking nursery nurse 5, Fife)

What this indicates is the ambiguity that we highlighted earlier (as well as some element of sectionalism) between the educational, play-centred and caring aspects of nursery nursing. These comments also demonstrate the juxtaposition of professionalisation and the intensification of work, which, we argue, is coming to define public sector employment for different groups of workers. But this is professionalisation without appropriate pay rewards. UNISON's initial claim was for £9.53 per hour for those new to nursery nursing, raising the annual salary for new starts from £10,000 to £14,000. For those with eight years' or more experience the demand was for an increase from £13,800 to £18,000 (rising to £21,000), or £11.94 per hour at the top of the grade. The offer made by employers was £7.35 per hour rising to £9.33. By the start of the national strike eight smaller councils had agreed local deals with UNISON but around 5,000 of 5,500 local authority nursery workforce undertook strike action, affecting 50,000 children across Scotland.

Central to the dispute were the nursery nurses' demands for better pay and a new pay scale. However, this soon became a battle for a national (Scotland-wide) pay agreement as CoSLA (Convention of Scottish Local Authorities, the local authority employers' body) argued from the start that the role of nursery nurses varied so much across Scotland that localised pay deals were more appropriate. Against such a view the striking nursery nurses fought for a unified framework of pay and conditions to match the increasing uniformity demanded by national childcare strategies and policy drives in terms of skills, knowledge and enhanced responsibilities. The struggle for a national settlement became a defining characteristic of the dispute, not least for the strikers themselves. Many of our interviewees viewed this as *the* key factor that generated resentment among the strikers as well as a willingness to continue the fight:

> 'They're [CoSLA] bringing in a national settlement for single status for council workers. The firemen have a national pay agreement and they're CoSLA. Even the CoSLA workers themselves have a national settlement. So why can the employers not have one for us?' (Striking nursery nurse 1, Fife)

> '[A national deal] was the whole point. Professionals get national pay. Teachers get national pay. That's the problem – they don't want to see us as professionals but they want us to be professionals. I'm not going to say that we are the same as teachers but it was CoSLA that tried to use this against us.' (Striking nursery nurse 3, Paisley)

> 'All we get is stuff about national this, national that, national care standards, national training and the like. Well what about national pay? Anybody who gets this job now has the same qualifications – why not pay us all the same?' (Striking nursery nurse 2, Glasgow)

We can see here how a language of professionalisation was utilised as a motivational tactic of the strikers, serving to indicate that employer and government-sponsored notions of professionalism can conflict with bottom-up worker ideas of what professionalism means. Indeed, we would add that the government and employers often play an active role in attributing a higher value to some professional work than others, particularly where professional qualifications are often accorded higher status than personal or emotional qualities (see Innes et al, 2006, pp 41-2).

The strikers also became acutely aware as the strike progressed that Labour-dominated CoSLA was determined to resist this central claim and were determined to break national pay bargaining, thereby allowing different councils to introduce different rates of pay depending on 'supply and demand' in different parts of Scotland. Hence this claim was rejected. This is very much in tune with New Labour's frequent hostility towards collective bargaining. Local settlements could both be spun as 'responsiveness' to an individual community's needs (and those of different customers) and allow individual local authorities to effectively manage often competing aims. Plainly, they could settle on what they were 'able' to afford as judged by those councils 'on the ground'. Policy and national strategies were the business of government, in London and in Edinburgh, not the local authorities. Therefore, while the Scottish First Minister Jack McConnell could refer to the dispute as a 'national disgrace' (quoted in *The Herald*, 31 March 2004), there was no official call for a national pay settlement and no public involvement by government. Ironically for New Labour and the Scottish Executive, the strike very quickly took on an explicitly political edge as the strikers seemed to become increasingly aware of crucial, if often obscured, links between the different layers of governance that arguably help characterise devolution in practice (see McCafferty, 2004). The strikers, with increasing public support, turned their attention to lobbying the Scottish Parliament and seeking out the active support of some of its Members. Alongside earlier demands, the strikers came to focus on political structures and those they saw as 'players', levelling sustained criticisms on the Labour leader of CoSLA and the Scottish First Minister.

## Legacies of the strike

The dispute officially ended in April 2004, with a series of local pay settlements imposed by employers. Nursery nurses were left with pay offers that varied considerably between local authorities, with a difference in pay as far apart as £8.76 and £10.46 per hour in some cases (see Findlay et al, 2005). In addition most of the offers made by local authorities were at the lower end of what was on offer. Strikes continued into early June in several council areas (including the largest,

Glasgow), the demand for a national agreement having been dropped by UNISON, much to the anger of many of its members. Therefore, by January 2006 annual salaries at the top of the scales varied between the equivalent of £17,436 and £20,168 across different local authority areas, an outcome still viewed with considerable anger and resentment among nursery workers. As noted above, this compares unfavourably with teachers' salaries, despite the open recognition on the part of the Scottish Executive that, in terms of Early Years education at least, 'there is not a clear boundary around the workforce[s]' (Scottish Executive, 2006b, p 1), as many of our respondents highlighted.

The nursery nurses strike helped to precipitate the Scottish Executive's national review of the Early Years and childcare workforce that was announced in June 2004 and published in August 2006 (see Scottish Executive, 2006b, 2006c). Alongside re-iterating and formalising the goals of 'developing the professional base – the skills, knowledge and values of the sector' (Scottish Executive, 2006b, p 53), the documentation produced as part of this review talked of improving the profile and status of childcare work. This is viewed as a key issue in recruitment and retention:

> The status currently afforded this workforce does not, in our view, accurately reflect the level of responsibility and importance that workers can have in child development. (Scottish Executive, 2006b, p 39)

While it contains a discussion of how to present this type of work to the wider public, this review makes little mention of pay, save to note that 'high pay' can contribute to increased status. This not only helps to illustrate the paradox of the low pay–high expectation proscription that helps define much public sector work currently. It also demonstrates the relatively few gains made by an increasingly crucial group of workers over nearly two decades. That these workers are overwhelmingly female presents specific challenges for the promotion of the sort of equalities agenda evident in government rhetoric (see Brown, 2004). The strike served to throw these issues – as well as wider issues about the state of public services – onto the political agenda in Scotland.

## Conclusions

In this chapter we have explored some of the key ways in which an apparently straightforward dispute about pay and conditions saw a group of hard-pressed workers increasingly challenge central elements of New Labour social policy. This meant that while the strike and the issues that surrounded it was presented by the Scottish Executive as a typical employer–worker disagreement, it is clear that national (in both Scottish and UK senses) childcare policy, together with the additional responsibilities brought about by other social policy initiatives, were also an important dimension of this dispute. However, this strike was also about control over the labour process of childcare work, about the restructuring of nursery work, and helps to highlight some of the ways in which such issues are at the heart of the reformed/reforming public sector more generally. As we have seen, the nursery nurses felt that they were being asked not only to do more work but increasingly to fulfil a range of often competing responsibilities, what we might term 'functional flexploitation'. However, to take this further, what are also apparent are the contradictory trends towards professionalisation, specialisation and the degradation of childcare labour: professionalisation in the sense that increasing pressures were being placed on nursery nurses to become more *formally* 'skilled' and substantively 'qualified' while simultaneously finding that 'more and more' was required from them (work intensification), but for 'less and less' reward.

We have argued throughout this chapter that this was also a dispute that brought a group of public sector workers into direct conflict with a government that increasingly sees them as an important vehicle through which important employment and social policies could be implemented. In taking strike action the nursery nurses considered in this chapter were explicitly making the point that they were not prepared to take on additional work without proper pay and improved conditions. In this respect they were challenging a central assumption of New Labour's social policy, that the expansion of childcare could be done 'on the cheap'.

The 2004 nursery nurses strike was Scotland's biggest all-out indefinite strike since the miners' strike in 1984-85. We have argued above that it would be mistaken to dismiss this as 'simply' a local dispute. In important respects this strike is representative of a recent trend in trade union militancy across the UK in that it involves public sector workers, it concerns workers who feel that their professionalism and autonomy is under attack and, as with other groups of welfare workers in recent years, there is a renewed and arguably more potent coming together here of employment relations policies along with diverse social policies and practices. Further, and importantly, following the UK-wide local government strike in 2002 and action over pensions in 2006 in particular, again which involved a significant number of female workers, strikers were able to tap into a wider reservoir of resentment about the thrust of New Labour policies, especially in relation to the modernisation of public services (see Wakefield, 2004).

In utilising this one example and the issues that have emerged since the strike took place, we are also able to critically explore some of the tensions and contradictions in New Labour's modernisation and social policy agendas, while highlighting that, for many public sector workers, social justice is what they are expected to deliver, not what they should expect to experience in their own working lives.

## Further sources

Findlay, P., Findlay, J. and Stewart, R. (2005) *Nursery nurses in Scotland 2005: A report for UNISON Scotland*, Glasgow: UNISON Scotland.

## References

Armstrong, H. (2006) 'The invisible generation: from picking up the pieces to predicting and preventing', Speech to IPPR North, Sunderland, 20 May.

Becker, G.S. (1975) *Human capital*, Princeton, NJ: National Bureau of Economic Research.

Blair, T. (1999) Beveridge Lecture, Toynbee Hall, London, 18 March, reproduced as 'Beveridge revisited: a welfare state for the 21st century', in R. Walker (ed) *Ending child poverty*, Bristol: The Policy Press, pp 7-18.

Braverman, H. (1974) *Labour and monopoly capital*, New York, NY: Monthly Review Press.

Brown, G. (2004) Speech to the Labour Party Conference, 27 September (http://politics.guardian.co.uk/print/0,3858,5025570-114255,00. html, 28/09/2004).

Cameron, C. (2001) 'Promise or problem? A review of the literature of men working in early childhood services', *Gender, Work and Organisation*, vol 8, no 4, pp 430-53.

Colley, H. (2006) 'Learning to labour with feeling: class, gender and emotion in childcare education and training', *Contemporary Issues in Early Childhood*, vol 7, no 1, pp 15-29.

Cook, D. (2006) *Criminal and social justice*, London: Sage Publications.

Davies, C. (2003) 'Introduction: a new workforce in the making?', in C. Davies (ed) *The future health workforce*, London: Palgrave Macmillan, pp 1-13.

DfEE (Department for Education and Employment) (1998) *Meeting the childcare challenge*, London: DfEE.

Ehrenreich, B. and Hochschild, A.R. (eds) (2003) *Global woman: Nannies, maids and sex workers in the new economy*, London: Granta.

Fairbrother, P. and Poynter, G. (2001) 'State restructuring: managerialism, marketisation and the implications for labour', *Competition and Change*, vol 5, no 3, pp 311-33.

Ferguson, I., Lavalette, M. and Mooney, G. (2002) *Rethinking welfare: A critical perspective*, London: Sage Publications.

Findlay, P., Findlay, J. and Stewart, R. (2005) *Nursery nurses in Scotland 2005: A report for UNISON Scotland*, Glasgow: UNISON Scotland.

Giddens, A. (1994) *Beyond Left and Right*, Cambridge: Polity Press.

Giddens, A. (1998) *The Third Way*, Cambridge: Polity Press.

Harman, H. (1997) Speech at the London School of Economics on the launch of the Centre for the Analysis of Social Exclusion, 13 November.

Harvey, J. (1995) 'Up-skilling and the intensification of work: the "extended role" in intensive care nursing and midwifery', *Sociological Review*, vol 43, no 4, pp 765-81.

*Herald, The* (2004) 'McConnell blames men for nursery strike', 31 March.

HM Treasury (2004) *Choice for parents, the best start for children: A ten-year strategy for childcare*, London: The Stationery Office.

Hochschild, A.R. (1983) *The managed heart: Commercialisation of human feeling*, London: University of California Press.

Hochschild, A.R. (2001) 'Global care chains and emotional surplus value', in W. Hutton and A. Giddens (eds) *On the edge: Living with global capitalism*, London: Verso, pp 130-46.

House of Commons Work and Pensions Committee (2003) *Childcare for working parents: Fifth report of session 2002-03*, London: The Stationery Office.

Innes, A., MacPherson, S. and McCabe, L. (2006) *Promoting person-centred care at the front line*, York: Joseph Rowntree Foundation.

Jones, C. and Novak, T. (1999) *Poverty, welfare and the disciplinary state*, London: Routledge.

Kelso, P. (2002) 'Angry women find a voice over pay that doesn't add up', *The Guardian*, 18 July.

Kessler, I., Bach, S. and Heron, P. (2006) 'Understanding assistant roles in social care', *Work, Employment & Society*, vol 20, no 4, pp 667-85.

Kofman, E. and Sales, R. (1998) 'Migrant women and exclusion in Europe', *European Journal of Women's Studies*, vol 5, pp 381-98.

Lister, R. (2003) 'Investing in the citizen-workers of the future: transformations in citizenship and the state under New Labour', *Social Policy and Administration*, vol 37, no 5, pp 427-43.

McCafferty, P. (2004) 'Working the "Third Way": New Labour, employment relations, and Scottish devolution', Unpublished PhD thesis, University of Glasgow.

May, J., Wills, J., Datta, K., Evans, Y., Herbert, J. and McIllwaine, C. (2006) *The British state and London's migrant division of labour*, London: Department of Geography, Queen Mary College, University of London.

Mooney, G. and McCafferty, T. (2005) '"Only looking after the weans?" The Scottish nursery nurses strike, 2004', *Critical Social Policy*, vol 25, no 2, pp 223-39.

Pearce, N. and Paxton, W. (eds) (2005) *Social justice: Building a fairer Britain*, London: Politico's.

Prime Minister's Strategy Unit (2002) *Delivering for children and families – Inter-departmental childcare review*, London: Prime Minister's Strategy Unit.

Prout, A. (2000) 'Children's participation: control and self-realisation in British late modernity', *Children and Society*, vol 14, pp 304-15.

Ridge, T. (2002) *Childhood poverty and social exclusion: From a child's perspective*, Bristol: The Policy Press.

Scott, G., Brown, U. and Campbell, J. (2000) *Visible childcare: Invisible workers?*, Occasional Paper No 1, Glasgow: Trade Union Research Unit, Glasgow Caledonian University.

Scottish Executive (2004) 'Review of Early Years workforce', Press release, Edinburgh: Scottish Executive, 9 June.

Scottish Executive (2006a) *Pre-school and childcare statistics 2006*, Publication Notice, 14 September (www.scotland.gov.uk).

Scottish Executive (2006b) *National review of the Early Years and childcare workforce: Report and consultation*, Edinburgh: Scottish Executive.

Scottish Executive (2006c) *National review of the Early Years and childcare workforce: Scottish Executive response – Investing in children's futures*, Edinburgh: Scottish Executive.

Scottish Office (1998) *Meeting the childcare challenge: A childcare strategy for Scotland*, Edinburgh: Scottish Office.

Scottish Parliament (2006) *Education Committee 7th Report: Ten year vision for universal care and education for Scotland's children*, June, Edinburgh: Scottish Parliament.

Simon, A., Owen, C., Moss, P. and Cameron, C. (2003) *Mapping the care workforce: Supporting joined-up thinking. Secondary analysis of the Labour Force Survey for childcare and social care work*, London: Institute of Education, University of London/Department of Health.

Thornley, C. (2006) 'Unequal and low pay in the public sector', *Industrial Relations Journal*, vol 37, no 4, pp 344-58.

UNISON (2003) *Working for local communities*, London: UNISON.

UNISON (2006a) *Qualifications, pay and quality in the childcare sector: UNISON submission to the Low Pay Commission 2006*, London: UNISON (www.unison.org.uk).

UNISON (2006b) *Raising the stakes: The link between pay and quality. UNISON submission to the Low Pay Commission 2006*, London: UNISON (www.unison.org.uk).

WAG (Welsh Assembly Government) (2002) *Childcare action plan*, Cardiff: National Assembly for Wales.

Wakefield, H. (2004) 'Women, modernisation and trade unions', *Soundings*, vol 27, Autumn, pp 44-56.

Wills, J. (2003) *On the front line of care: A research report to explore home care employment and service provision in Tower Hamlets*, London: UNISON/ Queen Mary College, University of London.

Wincott, D. (2005) 'Devolution, social democracy and policy diversity in Britain: the case of early-childhood education and care', in J. Adams and K. Schmueker (eds) *Devolution in practice*, Newcastle: IPPR North, pp 76-97.

# NINE

# Social work today: a profession worth fighting for?

*Michael Lavalette*

## Introduction

> There are some services which ... [are] recognised as being
> intrinsically suited to organisation on the welfare principle,
> as public, non-profit, non-commercial services, available to
> all at a uniform standard irrespective of means. They include
> ... the personal social services. (Marshall, 1981, p 134)

Social work, as many writers have noted, is a profession in crisis (Clarke,
1996; Jones, 1998; Jones and Novak, 1999; Asquith et al, 2005). As a
work activity, it has been increasingly dominated by managerialism,
by the fragmentation of services, by financial restrictions and lack of
resources, by increased bureaucracy and workloads, and by the increased
use of the private sector. While these trends have long been present in
state social work, they now dominate the day-to-day work of frontline
social workers and shape the welfare services that are offered to service
users. As Harris (2003) has so eloquently argued, social work has become
more business like – shaped by the priorities of neoliberal welfarism
that increasingly dominate the British welfare system.

But as well as impacting on the work tasks of social workers, the depth
of the neoliberal assault has started to pose questions about the very
nature of social work as an activity. Social work is a career that most
people enter because they believe that it will offer them the opportunity
to work with and/or help the very poorest and most marginalised
people in society. Many practitioners see themselves as workers who
have been educated and trained to act 'professionally', to adhere to a set
of values that involves them building relationships with service users and
carrying out a range of techniques and practices aimed at improving the
lives of those they work with. The International Federation of Social
Workers (IFSW) defines social work as an activity that

> ... promotes social change, problem solving in human
> relationships and the empowerment and liberation of
> people to enhance well-being. Utilising theories of human
> behaviour and social systems, social work intervenes at
> the points where people interact with their environments.
> Principles of human rights and social justice are fundamental
> to social work. (IFSW, 2000)

The scale of the neoliberal attack in Britain poses serious questions
about the ability of social workers to practise in ways that match the
IFSW definition of social work activity that challenge the very existence
of the social work profession.

This indicates that social work is shaped by two interconnected
dynamics. On the one hand, there are what we might consider
'economic' considerations concerned with the operationalisation of
the 'labour process': how the work is set, carried out, controlled and
regulated, the conditions of employment and the remuneration workers
receive for their labour (and the various manager/worker/service user
responses to all this). Social workers, as workers, join unions and take
various forms of industrial action to protect and improve their pay and
employment conditions. In part this chapter will consider the immense
deskilling pressures currently facing state social work and the response
of social workers in one part of the country (Liverpool) to the impact
of this deskilling.

On the other hand, as the Liverpool case study will suggest, the
grievances that shaped the strike partly reflected social workers'
concern that a new work regime and cuts in service provision were
having a negative impact on their ability to provide an appropriate
service for service-users – like nearly all social work clients, some of
the most vulnerable people in society. This is the second crucial aspect
to social work (indeed to all welfare work): its 'ideological' or 'political'
dimension. This notion is captured in the quotation from Marshall at
the start of the chapter – the idea that workers are providing a service
that cannot be reduced to the cash-nexus. It reflects the fact that many
people take up this type of work with, at least in part, a commitment
to a set of values and beliefs about their role as welfare professionals,
and to providing a service aimed at improving the lives of service users
(*The Guardian*, 2001).

The scale and the nature of the changes to social work practice
initiated by the new managerialist and neoliberal priorities throw
into question much of the value base of many social workers who had
traditionally viewed themselves as 'mainstream professionals'; indeed

it throws into question their ability to be 'professional'. It opens up questions about the nature of social work, the needs of service users, the nature of poverty and inequality and – more generally – the direction of Britain's welfare regime.

Furthermore, as many social workers struggle to come to terms with being a 'professional' within the present social work regime, they are confronted by social services directorates that increasingly question the need for local authorities to employ qualified 'professional' social workers. The Liverpool dispute was also partly about the attempt by local employers to remove the word 'qualified' from job adverts for social workers. It was clearly about deskilling but also an attempt to undermine social work 'professionalism', issues that are also raised elsewhere in this book (see Chapter Eight).

Mainstream social work in Britain formed its standards of 'professionalism' during the 20th century and particularly in the post-Second World War period. It reflected a conscious attempt to carve out a role for social workers within the developing welfare state (cf Younghusband, 1951; Jones 1983). As Parton puts it:

> The establishment of modern social work was a small, but significant, element of the 'welfarist' project as it developed in the twentieth century. (1996, p 7)

At the heart of this 'modern' social work was an optimism that held to the notion that 'measured and significant improvements could be made in the lives of individuals and families by judicious professional interventions' (Parton, 1996, p 8).

Social work's pre-eminent values reflected the dominant 'social democratic consensus' of the postwar settlement – values of citizenship, poverty alleviation, need fulfilment and of providing a caring, human face within faceless welfare bureaucracies. In the 1970s and 1980s these expanded to include notions of anti-oppression and closer alliances with service users (Penketh, 2001).

The development of a clearer social work value base brought with it a notion of 'professional independence'. The worker was not merely a mouthpiece of government policy (either national or local government) but someone who used social scientific knowledge and social work training to analyse, understand and confront the problems facing service users, utilising a range of methods and approaches to improve clients'/service users' lives (Jones, 1996). It is this notion of 'clear values and independence' that is at the heart of conceptions of social work professionalism.

But this raises two points. First, over the past 25 years the ideological assumptions of the postwar welfare state have come under sustained critique from New Right ideologues (see, for example, Bartholomew, 2004) and large sectors of state welfare provision have been privatised (see Clarke et al, 2001; Powell, 2002; Mooney, 2006). This has not improved the position of the very poorest – whose average life expectancy in parts of our inner cities is almost 20 years lower than it is for those in more affluent locations in Britain (Wilkinson, 2005) – but it has created a situation where many of the basic values of traditional social work find themselves in conflict with the 'new mandarins' of welfare whose language (and values) are based around such themes as 'what works', choice, consumerism and 'personalisation' embedded within a commitment to market methods of service delivery (see Ferguson, 2008). These values are expressed in a new 'anti-professionalism' captured in the following quotation from Cullen and Gendreau:

> The hegemony of professional ideology has outlived its utility and has become counter-productive. The challenge that lies ahead is to use science to develop, evidence-based ... [measures] that not only tell us what not to do but what to do. (2001, p 314)

This raises some profound questions: what is left of social work's traditional 'social democratic' values? How can these values be 'squared' within the neoliberal circle? How far does 'professional independence' exist within the modern 'social work business'? And to what extent does professionalism require that social workers speak out (and act) against government policies that clash with the profession's value base?

But there is a second important issue that relates to our understanding of both 'professionalism' and 'values'. The creation and development of social work professionalism in the post-Second World War period involved a particular interpretation of social work's history. This excluded – or at best marginalised – alternative, more radical social work practices from earlier in the 20th century (Jones, 1983). Michael Reisch and Janice Andrews (2002) have written of the radical 'road not taken' within social work in the US. Two important themes that come out of this work are that, first, there have been other forms of social work practice than those that now dominate the profession – models of practice that explicitly link the pain and problems of service users to the exploitation and oppression embedded within dominant social relations and see the need for practice to address both 'private troubles and public issues'.

The second clear theme to come out of their work is that the radical impulse within social work practice is intimately connected to the rise and fall of social movement activity. Radicalism within social work has grown and taken hold at those periods when there are more generalised 'waves of protest' against the iniquities of the modern world. A number of writers (for example, Harman, 1988, 1999; Tarrow, 1989) have noted that history is punctuated by periods of intensive protest when the very nature of society is thrown into question and movement actors contemplate the possibility of another world. Social movement activity – especially during deep protest waves – creates new possibilities, new conceptions of the world, new ways of seeing and new ways of acting. And all this has filtered into the practice of social work activists, suggesting new ways of conceptualising social problems and offering new solutions to the problems of everyday life.

Elsewhere (writing with Iain Ferguson) I have argued a similar case for social work development in Britain: that social work's own history has been narrowly drawn to exclude radical alternatives and that radical impulses into social work emerge from social movement activity (Ferguson and Lavalette, 2007).

All this suggests that the start of the 21st century marks a period both of great uncertainty and of hope for social work. On the one hand, welfare retrenchment, deskilling of social work and the demonisation of social workers threatens to reduce social work to a shallow labour process, with few resources available for workers to address service users' needs, and little time available to build meaningful relationships with service users. Here 'social work might continue as an occupation but perish as a caring and liberal profession' (Jones and Novak, 1993, p 211).

On the other hand, the growth in recent years of the great social movements against war and neoliberalism offer a vision of an alternative world, shaped by different priorities from those that dominate the present phase of neoliberalism. The Global Justice Movement – sometimes referred to as the 'anti-capitalist movement in Britain – is a movement against the disastrous impact of neoliberalism across the world, about its impact on the poor, on our environment and on our public services. It offers hope that 'another world is possible' and – within this – that 'another social work is possible', one that defends, deepens and extends the existing value base of the profession.

And this brings us back to our starting point: although it is 'in crisis', there is a project called 'social work' that is worth defending. At its best, social work can improve people's lives; can help them make sense of, and deal with, their pain, distress and problems; can challenge stigma and discrimination; and can be part of the struggle for social justice. Nevertheless, the scale of the assault on social work is deep. The following section looks at what is happening to the world of work inhabited by social workers.

## Deskilling of social work

In 2001 Chris Jones published an article in the *British Journal of Social Work* that reported the findings of research he had conducted into the experiences of frontline social workers (Jones, 2001). The story he told was traumatic: 'The manifestations of stress and unhappiness in today's local authority social services departments were various, serious and pervasive' (2005, p 98). He revealed a profession that was over-stretched to crisis point. Workers were working longer and harder – a process that left them emotionally and physically drained. They were highly regulated and increasingly controlled by computer technology – some workers reported that when they turned on their computers when they entered their offices they were presented with a list of tasks and reminders of reports that were due for submission. Jones found that many of his interviewees were spending more time at their desks, filling in forms, rather than being with clients. Thus this was increasingly a 'caring profession' where workers had less time to spend with service users – less time to form meaningful relationships, to understand the problems service users face and the situation they found themselves in. The consequence, Jones argued, was that worker–client relationships were becoming 'much more mundane and routinised' (2001, p 552).

Social workers' working lives were increasingly dominated by meeting 'targets' – to process clients, to close cases – and that target meeting was part of the routine of management pressure. Howe (1996) has described this process as part of a shift from a social work of 'depth' (an approach steeped in the idea that we can find meaning within and understanding of service users' lives) to one of 'surface' (where there is little attempt to understand clients' lives and the main thrust of policy is to manage and control clients). One of Jones' interviewees told him what work was like:

> Our contact with clients is more limited. It is in, do the assessment, get the package together, review after a spell and then close the case and get on with the next one as there [are] over 200 cases waiting an assessment. (quoted in Jones, 2005, p 101)

There was little space within social work teams to discuss cases and share experiences – leaving workers feeling isolated. There was constant downward pressure of resources. Service provision for clients was declining. The emphasis was on providing care management packages, where it seemed the main concern was not client need but budget control. Again, a frontline worker reported:

> Being a care manager is very different from being a social worker as I had always thought of it. Care management is all about budgets and paperwork and the financial implications for the authority, whereas social work is about people. (quoted in Jones, 2005, p 100)

In response to all this, both high worker turnover and sickness were pervasive within the system; indeed those who stayed in the job longer than five years were considered 'veterans' (Jones, 2001, 2005).

The gap between frontline staff and managers was growing. Social work – like other welfare professions – was in the grip of 'managerialism', a tool to introduce market methods of service delivery, competition and control over employees and their work tasks. As Jones reported: 'the depth of the division between front-line practitioners and their managers surprised me' (2005, p 106). One of his interviewees gave a sense of what was happening on the ground:

> Much of the stress at work is fear; social workers are scared of their managers, scared of all the monitoring stuff. We get no help and if we can't manage our work we are told that we are poor time managers. There is no solution offered. Most managers now are only interested in allocating work irrespective of the pressure on us the social workers. We will be blamed for the problems which are due to a lack of resources. This is the attitude of quite a few of the managers who are also being pressed by the senior management group to take on more and more work. The pressure is always downwards. (quoted in Jones, 2005, p 107)

Harris (2003, 2005) has similarly drawn attention to the deskilling of social work. He has noted that since the late 1970s (and with increased intensity since the late 1980s) social work has been under attack from government, from the national media and as a consequence of the privatisation of the welfare state.

There is no space here to trace in detail the shifting history of state welfare and social work over the last 30 years of the 20th century (see Lowe, 1993; Parton, 1996; Adams et al, 1998, 2002). Nevertheless it is worth noting that while the establishment of integrated social services departments (social work departments in Scotland) in the aftermath of Seebohm's *Report of the Committee on local authority and allied personal social services* (1968) marked the high-point of the profession's 'self-confidence', this development occurred at a time when the welfare state was increasingly viewed as being in crisis. The long postwar boom had ended. Poverty had already been 'rediscovered' and, suddenly, the welfare state was facing massive budgetary constraints. First under the Labour government of 1974-79 (especially after 1976) and then more significantly under the various Conservative governments of 1979-97 social services budgets were restricted, unemployment increased and the ethos of state welfare changed. To put it crudely, the argument ran: 'We are spending too much money on welfare; this is unsustainable and is undermining the efficiency of the British economy. Welfare spending is increasing because a culture of dependency has developed where sections of the poor expect something for nothing. The welfare state has created this moral and economic problem. Social workers, in particular, are responsible for this malaise.'

From 1979 onwards the public sector in Britain was subject to intense critique and the welfare state was subjected to attack on both ideological and economic grounds. Privatisation and the extension of market principles were promoted as the solution to a variety of welfare state-induced ills. Social work found itself regularly attacked by politicians (perhaps most famously is the case of John Major, during the immediate furore of the killing of James Bulger, who suggested that we needed to 'understand a little less and condemn a little more') and the media. In the media, social workers were portrayed as politically motivated, ex-hippies who were both 'politically correct' and easily manipulated by their underclass clients. They were attacked for heavy-handed interfering in family life and, at the same time, failing to intervene to protect children from violence and abuse. As the 1980s came to an end it certainly felt like a profession under siege (Midgley and Jones, 1994; Jones and Novak, 1999; Penketh, 2001).

In this general atmosphere of state welfare restructuring and restriction, Harris (2003) suggests that workers within the 'social work business' have been the victims of a 'managerial coup': that the 'bureau-professional regime' established post-Seebohm – which allowed a significant degree of professional discretion to workers in dealings with service users – has been subjected to systematic transformation.

The key moment in this process, he suggests, was the instigation of the purchaser–provider split embedded within the community care legislation that 'imposed an immediate reduction in both [social worker] discretion and autonomy' (Hadley and Clough, 1996, p 186).

The consequence was that 'social work has been transformed from a self-regulating professional activity into a managed and externally regulated set of tasks' (Jones and Novak, 1999, p 38).

Nevertheless, as we would perhaps assume from what is now more than 30 years of the 'labour process debate', the attack on social work has not meant that we are left with a work task where individuals have no discretion, or that, even in these difficult times, there is nothing social workers can do. As Evans and Harris (2004) point out, the practitioner still has a little room to make a difference. This is important. There is no doubt that managerialism and neoliberalism have had a significant and detrimental impact on social work but the skills of a practitioner cannot be completely wiped out, or performed by a computer. There is still a space – although it is shrinking – for the practitioner to act in ways that benefit the service user. This is also a space where opposition to the new managerialism can take hold – an opposition that can express anger and frustration at the working conditions of the labour process but also, crucially, that can reflect the attack on the professional values at the heart of the social work project. The strike by social workers in Liverpool in 2004/05 was precisely such a strike, motivated by anger at what was happening to social services provision for some of social work's most vulnerable service users across the city.

## Liverpool social workers on strike

### *The background to the strike and the research*

In August 2004 social workers from Liverpool City Council's emergency and children and families teams found themselves on strike. It was to be a long strike, lasting over six months, and it was ultimately unsuccessful. Yet it was important not only because it once more raised significant issues about the nature and future of social work activity, not just in Liverpool but across the UK, but because it also raised the question: 'what forms of action and activity are necessary to defend social work?'.

During the strike I spent a considerable amount of time with the strikers, visiting the shop stewards, attending the weekly mass meetings and interviewing some of those on strike. Short interviews with the strikers were conducted at the time of the strike; longer set interviews were conducted after the strike was finished. Of the latter a total of 10 leading strikers took part in interviews held at the Liverpool UNISON office and the University of Liverpool. Each lasted for approximately 45 minutes and covered the background to the dispute and details over how the dispute was conducted and run. In the aftermath of the dispute a number of strikers faced disciplinary action from both Liverpool City Council and UNISON. For this reason I do not give the names of those whose responses I quote.

## Issues

The strike was not concerned with 'economic' issues. It was not about pay or general working conditions – something the strikers were very keen to emphasise to all who would listen. Rather, the strike was concerned with the nature of the service they were able to provide to clients and service users. In essence it was a strike about the kind of social work workers wanted to practise. It reflected their concern that the profession was being changed, that it was turning into an activity that clashed with what they thought were some of the basic values of social work – based around a commitment to social justice.

In line with what we saw in the last section the strikers felt that the job was increasingly dominated by 'care management' approaches and by financial restrictions. It was increasingly marked by reduced contact with service users and contact itself was increasingly framed in terms of controlling the behaviour of 'difficult' clients (Hilditch, 2004; Jones et al, 2004). Against this background the strike focused on three main issues.

First, Liverpool City Council has firmly established itself as one of the key advocates of 'one-stop' call centre services, called *Liverpool Direct*. This means that anyone in Liverpool who has a problem or requires a service must first access a single-point call centre. Whatever the problem – housing, refuse collection, schooling and educational issues, or the needs of the full range of social work service users – the first point of access to services is the call centre. Lines are often busy. Many callers give up before they get the chance to speak to an operator. Those that do get through will be dealt with first by a call operator – a gatekeeper – who will make the first decision about the urgency of the call and where it should be directed. For social workers in the emergency team, in particular, this was not an appropriate service to be offering often troubled individuals. It was a system of processing individuals not dealing with their problems. It was a system that militated against quality contact with service users, against relationship building and against worker/client closeness and the establishment of 'empathy' with clients (Jones and Lavalette, 2004). As one of the strikers argued:

> 'Liverpool Direct has made things worse. What kind of service are we giving vulnerable people? I mean can you imagine – your son or partner is feeling suicidal, the situation is desperate and you have to pick up the phone and dial a call centre. At busy times you'll just be put on hold! There is a disaster waiting to happen here. And when it does you know who they'll blame, don't you?' (Striker 1, November 2004)

Second, workers were also expected to ring into the call centre to pick up new cases. There was no system of caseload allocation. Increasingly social workers in the city were operating out of their cars on mobile phones provided by the authority. There were few team meetings where complex cases could be discussed. Workers in some teams found themselves sharing desks. There was growing distance between senior team managers and frontline workers. Rather than being members of a team they increasingly felt themselves to be isolated, alienated workers – abandoned care workers, providing an inadequate service to abandoned service users.

> 'We rarely meet as a team any more. There is no time to stop and talk things over. We are just out on cases, back in the office, do the paper work, out again.' (Striker 2, December 2004)

Finally, these issues came to a head when the authority announced plans to introduce significant restructuring and replace staff and fill vacancies with workers who would be called 'social workers' but who would not necessarily have a professional social work *qualification*. One of the strikers put it like this:

> 'We became social workers because we care. And we are principled enough and brave enough to speak out. We have come to a stalemate with the employers over the word "qualifications" remaining part of the job description.
>
> Social workers normally only come to people's attention when there is someone to blame. Speaking out may be dangerous, but not speaking out is more dangerous. What is at stake is children's futures. And if speaking out

is whinging then I am proud to be a whinger. We are on
strike for professional, moral and ethical reasons.' (Quoted
in Hilditch, 2004, p 10)

Qualification and profession are inextricably linked. One is not possible
without the other. The attempt to introduce 'unqualified' social workers
therefore opened up some fundamental questions about the nature of
the social work project in Britain and the future direction of social
work activity. One social work union steward explained:

> 'This strike is about the clash of two different value
> systems. On the one hand the business drives and values
> of management and Blairism – even in the guise of a Lib
> Dem council – and on the other the values of humanity
> and social justice of the childcare social workers.' (Striker 3,
> December, 2004)

By refusing to give ground on the word 'qualification', the Liverpool
managers were indicating how important it was for them to manage
a social welfare service that was not bothered by a troublesome
professional presence; by social workers who legitimated their questions
and criticisms of a service unable to meet the needs of one of the
most impoverished cities in England by reference to their professional
obligations. Social work 'professionalism' was not a label used to secure
status, privilege and high salaries. Rather it reflects a professionalism
that speaks to service, to ethical practice, to social obligations and that
recognises that the issues and difficulties that confront clients deserve
skilled and expert interventions. And that clients have a right to expect
help from social workers who know that they have a professional duty
to speak out on their behalf when the agency fails to provide the
necessary service.

The strikers organised themselves via their shop steward committee
and weekly mass meetings. They went on delegation visits to other
workplaces (where they received a sympathetic hearing, particularly
from other public sector workers and especially from other social
workers). Their national demonstrations were well attended and
discussion in the national press indicated a significant level of support.
A senior steward told us:

> 'The financial support we have received has been great. The
> council wants to starve us back to work, but the support
> of trade unionists and supporters across the country means
> that isn't going to happen. This strike is so important. If we

win it will be a huge victory for social workers and service users everywhere.' (Striker 4, November 2004)

Interestingly, therefore, 'professional values' do not necessarily clash with collective organisation. Indeed the resistance on show in Liverpool was rooted in both trade unionism and 'professionalism'. The structure of resistance was the union and the history of union organisation within social work; the mobilising factor was their commitment to social justice and protection of services for the most vulnerable. Interestingly it was the power of this combination that meant that the social workers all looked to their union, rather than the professional association BASW (British Association of Social Workers), to express their collective demands and concerns.

## Outcomes

By the end of January 2005 the strike in Liverpool was over. The immediate demands of the strikers had been lost but it did suggest lessons for the future. First, it emphasised that 'professional' welfare workers – who have a political and ethical commitment to their job – are often willing to express this through industrial action in defence of services. At the start of 2007 healthcare professionals and civil servants have been involved – through their unions – in political campaigns against the privatisation of public services (see, for example, the campaign of the Public and Commercial Services Union [PCS] 'Public Service Not Private Profit': www.pcs.org.uk; see also Chapters Ten and Twelve, this volume). In this sense 'professionalism' is not a barrier to collective action; indeed, at times, it can be a mobiliser of protest and discontent.

Second, it also has lessons for the development of trade unions. A trade unionism that simply focuses on 'economic issues' (like pay and conditions) will at best only partially represent the interests and concerns of their members who are welfare workers. What is needed is a fuller, more engaged 'political unionism' that addresses both the economic concerns of members and the iniquities and injustice that fracture the modern world in which their members live and work. It means addressing the 'political' or 'ideological' dimension to public service employment and campaigning and acting to protect the value base at the heart of so many welfare jobs.

## Conclusions: resources of hope for a re-engaged social work

Social work is a contested activity. The heart of that contestation is political – it resides in the contradiction between social work's *caring* and *controlling* roles. The 'care/control' dichotomy has become rather cliched in much of the social work literature – an empty phrase with little real explanatory power. Nevertheless as a conceptual tool it takes us to the heart of the contradiction that runs through social work; it usefully refers to a real – and shifting – tension at the heart of competing definitions of social work, a tension that infuses every aspect of practice. The vast majority of practitioners become social workers because they want to help people in some (unspecified) way; they do not become practitioners because they have an intense commitment to care management, service rationing and/or moral policing.

Thus, most social workers hold onto 'professional values' that are steeped in 'social democratic' or reformist conceptions of the world. They include notions that service users – our 'clients' – deserve respect and understanding, rather than castigation and demonisation, and that it is possible to instigate and bring about change in people's lives and behaviours. That rehabilitation is possible and valuable. To grasp the full complexities of people's behaviour and problems we need to understand their lives – both the specific circumstances in which they live and the general context within which their lives are led. Hence social explanations are much more useful and powerful than individualist 'victim-blaming' accounts of the world. And that social work, as an ethical career, is also committed to social justice – to addressing the vast inequalities that shape our world and detrimentally impact on the lives of the poorest and the most disadvantaged.

Yet these values are under intense pressure both ideologically (from politicians, opinion formers, the media and local government managers) and materially (as a result of budget restrictions and managerialism). The impact of neoliberalism on social work, then, is throwing the whole nature of social work into question. In the process it is producing tremendous anxiety within social work, and this can be the seed bed of resistance.

Over the past few years I have been involved in a number of meetings where social workers, students, service users and academics have come together to express concern that there is something seriously wrong with the direction being taken by state social work in Britain. The first meeting took place in Glasgow in December 2003. It was organised under the title 'I didn't come into social work for this', and attracted over 60 people who came to listen, to debate and to express their anguish at what was happening to social work. It offered a space for social workers to discuss the problems they were facing and debate the possibilities for the future. But it also opened up a debate about where the 'resources' to defend social work were located. In my opinion it suggested a two-pronged strategy was necessary.

First, that social workers had to be members of their trade unions. This was the lesson social workers had learned in the late 1960s and 1970s, in particular during the first national social workers strike in 1979 (Joyce et al, 1988). It was also the lesson learnt from the dispute in Liverpool. The only collective organisation available to express the concerns and grievances of social workers was UNISON, the local government workers union. Union membership also brought solidarity from other sections of the labour movement and meant that, even in the most difficult periods of the strike, the strikers were not isolated.

But this on its own is not enough. The Liverpool experience suggests that if the unions are to attract and hold on to welfare and public sector workers they need to offer more than a commitment to protect pay and working conditions. It is clear that the Liverpool strikers were motivated by concern at what was happening to services and their ability to meet clients' needs. In this context, rather than a simple 'economic unionism', fuller 'political unionism' is required – that the unions should become the site for debate and action over defence of services and 'professional' concerns about the value base of social work.

Second, I suggest that a more radical, more engaged social work can emerge and gain confidence from a deep engagement with the Global Justice Movement and the movement against war that have – together – shaken the world over the past decade. These movements of the street have combined political protest and activism with an increasingly sophisticated critique of the priorities of global neoliberalism and imperialism, their social and environmental costs and their impact on the poor and dispossessed across the globe. But as well as critique, the movement has had to address the more difficult questions: 'what is the alternative?' and 'what is to be done?' (see, for example, George, 2004).

These form ongoing debates that are beyond the scope of this chapter, but one theorist has argued that the movement is based on four key interlinked values: justice, democracy, sustainability and, more controversially, efficiency (Callinicos, 2003).

Justice is a key social work value. By 'justice' Callinicos refers to the egalitarian principles of justice derived and developed from the work of philosophers like John Rawls, Ronald Dworkin and Amartya Sen

(Callinicos, 2000). This essentially asserts that resources should be made available to enable people to secure equal access to the advantages they need in order to be able to live the life they value. Equality and liberty are intimately related (inequalities necessarily impinge on liberties), so justice necessarily requires equality and liberty. Finally these values need more than a mere 'social structure'; they require an established social ethos that motivates people to behave justly towards, and provide support for, others – thus it requires solidarity. So for Callinicos the value of 'justice' necessarily brings a commitment to equality, liberty and solidarity – concepts and values with which many social workers will concur.

So how might this translate to debates about social work? Essentially it is framed in such a way that it involves a commitment to establishing a world where service users have access to the resources needed to allow them to engage with society, to choose freely to live the lifestyle they wish to follow and to have the appropriate support mechanisms in place to help and support them with the choices they make.

For Callinicos, 'democracy' refers to democratising the political process, but also to economic democracy and the decentralisation of power. But, applied to social work, democracy also means more open and equal relationships between practitioners and service users, more control by service users over the services they use, of political unity between service users and practitioners (Beresford and Croft, 2004).

'Sustainability', for Callinicos, primarily relates to the sustainability of the planet and the need for the world and its resources to be sustainable. These are issues that affect us all at the level of economy and the ecological system. But sustainability can also be usefully applied to our practice – the need to establish long-term, sustainable working relationships with service users and service user organisations.

'Efficiency' is the most controversial value identified by Callinicos. At the present moment there is no doubt that for many social workers the word 'efficiency' will be considered with, at best, ambivalence. For the past 30 years the 'efficiency' of the market has been claimed by governments and used as a justification for the privatisation of social care (and a whole range of other public sector services). But in government discourse the criteria by which 'efficiency' is judged are limited to questions of economic cost and profitability (so, for example, long-term social and ecological costs are not normally included in assessments of the efficiency). What Callinicos means is that it is necessary – given the demand of sustainability – to work out and plan the most efficient use of resources available to meet human need and to create the conditions for the controlled expansion of human society.

But perhaps we should not necessarily leave this to those who discuss things at this more abstract level. For example, a detailed analysis of government policy on incarceration, for example, would point out that this is a very inefficient system – both in terms of economic cost, its ability to stop recidivism and in terms of the social and human costs to those who are locked up and their families (thus incarceration is both inefficient in this broader sense, as well as breaching the commitment to 'justice'). Finally, let us re-stress that these values are interlinked. That 'efficiency' has to complement the demands of 'justice' and 'democracy', for example.

Callinicos' case is that the fulfilment of these values is impossible within the confines of neoliberalism. The case made here is more straightforward: I believe these core values of the Global Justice Movement match, in many key respects, the essential values of social work. The examples above are merely given to indicate the ways in which these values can also be applied to social work thinking. I suggest that this indicates that within the Global Justice Movement space exists for social workers to consider how we can best defend the social work project. Certainly it is my belief that a full engagement with this movement offers the best chance for rigorous intellectual defence of, and political support for, social work.

Thus by combining elements of traditional social work, radical social work and the experience of new social movements, both the user-led movements and the Global Justice and anti-war movements, it may be possible to establish a newly invigorated social work profession. It is certainly something worth fighting for.

**Further sources**

Harris, J. (2003) *The social work business*, London: Routledge.

Ferguson, I., Lavalette, M. and Whitmore, E. (2005) *Globalisation, global justice and social work*, London: Routledge.

Lavalette, M. and Ferguson, I. (eds) (2007) *International social work and the radical tradition*, Birmingham: Venture Press.

Reisch, M. and Andrews, J. (2002) *The road not taken*, London: Brunner-Routledge.

www.ifsw.org/home – International Federation of Social Workers

www.resist.org.uk/ – Globalise Resistance

www.scotland.gov.uk/Publications/2005/12/1994633/46334 – Social Work in the 21st Century

www.socialworkfuture.org/ – Social Work Action Network

# References

Adams, R., Dominelli, L. and Payne, M. (1998) *Social work: Themes, issues and critical debates*, Basingstoke: Macmillan.

Adams, R., Dominelli, L. and Payne, M. (eds) (2002) *Critical practice in social work*, Basingstoke: Palgrave Macmillan.

Asquith, S., Clark, C. and Waterhouse, L. (2005) 'The role of the social worker in the twenty-first century' (www.scotland.gov.uk/Publications/2005/12/1994633/46334).

Bartholomew, J. (2004) *The welfare state we're in*, London: Politico's.

Beresford, P. and Croft, S. (2004) 'Service users and practitioners reunited: the key component of social work reform', *British Journal of Social Work*, vol 34, pp 53-68.

Callinicos, A. (2000) *Equality*, Cambridge: Polity.

Callinicos, A. (2003) *An anti-capitalist manifesto*, Cambridge: Polity.

Clarke, J. (1996) 'After social work?', in N. Parton (ed) *Social theory, social change and social work*, London: Routledge, pp 36-60.

Clarke, J., Gewirtz, S. and McLaughlin, E. (eds) (2001)) *Reinventing the welfare state: From New Right to New Labour*, London: Sage Publications.

Cullen, F. and Gendreau, P. (2001) 'From nothing works to what works: changing professional ideology in the 21st century', *The Prison Journal*, vol 81, no 3, pp 313-38.

Evans, T. and Harris, J. (2004) 'Street-level bureaucracy, social work and the (exaggerated) death of discretion', *British Journal of Social Work*, vol 34, pp 871-95.

Ferguson, I. (2008, forthcoming) *Reclaiming social work: Challenging neo-liberalism and promoting social justice*, London: Sage Publications.

Ferguson, I. and Lavalette, M. (2007) '"The social worker as agitator": the radical kernel of British social work', in M. Lavalette and I. Ferguson (eds) *International social work and the radical tradition*, Birmingham: Venture Press.

George, S. (2004) *Another world is possible if ...*, London: Verso.

*Guardian, The* (2001) 'The common good', 20 March.

Hadley, R. and Clough, R. (1996) *Care in chaos: Frustration and challenge in community care*, London: Cassell.

Harman, C. (1988) *The fire last time: 1968 and after*, London: Bookmarks.

Harman, C. (1999) *A people's history of the world*, London: Bookmarks.

Harris, J. (2003) *The social work business*, London: Routledge.

Harris, J. (2005) 'Globalisation, neo-liberal managerialism and UK social work', in I. Ferguson, M. Lavalette and E. Whitmore (eds) *Globalisation, global justice and social work*, London: Routledge, pp 81-94.

Hilditch, K. (2004) 'This battle's for the vulnerable', *Socialist Worker*, 13 November.

Howe, D. (1996) 'Surface and depth in social work practice', in N. Parton (ed) *Social theory, social change and social work*, London: Routledge, pp 77-97.

IFSW (International Federation of Social Workers) (2000) *Definition of social work* (www.ifsw.org/en/p38000208.html).

Jones, C. (1983) *State social work and the working class*, Basingstoke: Macmillan.

Jones, C. (1996) 'Anti-intellectualism and the peculiarities of British social work education', in N. Parton (ed) *Social theory, social change and social work*, London: Routledge, pp 190-210.

Jones, C. (1998) 'Social work: regulation and managerialism', in M. Exworthy and S. Halford (eds) *Professionals and the new managerialism in the public sector*, Buckingham: Open University Press, pp 28-45.

Jones, C. (2001) 'Voices from the frontline: state social work and New Labour', *British Journal of Social Work*, vol 31, pp 547-62.

Jones, C. (2005) 'The neo-liberal assault: voices from the front-line of British state social work', in I. Ferguson, M. Lavalette and E. Whitmore (eds) *Globalisation, global justice and social work*, London, Routledge, pp 97-108.

Jones, C. and Lavalette, M. (2004) *Social work: Qualification and professionalism. A submission to UNISON Industrial Action Committee*, 21 December.

Jones, C. and Novak, T. (1993) 'Social work today', *British Journal of Social Work*, vol 23, pp 195-212.

Jones, C. and Novak, T. (1999) *Poverty, welfare and the disciplinary state*, London: Routledge.

Jones, C., Ferguson, I., Lavalette, M. and Penketh, L. (2004) 'Social work and social justice: a manifesto for a new engaged practice' (www.liv.ac.uk/ssp/Social_Work_Manifesto.html).

Joyce, P., Corrigan, P. and Hayes, M. (1988) *Striking out: Trade unionism in social work*, Basingstoke: Macmillan.

Lowe, R. (1993) *The welfare state in Britain since 1945*, Basingstoke: Macmillan.

Marshall, T.H. (1981) *The right to welfare and other essays*, London: Heinemann.

Midgley, J. and Jones, C. (1994) 'Social work and the radical right: the impact of developments in Britain and the United States', *International Social Work*, vol 37, pp 115-26.

Mooney, G. (2006) 'New Labour and the management of welfare', in M. Lavalette and A. Pratt, *Social policy: Theories, concepts and issues* (3rd edn), London: Sage Publications, pp 255-73.

Parton, N. (1996) 'Social theory, social change and social work: an introduction', in N. Parton (ed) *Social theory, social change and social work*, London: Routledge.

Penketh, L. (2001) *Tackling institutional racism*, Bristol: The Policy Press.

Powell, M. (ed) (2002) *Evaluating New Labour's welfare reforms*, Bristol: The Policy Press.

Reisch, M. and Andrews, J. (2002) *The road not taken*, London: Brunner-Routledge.

Seebohm, F. (chair) (1968) *Report of the Committee on local authority and allied personal social services,* Cmnd 3703, London: HMSO.

Tarrow, S. (1989) *Power in movement,* Cambridge: Cambridge University Press.

Wilkinson, R. (2005) *The impact of inequality*, London: The New Press.

Younghusband, E. (1951) *Report on the employment and training of social workers*, Edinburgh: T.A. Constable.

# TEN

# Working 'for' welfare in the grip of the 'iron' Chancellor: modernisation and resistance in the Department for Work and Pensions

*Tricia McCafferty and Gerry Mooney*

## Introduction

In his Budget Statement in March 2004 Chancellor Gordon Brown announced what many civil servants had long felt was just a formality: that the modernisation of the civil service would result in swingeing cuts in jobs across many government departments, especially, although not exclusively, those related to 'welfare-focused' services. Furthermore it became increasingly apparent that, despite media claims of a long-overdue cull of 'bureaucrats in bowler hats', a largely low-paid, increasingly angry group of workers would not only be at the frontline of delivering the central elements of New Labour's policy thrust in welfare reform, they would also bear the brunt of 'efficiency' drives to cut spending on public services.

Elsewhere in this book the key New Labour principle, that the 'best welfare policy of all is work' (Hutton, 2006), has been highlighted as pivotal to welfare reform. Yet, save their representation (alongside other public sector workers) as 'wreckers' (Blair, 2002) or as part of 'the forces of conservatism' (Blair, 1999, 2002), what are often overlooked are the very workers whose job it is to facilitate the transformation of welfare and public services. And all too often with fewer resources. A key aim of this chapter is to explore the impact of New Labour's attempt to drive down welfare costs on one group of workers at the very heart of service delivery: those in the Department for Work and Pensions (DWP).

In this department, which counts Jobcentre Plus, the Pensions Service and the Child Support Agency among its 'businesses' (DWP, 2006a, p 1), it quickly became clear to workers that 'releasing resources to the frontline' (Gershon, 2004) would mean an unprecedented overall loss of 30,000 jobs in under four years and radical organisational, infrastructural and procedural changes. At the same time, government ministers and DWP bosses are increasingly charging these same workers with promoting 'opportunity and independence for all through modern, customer-focused services ... end[ing] child poverty by 2020 ... [being part of] building a fair and inclusive society' (DWP, 2006a, p 1).

In our view the study of this key group of workers gives us crucial insights into the central trajectories of welfare reform and the impact of New Labour policies on frontline workers. This chapter therefore outlines key developments in this respect over the past few years and details more recent changes, as well as some of the key plans at the time of writing in early 2007, including those associated with the spending and efficiency review conducted by Sir Peter Gershon in 2003/04 that both forms the basis of key changes already enacted and continues to act as a springboard for further reforms.

Importantly, it is also possible to understand more fully how government policy affects workers at the frontline of service delivery where more and more is expected *with* fewer and fewer workers. Moreover, exploring the experiences of workers in the DWP allows us to develop a more nuanced awareness of important responses to New Labour policy in the shape of resistance to the changes that are transforming the lives of both groups who rely on the benefits and other forms of welfare support and, of course, those who rely on those systems for their livelihood. Hence this chapter will also outline how these workers have struggled against reforms and their impact on working conditions in the department and, crucially, how they feel forced to take action to defend services.

We seek to fully demonstrate from the outset the interconnectedness of the impact of the reform and modernisation on employment relations on a key 'welfare delivering' department and their effects on relations between such departments and their 'customers' – as we hope the title of the chapter helps to highlight. Hence DWP 'customers' are increasingly pressed to work 'for' welfare and, put simply, DWP employees are, of course, working 'for' welfare. But we hope to show that they also work 'for' welfare as an ideal, as a form of state support for vulnerable and disadvantaged groups of the population – something rarely recognised in media caricatures and political representations. That they are able and willing to do this is testimony, in part at least, to the impact of developments in trade unionism in the civil service more generally, outlined below.

Therefore we also illustrate how, despite the increasingly tight grip of the 'iron' Chancellor, DWP workers seek to deliver the 'quality services' that are promised in New Labour policy making, paradoxically in the face of cuts in real terms in spending and in personnel that expose the ideological underpinning of the programme of 'radical and beneficial' modernisation of the welfare state in the early 21st century. Overall, we explore three central and interconnected features of working in the DWP currently: the decimation of the workforce, the transformation of the organisation and infrastructure, and, of course, the radical overhaul of welfare benefits provision. Importantly, drawing on interviews with DWP strikers carried out on picket lines and at a national rally during the civil service-wide one-day strike in 2004 and thereafter, we also set out to link these features with a fourth: struggle and resistance on an unprecedented scale. We have been able to utilise political speeches and official documents as secondary sources as well as the welter of news stories covering the issues discussed here.

## 'Modernisation' and 'reform': the vision of a 'true opportunity society'

To begin our examination of the 'transformation' of welfare and its impact on DWP workers, it is important that we explore first the thrust of New Labour's drive to modernise welfare and its ideological underpinning (see also Chapter One, this volume). What this is premised on, as frontline welfare workers are increasingly discovering, is the deconstruction of what New Labour sees as a monolithic state and the vilification of those who seek to defend it. Hence despite the welfare state being 'Labour's proudest twentieth century boast' (Blair, 2004a), a critique of the institutions of postwar welfare forms the basis of a 'modernisation' programme that sees them represented as a 'one-size-fits-all' solution that is no longer appropriate:

> ... our 1945 Government created the welfare state and did more than any other Government of the century to attack poverty, promote equality and unify the country....Yet the institutions they created 60 years ago were rooted in social conditions and assumptions radically different to those of today.... (Blair, 2004a)

Moreover the New Labour perspective on 'modernisation' means the removal of apparent constraints on creativity and individual responsibility and, unsurprisingly, becoming selective about welfare provision in terms of cost and methods of delivery. This makes it possible to re-assert a commitment to central values of the postwar welfare state while 'reforming' the structures and organisation in such a way that, in the longer term, could render it unrecognisable. Reform is not piecemeal therefore, nor 'minimalist':

> We are engaged not on a set of discrete reforms, area by area, but a fundamental shift from a 20th century welfare state with services largely collective, uniform and passive, founded on low skills for the majority, to a 21st century opportunity society with services that are personal, diverse and active, founded on high skills. The purpose is however entirely traditional: social justice.... (Blair, 2004a)

Arguably, however, this is a commitment to an ambiguous social justice and, first and foremost, one that rejects the notion that the state can or should deliver it. This has been represented as Old Labour folly: 'heavy handed government is a thing of the past', says Giddens, a key player in the development on New Labour's Third Way (Giddens, 2002). The state, for New Labour, is an enabler, a facilitator. The task is not to provide social justice but to provide *for* it through modernising structures and, crucially, as workers have found, 'modern' attitudes – both their own as well as in the people they provide services for.

This, then, alerts us to some of the underlying motivations and guiding principles that have helped steer existing and emerging 21st-century welfare: the re-formulation of the state; the re-casting of its central values and assumptions; reforming its structures and, ultimately, a reduction in its reach. By the time of New Labour's second term in government in 2001, the impact of the policies and processes that emerged from these was already being keenly felt in key areas in the public sector. Notably, a central foundation for the programme of welfare reform that resulted in the development of flagship policies like the 'New Deals', 'Sure Start', the reform of in-work benefits as 'tax credits' was that it was to be 'customer-focused' and very different from the 'passive, dependency-creating system of the past' (DWP, 2005). This has continued apace with, as we shall see below, a clear concern to create 'co-ordinated, streamlined' organisations that are 'more outward looking' to fit with New Labour's vision for social justice (DWP, 2006b).

The central commitment, rhetorically at least, to 'achieving a fairer, more inclusive society where nobody is held back by disadvantage or lack of opportunity ... tackling child poverty [and] working towards employment for all ...' (DWP, 2005) can be specifically related to the role of work in the 'transformation' of welfare. As has been highlighted elsewhere in this book, work as the panacea to turn around lives and communities was both the key and best known element of the reform of welfare in its 'first phase'. This became clear from references to work and 'worklessness' in the speeches of New Labour politicians, with this claim in 1997 from the then Social Security Minister, Harriet Harman, being among the most widely quoted:

> Work is central to the government's attack on social exclusion. Work is the only route to sustained financial independence. But it is also much more. Work is not just about earning a living. It is a way of life ... work helps to fulfil our aspirations – it is the key to independence, self respect and opportunities for advancement ... work brings a sense of order that is missing from the lives of many unemployed young men. (Quoted in Fairclough, 2000)

Hence work is centre stage. For the government, several purposes are served via a renewed focus on work. First, there is a, largely forced, shift away from benefit 'dependency' towards self-supporting, responsible, rather than 'rights-claiming', activity. Second, 'imaginative workfare programmes are the key to ending the scourge and waste of social exclusion' (Mandelson, 1997). However, while 'reform' is couched in terms of 'fairness' and 'incentives' to work, we note that there is little recognition of problems of in-work exclusion through persistent low wages and the 'scourge and waste' of government-sanctioned, worker dispensability in the name of flexibility (see McCafferty, 2004). Moreover, in the 'work-as-the-cure-all' model promoted by New Labour even before they took office (see, for example, Commission on Social Justice, 1994), there is a lack of understanding that for many people work is *not* the answer to the poverty that remains endemic to their lives. This is summed up well in the following comment from Helen Dent, Chief Executive of the Family Welfare Association:

> One of the things we haven't tackled as a society is security for those who cannot work and improving incomes of the very poorest. The long term poor have particular problems, for example, if they have disabled children or live in a rural area. You have to take account of the very poorest of those for whom work is not a realistic prospect in the near future or at all. (Quoted in *The Observer*, 2005)

While this is rarely, if ever, countenanced by the government, as we note below it is not lost on welfare workers in the DWP themselves.

Third, the focus on work means changes in welfare can be portrayed as contributing to a successful economy (see DWP, 2005) through welfare budget cuts and prudent public spending, and a larger in-work population. Hence the successes that are attributed to the ongoing 'transformation' of welfare, for example, over two million more people working than in 1997 and a drop in the number of lone parents on Income Support of 230,000 are seemingly obvious and readily conveyed as an indication of how far New Labour has progressed its 'modernised welfare state' goals (DWP, 2006c, pp 7, 10).

What should also be clear is that, alongside policy developments, the restructuring of how services are delivered has also played a central role in welfare, particularly the creation of the DWP and especially its Jobcentre Plus 'business', which, at a cost of £2 billion, brought together for the first time the functions of the Benefits Agency and the Employment Service (DWP, 2006c, p 9). Hence the administration and payment of benefits, labour market participation and employer involvement is coordinated under one overarching department. This is a clear indication of the government's commitment to forging and consolidating the relationship between welfare and work. And also, from our point of view, alongside the reform of the pensions and child support systems, and disability and carers services, it demonstrates the centrality of DWP workers in the transformation of the welfare state and its apparent successes thus far. Yet, as we discuss below, this does not necessarily bring forth the 'rewards' that have been promised. Indeed, this closeness to the frontline of the delivery of welfare reform sees groups of workers both administer some of the harshest changes to the welfare state since its creation and, paradoxically perhaps, bear the brunt of them.

## 'Prudence for a purpose': review, rationalisation, reform

This chapter does not set out to offer a fully comprehensive account of welfare in its entirety since New Labour's election in 1997. Similarly, it is not possible to discuss all of the changes and the political pronouncements that have emerged in relation to public spending. However, we believe it is possible to pin-point key events that have helped to shape central government welfare work and that indicate the nature and contours of the structures and organisation that will define 21st-century welfare and work within a key sector of the welfare state. Also, from the perspective set out in the introduction, it is also possible to outline an important catalyst for resistance and struggle against modernisation and its impact.

First, however, it is important to note how, on the one hand, welfare changes thus far have been constructed, in government rhetoric at least, as a success in terms of effectiveness. Indeed, claims like 'youth unemployment has virtually been eradicated' (Hutton, 2006) are seemingly testament to the efficacy of 'reform' and to the apparent prescience of government commitments. Yet, on the other hand, it must also be noted how this is increasingly framed, first and foremost, in terms of economic efficiency and the fundamental impact of this focus. Thus policy changes and government welfare initiatives are presented as a key driver for overall economic success and investment in public services:

> Britain can continue with historically high and rising investments in … our public services…. Investments made possible because since 1997 … unemployment which, in 1997, cost 1 per cent of national income now costs a third of that, just 0.3 per cent – the lowest of our major European competitors…. (Brown, 2004)

As noted earlier, 2004 was a 'watershed' year in respect of these issues with the March Budget statement and the Spending Review announced in July. The former represented the first formal announcement of serious cutbacks in the welfare workforce. Despite being couched in terms of 'slashing the foot soldiers of Whitehall' (BBC News, 2004c) and being presented as cuts in ambiguously named 'administrative costs' (BBC News, 2004b; Brown, 2004) of 2.5% annually over three years across all government departments, it was clear that the majority of the 40,000 jobs to be lost in the civil service would be in the DWP. While claiming that the UK was 'enjoying its longest period of economic growth since the Industrial Revolution' (BBC News, 2004c), the Budget Statement heralded the introduction of 'efficiency measures', which resulted in a 'day of the long knives for public servants across the UK', according to the Public and Commercial Services Union (PCS) (BBC News, 2004c). The job cuts, as the Chancellor subsequently made clear, were one of 'the three major drivers of change, the three sources of new resources … releasing substantial new money for frontline services' (Brown, 2004).

In addition to recognising what was, in effect, a very public and, it has to be said, enthusiastically delivered redundancy notice without any consultation with employees or unions, we must also note an apparent lack of regard for potential human costs in terms of both the workers involved and, as we discuss below, for public sector 'customers', especially welfare recipients. The Budget Statement also laid the foundation for and indicated the nature of the government's July Spending Review that was even more comprehensive and potentially damaging from the perspective of public sector workers.

This review was principally based on the Brown–Blair commissioned, 'independent' investigation of public sector efficiency by former 'captain' of the information technology (IT) industry and the first chief executive of the Office of Government Commerce, Sir Peter Gershon, that took 'efficiency' much further, proposing £20 billion worth of 'efficiency gains in the year 2007-08' (Gershon, 2004, p 3). The 'gross reduction of over 84,000 posts in the Civil Service and military personnel in administrative and support role' (Gershon, 2004, p 3) claimed to be premised on the re-direction of resources from 'back office' functions to 'frontline' public service delivery and cutting the 'unproductive' time spent on 'serving the organisation rather than [their] customers' (Gershon, 2004, p 38). This review, and its enthusiastic embrace by both Blair and Brown, demonstrated in sharp relief the 'modernised' structure and organisation that would 'deliver improved public services'. In addition, it made clear who would be on the receiving end of the negative effects of the apparent strive to 're-direct resources' in order to keep spending down: those charged with delivering public services that 'exude[s] pride, pace, passion and professionalism' (O'Donnell, 2006) in the civil service, especially workers in the DWP where the majority of cuts were to be targeted. Hence this review and its subsequent impact have brought civil servants in general and DWP workers in particular into direct conflict with the government. It is important, therefore, before considering the effects of the changes proposed by Gershon in terms of welfare work and resistance to them by welfare workers, to briefly outline some of the changes his review enacted.

One of the most important elements of the review is its clear articulation of the whole concept of 'efficiency'. Unsurprisingly, at one level, this means a potentially vague commitment to the better utilisation of resources including the workforce (Gershon, 2004, p 6). However, what is clear from our point of view is that efficiencies implicitly meant cuts based on '*reduced numbers* of inputs (eg people or assets), whilst maintaining the *same level* of service provision; or *lower prices* for the resources needed to provide public services or *additional* outputs, such as enhanced quality or quantity of service, for the *same level* of inputs; or *improved* ratios of output per unit of input ...' (Gershon,

2004, p 6; emphasis added). Fundamentally this translates as more and more *with* less and less.

Additionally, as with the Spending Review, Gershon's efficiency cuts were based on earlier and proposed investment in information and communication technology (ICT) (Gershon, 2004, pp 7, 19). Gershon noted in particular the apparent success, in efficiency terms of course, of the shift to a Direct Payments system in the DWP that pays all benefits into its customers' bank accounts that was 'on track to deliver savings of £400 million a year by the end of 2006' (Gershon, 2004, p 7). We would also note the increasing likelihood that these are implemented on a public–private partnership (PPP) basis, especially given the background of Gershon himself, his view that service provision by the 'independent sector' (in the NHS, for example; see also Chapter Four, this volume) helped 'to develop a new market for quality and efficient private sector capacity in the UK ...' (Gershon, 2004, p 14), and the fact that around half of his review team were drawn from private sector firms including IBM and Hewlett Packard (Gershon, 2004, p 59). Moreover, as one report pointed out, 'wiping out a large percentage of the workforce could affect service levels', that is likely to leave the sort of gaps to which the answer, for some at least, is 'outsourcing' (eGov Monitor, 2005).

Yet given the focus just outlined in relation to 'modernisation' through ICT and proposed cut-backs on 'non-productive' and 'repetitive' functions, it is perhaps surprising that Gershon's cuts were disproportionately borne in the DWP – the key deliverer of welfare reform that serves millions of people across the UK including many of the most disadvantaged (Gershon, 2004, p 16). In order to achieve £960 million in 'efficiency gains', 30,000 jobs were to be lost and, in line with the drive to make savings on estates, property and staff turnover costs, at least 4,000 DWP jobs were to be relocated from London and South East England (Gershon, 2004, pp 19, 30, 54). Such measures, arguably like none other in the spending and efficiency reviews of recent years, give by far the clearest indication of the direction and indeed the underpinning ethos of welfare reform. Hence it is important to bear both of these in mind when we consider how change has impacted on the lives of DWP workers. Moreover, rather than the bureaucrat with bowler hat stereotype, one estimate suggested that 75% of civil service workers at the time of the publication of Gershon's report were employed 'in the administration and distribution of benefits and tax [and] the delivery of the Government's social and labour market programmes ...' (TUC, 2005, p 8).

## Transforming welfare: transforming welfare work

In discussing the relationship between the 'transformation' of welfare and of welfare work it is important to remind ourselves that ideas of 'piecemeal' and 'minimalist' reform are rejected (Blair, 2004a). However, before moving on, it is also important to unpack the idea of 'transformation' a little further. First and foremost, it is necessary to make clear that we would seek to problematise New Labour's notion of 'transformation'. Despite the promotion of what are presented as 'new' ideas for the public sector, for instance the emphasis on 'putting customers in the driving seat' (Osborne and Gaebler, 1993), we must remain fully alert to continuities with the past, not least in relation to the construction of 'welfare dependency' as problematic, and along with this an often stigmatising and condemning approach to people defined as poor (see Levitas, 2005). That said, however, we would suggest that there is already evidence that welfare work is in the process of being 'transformed' as a result of part of the programme of 'modernisation' and 'reform' already discussed. In this brief section we seek to outline what we believe to be the key areas of transformation and to briefly examine some of the connections between these and the proposals of the reviews of 2004 and working in the DWP in particular. However, we first consider some important civil service-wide issues.

One 'concern' that frequently exercises bosses, politicians and the media is sick leave. This is frequently represented as a widespread and persistent problem across the public sector. Unsurprisingly, creating the conditions for the development of Gershon's 'culture of efficiency' and reducing the cost of 'unproductive' time presents departments with the opportunity to reduce sick absence through the reform of procedures (Gershon, 2004, p 19). Also of particular interest to Gordon Brown was the civil service regulation that the majority of absences are 'self-certified', with the necessity for medical certificates only being triggered after around a week of time off, leaving the system, according to the Chancellor, open to abuse (Brown, 2004). Hence this was to be reviewed and plans developed to reduce 'unplanned' absence, despite the fact that short-term absence in the public sector is actually lower than in the private sector (Cabinet Office/DWP/HSE, 2004, p 2). Alongside subsequent plans to increase the civil service pension age from 60 to 65, this represents the potential transformation of the best of civil service working conditions. And these proposals, together with the cuts already outlined, have been a central element of campaigning, lobbying and more militant action (see below) across the whole service, especially in the DWP.

Although there is little scope to develop them here, two further points are worth noting in relation to sick absence. First, such moves can be connected to what we might term the 'Tesco-isation' of public sector work, that is, the adoption and adaptation to what the government sees as the 'best' practices of companies like Tesco, particularly related to issues represented as damaging to customer services, especially if they can address these in 'partnership' with an acquiescent union. For example, the supermarket giant declared the introduction of sickness schemes, where the first three days of absence are unpaid, a success (see Corporate Watch, 2006). It was praised in the government's 2004 public sector sick absence review for a training programme of more than 12,000 managers that sought to encourage them to have 'the confidence to make decisions ... on the action to take to manage unplanned absence issues ...' (Cabinet Office/DWP/HSE, 2004, p 14). This is, arguably, further demonstration of the import of the ethos and managerial culture of the private sector into public sector service delivery.

Second, there is a sense in which the issue of sick absence represents the nexus of the relationship between DWP workers and their customers. The continuing concern to reduce the numbers of claimants on Incapacity Benefit, for example, is a persistent and key feature of 'modernising' welfare (see DWP, 2006c). But it is now also a feature of concerns in relation to sick absence in the public sector that are being raised in terms of getting people back to work, keeping them in the labour market and 'responsible certification from GPs' (Cabinet Office/ DWP/HSE, 2004, p 1) – in ways similar to those that are directed to DWP customers. This is an important development and elicits more in-depth analysis and understanding than a perhaps slightly superficial, although no less important view, that 'reform' is made complex because public sector workers are both consumers and producers of services (see McCafferty, 2004).

With regard to other elements of the modernisation programme, the much-vaunted transformation of public services through significant changes to ICT delivery has been beset with problems, not least in the DWP, where the government has spent 'billions on [an] ill-conceived and abortive' computer system at the Child Support Agency (BBC News, 2004b). Moreover, also in the DWP, both the PCS and a House of Commons Select Committee in 2006 blamed the introduction of a new customer management system (CMS) in Jobcentre Plus as precipitating a 'catastrophic failure' of its services in the summer of 2005 (*The Guardian*, 2006a, 2006b). In addition, concerns about the introduction of outsourcing and off-shoring are not, it seems, without foundation, since more than 200 jobs from National Savings have been moved to India (with 200 more planned) and some DWP work is already being performed in Asia (PCS, 2006a).

However, where the most notable change has occurred is in relation to how DWP workers conduct their 'traditional' business and a shift away from 'shop-front' interactions to processing and call (contact) centres. Although there is not the scope here to fully develop a discussion of call centres (an issue that also emerges in other chapters in this volume), it is important to briefly note that these are a central element of the DWP's overall welfare transformation strategy as the intention is to have almost all non-face-to-face contact handled through its call centres (NAO, 2006, p 2). The point to touch on here is this element of organisational and 'transactional' reform, highlighting how it relates to the 'transformation' of welfare work (as well as to the 'customer-focused' service). First, it should be noted that the shift to call centres pre-dates those 2004 reviews that have already been discussed and in three of the DWP key businesses more than 33 million incoming calls and 7 million outgoing calls were handled by nearly 6,000 operatives at 70 call centres in 2004-05 (NAO, 2006, p 2). Second, despite clear increases in the scale of DWP business conducted in call centres in recent years (they have been central to the roll-out of Direct Payments, for example, moving 9 million customers to this method by 2002 and processing hundreds of thousands of calls from benefits claimants who would traditionally have appeared in person), a number of the centres handling these calls were closed by 2005 (NAO, 2006, p 2). Paradoxically, the establishment of call centre networks in key DWP agencies like Jobcentre Plus and the Pensions Service has helped facilitate the closure of many local offices, therefore contributing to both staffing and estates' costs savings (NAO, 2006, p 5). Hence this key element of rationalisation is helping to change the nature of working 'for' welfare dramatically not least in the day-to-day contact with some of the most vulnerable people in society, such as poor single parents and pensioners.

Call centre working has proved problematic for employees who receive little training and whose skills and aptitudes in DWP-specific knowledge are under-valued in the face of the need to meet the demands, competencies and approaches of call centre work, including the use of 'mystery shoppers' and routinisation and repetition (NAO, 2006, pp 8, 10, 13). It has also been a difficult transition for the DWP's millions of customers who have faced delays in the processing of claims because of the failure of IT systems and call centre procedures generally, where rates of response have been drastically off-target (NAO, 2006, p 7; see also *The Guardian*, 2006a, 2006b). Overall, these have resulted in high staff turnover in DWP call centres and low-level customer satisfaction. Thus efficiency gains have been made, but at a cost. Closures in job centres around the country and their replacement with call centres has proved highly problematic for disadvantaged individuals and groups, with staff cuts also resulting in tens of thousands of calls going unanswered (*Socialist Worker*, 27 January 2007).

## Resistance and struggle: striking 'for' welfare?

Before outlining in some detail how DWP workers, often alongside other civil service colleagues, have sought to challenge key reforms, it is necessary to discuss some important developments concerning their representation over the past decade. Clearly, in any account of how groups of workers are affected by policy shifts and ideological developments we should at least note the nature and contours of workplace relations (Darlington, 1994), particularly in relation to trade union representation. However, the case of the DWP workers and, to a lesser extent, civil servants in general, helps demonstrate how an arguably radical shift in both how they have been represented and by whom is a critical element of resistance.

As noted earlier, the main union in the DWP is the Public and Commercial Services Union or, more commonly, the PCS. The union was created in 1998 out of a merger between the Civil and Public Services Association (CPSA) and the Public Services, Tax and Commerce Union and with a current membership of around 325,000 is the sixth largest union in the UK. This figure represents an increase from 280,000 in 2001 and it includes 97,000 members in the DWP, who have taken more than one-and-a-half million strike days between 2001 and 2006 (*The Socialist*, 2006). This figure is a clear indication of growing militancy and evidence of the preparedness to initiate action in the face of job cuts and reductions in services but, as alluded to above, it is also linked to the type of union that the PCS has emerged as in the years since 1998.

On the one hand, it is perhaps unsurprising that the government's whole approach to the transformation of welfare has precipitated militant action. Yet, on the other hand, it is worth noting how the scale of this action stands in stark contrast to the near (although not total) 'silence' of key groups of welfare workers in the years since the 1978/79 'winter of discontent'. The fact that this was the case in the face of sustained attacks on poor and unemployed people carried out by previous Conservative administrations and changes to workers' terms and conditions helps alert us to the unprecedented nature of contemporary action. Moreover, clashes between DWP workers and the New Labour government have, to a large extent, been about the whole nature of welfare reform and its impact on 'customers' and workers alike:

> 'Of course we care about jobs but we care about the sort of services we will be providing for people when it's all processing centres....' (DWP striker, Greenock 1)

Crucially, we would argue that, above all, an analysis of these relations gives us an invaluable insight into the fundamental fault line that exists at the heart of New Labour's programme of 'modernisation' whereby the very people needed to deliver welfare change are at risk from its negative effects. Before discussing this in more detail, however, it is important to briefly explore key changes that have occurred at the level of trade unionism in order to fully understand the nature of resistance in the DWP and, as a result, to allude to some crucial methods and perspectives through which the 'hard labour' edge of New Labour can be challenged.

Arguably one of the most important changes that has occurred in the history of civil service trade unionism is relatively recent in origin. In July 2002 the High Court ruled that Left-winger Mark Serwotka was legally the General Secretary of the PCS after more than two years of wrangling since his election by the membership of the union in 2000. The fight for the leadership of the PCS had been a defining feature of the union since its creation, and Serwotka's election represented a significant defeat for the group of so-called 'Moderates' that had controlled its fore-runner, the CPSA, for more than two decades. The 'National Moderate Group' had evolved from the 'Daylight Group' that then CPSA President, Kate Losinska, admitted in 1978 took money from the infamous Movement for True Industrial Democracy (TRUEMID), run by David Stirling (the notorious founder of the British Army's elite SAS forces), and that operated a private strike-breaking force in the 1970s (see Jamieson, 2002; Osler, 2002). By the time of the creation of the PCS, the CPSA was effectively in the control of two key 'Moderate' figures, President Marion Chambers and General Secretary Barry Reamsbottom, whose supporters initiated a coup at a 2002 National Executive Committee meeting that sought to overturn Serwotka's election and re-install Reamsbottom in the position of General Secretary. The same action also sought to sideline Janice Godrich, the PCS President and high-profile former member of the Scottish Socialist Party (*Socialist Worker*, 2002). Hence, the affirmation of the election of two declared socialists into key positions not only represented simply loosening the grip of the Right on the union, it also represented a historic fissure with the union's recent past. This event also dashed the hopes of the Trade Union Committee for European and Transatlantic Understanding, a NATO-sponsored (North Alliance Treaty Organisation) think-tank of which Reamsbottom was a Vice-President (Jamieson, 2002; Parks and Dropkin, 2002), and those of Blair and New Labour that the Left in the PCS could not consolidate its hold. Moreover, it has arguably helped to shape workplace trade unionism in departments like the DWP and to facilitate the sort of militant action that we have witnessed in recent years.

Connected to this is a second, crucial and recent change that concerns the nature of the political approach that has developed at the heart of the PCS leadership. As noted above, PCS President Janice Godrich was, until recently, one of a few key trade union leaders in the Scottish Socialist Party (SSP) (since October 2006 a member of Tommy Sheridan's breakaway Solidarity Party) and was de facto leader of a relatively strong group of PCS militants within the SSP that represented a number of government departments including the Scottish Executive and, unsurprisingly, the DWP. Clearly this has had an important politicising effect, although this is uneven in character and its impact has been far from uniform. But it is the political approach of former benefits worker, Mark Serwotka, that has drawn most attention as one of a new generation of so-called 'awkward squad' union leaders that were avowedly anti-New Labour-style 'partnership' and 'modernisation', and key supporters of the emerging social movements of the late 20th and early 21st century like the Anti-Capitalist Movement and Stop the War (for a fuller discussion, see Smith, 2003).

However, it is also possible to distinguish Serwotka from most of his 'awkward squad' colleagues in that his approach is not underpinned by a concern to wrestle the Labour Party, and the trade unions' link with it, from New Labour. He was, rather, a member of the Socialist Alliance, central to its campaign to 'democratise trade unions' and, in particular, to initiate real debate over the dominance of Labour as a recipient of their political funds (Socialist Alliance, 2002), latterly offering support to the Respect Coalition in England. In fact, in another key political development that is arguably both evidence of a new outlook and a key factor in helping to shape it, the PCS membership in 2005 took the historic decision to create a political fighting fund. This leaves the union in a strong position to initiate campaigns both on their own account and also against service cuts. Crucially it is not affiliated to the Labour

Party although PCS is a member of both the Trades Union Congress (TUC) and the Scottish Trades Union Congress (STUC).

Overall, two things need to be drawn out here, before moving on. First, it should be clear from this, and from the other chapters in this volume, that the public sector remains a key battleground and New Labour 'modernisation' and 'reform' has done little to assuage this. In terms of limited improvements in services, increasing costs, pressure to convince the public on its real aims in relation to 'modernisation', and a growing resistance to its objectives by workers, the public sector remains an 'Achilles heel' for New Labour. Second, the PCS has no Labour affiliation to hinder its struggle in opposition to New Labour government policy (unlike UNISON; see Chapter Four, this volume). and therefore no party political pressure to 'toe the line'. This results in the union representing a central force in the battles that have helped to define both second- and third-term New Labour. Importantly in the 'cull' of civil servants, a key force both shaping *and* exemplifying the restructuring of welfare, New Labour has set its face against a very different civil service union leadership than that faced by the Conservatives in the 1980s and 1990s. As a result of this, and cuts in jobs and terms and conditions, it faces a very different civil service, especially in frontline welfare services. Clearly, as the largest government department and *the* key deliverer of welfare, the DWP is critical in relation to New Labour achievements and, of course, the success of trade union militancy against modernisation and its resultant cutbacks.

It is clearly evidenced in the extent and the nature of the industrial action that has taken place in recent years that the workers therein have risen to the challenge of resisting both. Indeed, even while the Chancellor was making the 2004 Budget Statement that heralded the 'largest attack on the civil service ever mounted' (*The Observer*, 2004), PCS members in the DWP were engaged in a battle against low levels of pay that resulted in a starting salary of around £10,000 and a 'divisive' performance development scheme (PDS), imposed in April 2003 (*The Guardian*, 2004).

The 'pay and PDS dispute' ended in February 2005. It lasted 16 months, involved six days of strike action, a year of non-cooperation with the PDS and a change of Secretary of State for Work and Pensions from Andrew Smith to Alan Johnson. Eighty-seven per cent of DWP PCS members voted for the deal that saw a rise of 15% for the lowest paid, a 20% rise in overall starting salaries (*The Guardian*, 2005) and 'substantial changes' to the PDS (Serwotka, quoted in PCS, 2005). For the union, this represented a 'positive move forward for some of the lowest paid' and significant change to 'the hated pay performance system in the face of a senior management saying the system was non-negotiable' (Serwotka, quoted in *The Guardian*, 2005).

However, from the point of view of our discussion of resistance in the DWP against reform and modernisation and their impact, the issues around this strike precipitated some important responses that continue to have significant effects. First, for the PCS leadership and Serwotka, the settling of this key dispute did not mean an end to the 'campaign against cuts in jobs and services and the attacks on [our] pensions' in the longer term (Serwotka, quoted in *The Guardian*, 2005). Second, this sustained dispute in the relatively new DWP 'that showed that [workers] would not be cowed' nor would they allow the imposition of 'unacceptable changes to ... conditions' (Serwotka, quoted in PCS, 2005) fully demonstrated that New Labour should not expect an easy transition to the big vision, replacement welfare state. Third, it brought to the fore the problematic nature of the employment relations that had developed in the DWP since its creation in 2002. For many welfare workers this entailed the import of a particular management style, characteristically and increasingly seen as:

> '... actively discouraging people from joining the union ...
> for the first time ever really.' (DWP striker, Greenock 2)

This then forced them to draw a distinction between this and previous experience:

> 'People were never scared or anything about being in the union – it was just an accepted part of working here. But new management are strict about facility-time and about us using the internal email system and phones to talk about union stuff. It's just a different atmosphere....' (DWP striker, Greenock 1)

It is perhaps understandable therefore why this style is also increasingly represented as 'senior DWP managers [were] out to smash the union' (Serwotka, quoted in PCS, 2005).

The last response to the 'pay and PDS dispute' worthy of our attention is that of DWP workers themselves and an arguably unprecedented embrace of trade unionism, exemplified in large-scale growth for the PCS. Thus from the time of the imposition of PDS and their third strike in the dispute in July 2004, the union could claim it had recruited 14,000 new members (*The Guardian*, 2004), and a further 4,000 had joined by the time the dispute was settled in February 2005 (Serwotka, quoted in PCS, 2005). Moreover in the national, civil service-wide 'anti-modernisation, pro-pension' strike on 5 November 2004 support was at its strongest in the DWP:

> 'The strike was solid here and we had more than a thousand on strike ... about 50 HEOs [managers] and above. I saw about 30 pickets.... People due for retirement had a dispensation, so did casuals but we had their verbal support. Some casuals wouldn't cross the picket line.' (DWP striker, Northgate 3)

This highly politicised, one-day strike was action in response to:

> The talk about cutting waste that involves real people ... the low paid who depend on jobs ... not faceless bureaucrats but the half of the civil service workforce that earn less than £13,750 ... the vilification, the distress, the insecurity ... to protect essential services ... against purely political decisions.... (Godrich, 2004)

With the first, most obvious, and harshest cuts being experienced in DWP local offices and the move to large-scale processing centres, as outlined above, it is understandable why workers there were among the most vociferous and militant. Moreover, willingness to take industrial action is also something that persists as members seek to defend services 'against a backdrop of the DWP refusing to acknowledge the damage being wrought by job cuts ...' (Serwotka, quoted in *Inside Public*, 2006) as demonstrated in the most recent round of strikes in the DWP in 2006. This also demonstrates the increasingly political nature of DWP disputes and how they strike at the heart of the New Labour project.

The most recent example of this has been the strikes and beginning of an overtime ban in January 2006 as the continuing formal response to the effects of the 2004 reviews. Importantly, however, the union made clear that this was also fundamentally a strike about 'deteriorating service levels' that were 'letting down some of the most disadvantaged in society' (Serwotka, quoted in PCS, 2006b) as well as their own jobs. This is a crucial twist in the responses of key groups of public sector workers in the face of modernisation in that disputes are increasingly and demonstrably 'double-edged' with an equal focus on the ill-effects on workers themselves and those for whom welfare services are critical. Importantly, this represents a challenge to the idea of 'wreckers' and is, of course, a world away from their portrayal as self-seeking, faceless, bureaucrats with bowler hats and 'skivers' by some politicians and sections of the media (notably *The Sun*) (see PCS, 2004).

Yet the DWP has still sought to represent the PCS and the strikers as resistant to any change, working against seemingly beneficial reforms:

> We have said throughout that we want to work with them through discussion, not industrial action. If we are going to meet our commitment to deliver the highest quality of service to our customers it is vital that we push ahead with our modernisation programme. It is therefore disappointing that the PCS appear to not be moving in the same direction and seem opposed to much of the change. We are absolutely committed to our service to the public.... (DWP, quoted in *The Guardian*, 2006c)

The distinct positions of the PCS and the DWP, with the former claiming a 'deterioration of services' through modernisation that will continue to 'let down' the 'most vulnerable members of the public ... as overstretched staff struggle to deliver' (Serwotka, quoted in *The Guardian*, 2006c) and the latter claiming that services would deteriorate if modernisation did *not* occur, became most obvious during this dispute. Crucially, this is also further evidence of the gulf between the government's position and that of a key group of public sector workers responsible for the delivery of the modernisation of welfare at the frontline. This has helped to set the tone of how this programme is to be both 'imposed' and 'enforced', and how it is to be resisted and challenged.

More recent action has focused on the intransigence of management and their lack of ability to conceive of the full and lasting impact of reform. This is illustrated in the union's responses to the publication of the latest welfare plans (DWP, 2006c), which were now characteristically premised on their own demands regarding cutting staff numbers and work intensification (PCS, 2006c) alongside campaigning on behalf of their customers – in this case those on Incapacity Benefit who were to be further pressed to return to work (DWP, 2006c). In addition, a few days ahead of the January 2006 DWP strike, the minister at the DWP, Margaret Hodge, confirmed 'Gershon-busting' closures of more than 100 further local offices (*The Guardian*, 2006d) despite warnings from both Gershon and Gordon Brown that to do so would put services at risk (Brown, 2004; Gershon, 2004). A further 48-hour strike at the DWP in May 2006 also highlighted the effects of efficiency reforms on staff (over 17,000 jobs had gone by this time) and the problems that continue to beset the technology of the welfare system and its organisational practices. Lastly, in January 2007 another civil service-wide national strike took place against the continuing programme of reform founded on what, on the evidence outlined above at least, are turning out to be the contradictory and competing demands of driving down costs and staff numbers while delivering improvements in 21st-century public services.

## Conclusions

This chapter reflects ongoing research into the developing tensions, anger and struggles that are increasingly characterising key areas of the civil service, given repeated New Labour commitments to 'driving on' with welfare and public sector modernisation and for more job cuts. Here we sought first of all to redress what we believe is an imbalance in researching the public sector in that, where this research does take place, it is all too infrequently focused on the frontline of local government welfare delivery. While we would not suggest that there is a general acceptance of the bureaucrats with bowler hats or 'skivers' stereotypes, importantly the role of the hundreds of thousands of central government welfare workers requires immediate and serious attention in a critical period both for New Labour and for work in the welfare industry. Workers in the DWP are both at the cutting-edge of welfare reforms *and* at the sharp end of their impact and are therefore crucial to our understanding of their full effects. Importantly, as we have detailed above, they are also at the forefront of militant responses to New Labour's modernisation programme and currently, alongside their colleagues in the wider civil service, present the government with its greatest public sector challenge. We have also sought to demonstrate how the DWP workers themselves have been forced to take action on their own behalf and also on behalf of the most vulnerable groups in society including pensioners and the chronically sick. They draw attention to essential flaws in the New Labour approach to both work and welfare: more and more seemingly cannot be done for less and less. Crucially, their challenges and experiences more generally alert us to the fault line that divides New Labour from the public sector workers whose ultimate consent they desperately need.

### Further sources

For a fuller examination of New Labour's valorisation of the citizen as consumer and how this is impacting on public services see Clarke, J.,

Newman, J., Smith, N., Vidler, E. and Westmarland, L. (2007) *Creating citizen-consumers: Changing publics and changing public services*, London: Sage Publications.

## References

BBC News (2004a) Report by Jenny Scott, 17 March (www.news.bbc.co.uk, accessed 20/03/2004).

BBC News (2004b) 'Is Brown right to wield the axe', 18 March 18 (http://news.bbc.co.uk/1/hi/business/3520138.stm, accessed 20/03/2004).

BBC News (2004c) 'Brown slashes 40,000 Whitehall jobs', 17 March (http://news.bbc.co.uk/1/hi/UK_politics/3518888.stm, accessed 20/03/2004).

Blair, T. (1999) Speech to the Labour Party Conference, 28 September (http://news.bbc.co.uk/1/low/UK_politics/460009.stm, accessed 09/07/2007).

Blair, T. (2002) Speech to the Spring Conference of the Labour Party, 3 February (www.guardian.co.uk/Archive/Article/0,4273,4349556,00.html, accessed 04/04/2002).

Blair, T. (2004a) 'Reforming the welfare state', Speech by the Prime Minister and Leader of the Labour Party, 11 October (www.labour.org.uk/ac2004news?ux_news_id=tbwelfare04, 11/10/2004).

Blair, T. (2004b) Foreword to the 2004 Spending Review by the Prime Minister (http://www.hm-treasury.gov.uk/media/C/A/sr2004_forecontents.pdf).

Brown, G. (2004) Statement by the Chancellor of the Exchequer on the 2004 Spending Review (www.hm-treasury.gov.uk/spending_review/spend_sr04/spend_sr04_statement.cfm, accessed 8/01/2005).

Cabinet Office/DWP (Department for Work and Pensions)/HSE (Health and Safety Executive) (2004) *Managing sick absence in the public sector: A joint review by the Ministerial Task Force on health, safety and productivity and the Cabinet Office* (www.hse.gov.uk/gse/sickness.pdf, accessed 30/11/2004).

Commission on Social Justice (1994) *Social justice: Strategies for national renewal: the Report of the Commission on Social Justice*, London: Vantage.

Corporate Watch (2006) 'Tesco and its staff' (www.corporatewatch.org/?lid=255#staff, accessed 12/11/2006).

Darlington, R. (1994) *The dynamics of workplace unionism – Shop steward organisation in three Merseyside plants*, London: Mansell.

DWP (Department for Work and Pensions) (2005) 'Principles of welfare reform' (www.dwp.gov.uk/welfarereform/legislation_principles.asp, accessed 28/11/2005).

DWP (2006a) 'About the Department' (www.dwp.gov.uk/aboutus/, accessed 31/01/2006).

DWP (2006b) 'Departmental framework' (www.dwp.gov.uk/aboutus/departmental_framework.asp, accessed 31/03/2006).

DWP (2006c) *A New Deal for welfare: Empowering people to work*, London: DWP/The Stationery Office.

eGov Monitor (2005) *The Gershon Report and the value of outsourcing*, 22 March (www.egovmonitor.com/node/163/print, accessed 11/11/2005).

Fairclough, N. (2000) *New Labour, new language?*, London: Routledge.

Gershon, P. (2004) *Releasing resources to the front-line: Independent Review of public sector efficiency*, Norwich: The Stationery Office.

Giddens, A. (2002) 'Don't go back to the bad old ways of tax and spend, Mr Blair', *The Independent*, 7 January.

Godrich, J. (2004) Speech to the PCS Rally, Glasgow, 5 November.

*Guardian, The* (2004) '90,000 civil servants strike against low pay', 29 July.

*Guardian, The* (2005) 'Benefits staff settle pay deal', 17 February.

*Guardian, The* (2006a) 'Two-day strike at job centres and benefit offices', 2 May.

*Guardian, The* (2006b) 'Strike threats over "catastrophic failure" of public services', 7 June.

*Guardian, The* (2006c) 'Benefits staff to join two-day strike', 16 January.

*Guardian, The* (2006d) 'Hodge confirms further job closures', 25 January.

Hutton J. (2006) *A New Deal for welfare: Empowering people to work*, Ministerial Foreword, London: DWP/The Stationery Office.

*Inside Public* (2006) 'DWP strikes go ahead', 7 January.

Jamieson, J. (2002) 'Spies, lies and the PCS: the road to Istanbul', 22 July (www.labournet.net/ukunion/0207/pcs7.html, accessed 31/01/2005).

Levitas, R. (2005) *The inclusive society* (2nd edn), London: Palgrave.

McCafferty, P. (2004) 'Working the 'Third Way': New Labour, employment relations, and Scottish devolution', Unpublished PhD thesis, University of Glasgow.

Mandelson, P. (1997) *Labour's next steps: Tackling social exclusion*, Fabian Pamphlet 581, London: Fabian Society.

NAO (National Audit Office) (2006) *Delivering effective services through contact centres*, London: NAO.

*Observer, The* (2004) 'Brown's blunder', 22 March.

*Observer, The* (2005) '£3 a day: the slim budget of Britain's hidden underclass', 5 June.

O'Donnell, G. (2006) 'A message from the head of the civil service' (www.civilservice.gov.uk/reform/message_from_gus.asp, accessed 01/10/2006).

Osborne, D. and Gaebler, T. (1993) *Reinventing government: How the entrepreneurial spirit is transforming local government*, New York, NY: Plume.

Osler D. (2002) 'PCS conspiracy flashback: TUCETU, IRIS, and TRUEMID', 18 July (www.labournet.net/ukunion/0207/pcs6.html, accessed 31/01/2005).

Parks, D. and Dropkin, G. (2002) 'Backing Barry: the NATO publisher and the PCS Coup', 5 July (www.labournet.net/ukunion/0207/pcs2.html, accessed 30/01/2006).

PCS (Public and Commercial Services Union) (2004) 'I'm not a skiver, I'm a striker', Press release, 4 November.

PCS (2005) 'General Secretary urges DWP members to vote yes in Pay and PDS ballot', Press release, 8 February.

PCS (2006a) *Campaigns update*, October.

PCS (2006b) 'Support for Work and Pensions strike grows', Press release, 27 January.

PCS (2006c) 'Union reaction to welfare reform Green Paper', Press release, 25 January.

Smith, M. (2003) *The awkward squad: New Labour and the rank and file*, London: Socialist Workers Party.

Socialist Alliance (2002) 'Member's bulletin', 11 June.

*Socialist, The* (2006) 'Delegates debate DWP strikes', June 8.

*Socialist Worker* (2002) 'This is a battle to defend democracy', 8 June.

*Socialist Worker*, (2007) 'Everyone must back our strike', 27 January.

*The Telegraph* (2006) 'Workshy must lose benefits', 19 December.

TUC (Trades Union Congress) (2005) *Bowler hats and bureaucrats – Myths about the public sector workforce*, March, London: TUC.

# ELEVEN

# Working in the non-profit welfare sector: contract culture, partnership, Compacts and the 'shadow state'

*Lynne Poole*

## Introduction

This chapter focuses on the impact of recent welfare restructuring and 'modernisation' agendas on the non-profit sector, now increasingly responsible for the delivery of a range of welfare services, and its welfare workers. Fyfe and Milligan (2003, p 272) note that the sector is generally seen to comprise independent, self-governing bodies that do not distribute profits but are run for the benefit of others and/or the community. They are perceived to be accountable to their membership, the people they serve and represent, and their funding bodies in relation to how they spend their funds. Some rely on volunteers, some on paid workers, some on a mixture of both, and they draw on a range of resources including individual and corporate donations, state grants and contract finance, tax relief and lottery funds.

Collectively these types of organisations are commonly referred to as the 'voluntary sector', reflecting their traditionally voluntarist nature. More recently government policy documents have drawn on the concept of a 'voluntary and community sector', which hints at the government's own neocommunitarian agenda and the place of non-profit organisations within that. Others have used the term 'third sector' to highlight the distinction between private, statutory and voluntary organisations and the relationship between them. However, given the recent changes in the sector and the blurring of the boundaries between different types of organisations and the roles and functions that they are now called on to perform, this chapter utilises the term 'non-profit sector' (Miller, 2002).

It is important to note from the outset that there is an incredible amount of diversity within the sector in terms of finances, human resources, functions, structure and organisational characteristics. Moreover, there is evidence that, in part as a consequence of the restructuring of the welfare system in Britain, there is a growing polarisation within the sector between those larger, more formal, more professionalised organisations and those that are smaller, who rely more on volunteers and community input and are more informally organised. This argument will be explored in more detail later in the chapter.

The chapter begins by situating the sector in its historical context before going on to outline the impact of social policy developments, and the emergence of a contract culture in particular, on non-profit organisations throughout the Thatcher and Major years. The chapter then examines the consequences of New Labour's welfare 'modernisation' agenda for these organisations. In doing so it highlights the implications of New Labour's take on partnerships, the development of *Compacts* and the extension of contract finance, especially for that section of the sector that seems to have embraced New Labour agendas uncritically and with enthusiasm. Here the focus is on the impact that the changing political and policy context has had on larger, more formal non-profit organisations in particular and, crucially given the remit of this book, on their employees. The chapter ends with a brief discussion of some preliminary findings that have emerged from the early stages of an ongoing piece of research that is exploring the shifting relationship between non-profit sector workers and their employees in a Scottish criminal justice setting.

## The non-profit sector and New Right welfare restructuring

The non-profit sector emerged strongly in the 19th century with a significant role in both welfare provision and social control (Lewis, 1995), but by the end of that century the tide was turning in the face of claims about 'voluntary failure' on the one hand, and the need to increase state activity and responsibility for welfare on the other. Of course, voluntary activity continued, largely supplementing, complementing and extending informal and statutory arrangements but also sometimes meeting new needs and using different approaches. Throughout this period claims were made for and on behalf of the sector in terms of its potential for innovation, giving rise to the notion of what Halfpenny and Reid (2002) have called 'philanthropic entrepreneurialship'. Nevertheless, particularly in the postwar boom period when the state's responsibility for welfare was arguably at its height, the non-profit sector was the junior partner in relation to social policy and provision (Taylor and Bassi, 1998).

However, in the 1980s the place of the non-profit sector in the provision of welfare was re-evaluated. In essence there was a call, particularly although not exclusively from the political Right, for a more pluralist system of welfare provision. This was seen to entail a shift in the state's role whereby it would relinquish much of its direct welfare provision to the for-profit and non-profit sectors, which it would in turn work to enable, finance and regulate. Halfpenny and Reid (2002) have argued that this renewed focus on the welfare role of the non-profit sector increased its visibility and ultimately its opportunities to mop up service provision for the needy through the development of a quasi-market-based mixed economy of welfare, which functioned through the application of competitive principles embodied in a new contracting culture. In essence, non-profit organisations were encouraged to bid for service contracts and, if successful, to step into the role of providing welfare services on behalf of the state (see also Lewis, 1999). This push for a more mixed economy of welfare was in part built on a number of positive assumptions made about both the for-profit and non-profit sectors. Concerning the latter, it was believed by some commentators, politicians and policy makers alike that non-profit organisations compared favourably with statutory agencies insofar as they were more flexible and responsive, more committed to the principles of community participation and user empowerment and more capable of being imaginative and innovative in their meeting of needs and solving of 'social problems' (see, for example, Wolfenden, 1978, and Hadley and Hatch, 1982, both cited in Halfpenny and Reid, 2002). Moreover, they were seen as capable of delivering services more cheaply than the statutory sector, principally as a result of the lower labour costs involved in relying on women, lower-paid professionals and volunteers. And, while the evidence in support of some of these claims has been contested (Leat, 1996; Halfpenny and Reid, 2002), the more positive representations of the sector were enthusiastically embraced by a Thatcher government, keen to discredit and 'roll back' the state and to use public dissatisfaction with public services to legitimate a restructuring of welfare in line with its own welfare agenda. Moreover, an increased shift towards a greater role for the non-profit sector in welfare service delivery was also used in a pragmatic way by central government in the 1980s to bypass resistant local authorities – if they refused the government's bidding it could contract services out to either a non-profit or for-profit organisation. Similarly, it could and did use its power to restrict the ability of local authorities to 'recruit' non-profit agencies to their own agendas and priorities, not least through the growing restrictions placed on local government finance (Taylor and Bassi, 1998).

As a result, grant giving and tax breaks in various forms continued under New Rightist governments, but increasingly contracts became a crucial source of funding support for the sector (Lewis, 1996). However, Harris et al (2001, p 3) note that while this resulted in an extension of the role of the non-profit sector throughout the 1990s, to include the delivery of mainstream services in place of statutory agencies, non-profit organisations remained 'at best "junior partners"' – they may have increasingly substituted for the state as service providers but still had little if any input into the policy process and the shape and direction of social policy either at the local or central level (Fyfe and Milligan, 2003). This is clearly illustrated in the period of local government reorganisation across the UK between 1995 and 1998, which saw the voluntary sector largely excluded during the consultation period and anxious about future funding arrangements (Craig and Manthorpe, 1999). Reduced to the status of service agent, non-profit agencies were effectively a pawn in the game of introducing market discipline into the provision of public services, with contracts as a vehicle for the pursuit of neoliberal agendas (Lewis, 2005).

Moreover, in this welfare pluralist framework where non-profit organisations were now 'providers', competing with one another for welfare contracts, they were under pressure from the state to demonstrate managerial efficiency and a 'business-like' ethos seen to be synonymous with 'value for money', in order to keep the funding coming in. As the least powerful actors in the contracting relationship, non-profit organisations were effectively being pushed into shifting their own organisational culture, modes of operation and priorities in the bid to secure government contracts. This particular development was the focus of a study by Wolch, who argued that in a contract culture context the state was increasingly influential in the sector's activities to the point that participating non-profit organisations were emerging as a 'shadow state', defined as 'a para-state apparatus comprised of voluntary organizations ... administered outside of traditional democratic politics ... charged with major collective service responsibilities previously shouldered by the public sector' and importantly, 'within the purview of state control' (Wolch, 1990, p 4). For Wolch the non-profit sector was being qualitatively transformed in terms of its shape and role, not least by the state's restructuring of the British welfare system through a combination of shifts in state welfare responsibilities, selective system dismantling, a decentralisation of service responsibility and the externalisation of service provision.

The new relationship between the state and non-profit sector was characterised by a growing penetration of the state into the activities of participating organisations that demanded more planning, increased accountability, an openness to external monitoring and evaluation and the implementation of a range of regulatory policies around health and safety and equal opportunities, to name but two. Indeed, Wolch argues that the accountability conditions attached to contracts effectively became the disciplining mechanism for the sector, and non-profit organisations that were unable to 'resist the imposition of incompatible state-mandated agendas' (Wolch, 1990, p 4) would, as a consequence, become more highly structured, formalised and professionalised. Indeed, as Wolch notes, contract requirements even incorporated guidelines regarding 'acceptable' political and campaigning activities.

While Wolch (1990, p 41) accepts that initially the sector maintained a degree of operational autonomy, he is keen to argue that insofar as non-profits carried out 'welfare state functions, providing essential human services, financial and in-kind benefits, and surveillance of clients ... enabled, regulated and subsidized by the state', they would be increasingly subject to both direct and indirect constraints on their autonomy. And in a bid to win contracts, they would become more reactive as opposed to proactive, conservative and cautious as opposed to innovative, exclusive as opposed to empowering and participatory, a process that would take them further from their community roots and perhaps even their original mission statements. Indeed, already at this stage, Wolch could identify a growing division between smaller more less formalised organisations that did not succumb to the lure of government finance dependency, preferring to continue their advocacy and campaigning work and maintain their commitment to client-centred, user-led strategies, and larger more formal organisations whose primary focus was increasingly on meeting government requirements in exchange for service contracts. Arguably, both in this period and later under the direction of New Labour, the latter are being subject to a process of 'isomorphism' – they are effectively being shaped in the image of the statutory organisations they are there to displace.

Crucially, Wolch also recognises the importance of the non-profits' response to the new pressures emerging out of this changing political and policy context – for him their decisions and activities matter. But he also claims that 'the ability of the voluntary sector to fulfill its progressive potential is currently limited by the internal structure and dynamics of many voluntary organisations themselves' (Wolch, 1990, p 221), citing the problems of 'excessive hierarchy and minority control' and the tendency for large, conventional non-profit organisations to become 'excessively oriented to internal operations' and more concerned with the 'self-serving objectives of internal advancement and power instead of collective group goals' (Wolch, 1990, p 221).

At this point it is important to emphasise that New Right restructuring of welfare did not impact evenly on the voluntary sector, which continued to be characterised by diversity. That said, change *was* significant for a section of the non-profit sector, and that change was to be built on following the election of New Labour in 1997.

## The voluntary sector and New Labour 'modernisation'

As was highlighted in Chapter Two (this volume), at the heart of the New Labour project is a stated commitment to the 'modernisation' of public services on the one hand (Powell, 1999; Clarke et al, 2000) and the 'modernisation' of the modes and structures of governance on the other (Newman, 2001; Glendinning et al, 2002). For example, the White Paper *Modernising government* (Cabinet Office, 1999) committed New Labour to developing a more 'joined-up', 'strategic' approach to policy making that would involve the government drawing a broader range of stakeholders and networks into the policy process through the activation of new partnership arrangements. In this way it sought to facilitate a process of 'national renewal'.

While the range of tools utilised by successive New Labour governments in the quest for 'modernisation' and 'national renewal' is broad, for the purposes of this discussion it is important to emphasise the construction of 'partnerships' in a range of forms, incorporating responsibilised stakeholders within a devolved administrative and political framework, in a bid to activate 'new' forms of governance seen as crucial to the legitimation of government. Partnerships with other welfare sectors are particularly important to New Labour as they are seen in broad terms to have the potential to deliver a regenerated, more active civil society through their commitment to community involvement, empowerment and responsibilisation.

Partnership strategies are not, of course, employed in isolation – a number of 'old' weapons have found their way into the New Labour armoury, not least marketisation, managerialisation and individual responsibilisation, all of which were central to the neoliberal project of the post-1979 Conservative governments. The employment of both 'new' and 'old' strategies can be seen as part of a New Labour emphasis on 'what works'. This idea speaks to a pragmatic concern with the effectiveness of policy and practice as well as efficiency and thus to a move beyond a simple replication of neoliberal strategies. Indeed, it is a discourse of the 'Third Way' that has been used most regularly to capture the ways in which Blair's Labour Party has worked to carve a path between the traditions of 'old' Labour, reflected in the welfare settlements of the postwar period, and those of the New Right, rooted in a commitment to market-based/led solutions.

In that vein, New Labour was outwardly critical of quasi-markets and the imposition of contract culture in a top-down manner, while accepting arguments that supported the introduction of competition and market-type mechanisms into the provision of public services. Subsequently, the post-1997 agenda was characterised by a focus on partnership as a tool for maintaining key aspects of the old competitive contract culture while at one and the same time reworking the role of the non-profit sector to take advantage of its assumed inherent positive qualities and hence deliver on community governance and active citizen involvement.

New Labour thus set about demonstrating its commitment to maintaining the non-profit sector at the centre of service provision, as illustrated by the growth of charitable agencies from 98,000 in 1991 to 153,000 in 2001, with expenditure increasing from £11.2 billion to £20 billion in that same period (NCVO, 2004), and the review of charity tax in the 1997 budget (Kendall, 2000). However, while continuing to require the sector to demonstrate 'efficiency and effectiveness and submit itself to close monitoring and regulation' (Harris et al, 2001, p 3), and utilising choice discourse to legitimise its commitment to welfare pluralism (Fyfe and Milligan, 2003), both reflections of a neoliberal agenda, New Labour also increasingly drew on neocommunitarian discourses, which highlighted the apparent decline in social participation and community involvement and, crucially, the role of the non-profit sector as a potential 'training ground' for active citizenship and civil responsibilisation. As Osborne and McLaughlin (2002) note, in this way New Labour was able to present the non-profit sector as capable of delivering a community governance strategy, meeting needs, tackling social problems and delivering those 'public' services that cannot easily be delivered by the depleted apparatus of central and local government (following decades of privatisation and contracting out, for example), and are not seen by the private sector as a viable profit-making option (Morrison, 2000), while also seemingly speaking to increased demands from a variety of stakeholders for increased choice, individual responsibilisation and a more active community. In order to operationalise this agenda New Labour looked to the concept of Compacts, and the activation of more meaningful stakeholder 'participation'.

## Compacts: a partnership or tool for mainstreaming voluntary providers?

Taking the Scottish experience as illustrative of developments across Britain, in 1995 the Convention of Scottish Local Authorities (CoSLA) and the Scottish Council for Voluntary Organisations (SCVO) came together to produce a guidance document entitled *Positive partnership* that laid out a set of principles for shaping the relationship between the non-profit sector and the new unitary authorities emerging from the process of local government reorganisation that was under way (Craig et al, 1999; Craig and Taylor, 2002; Scottish Executive, 2003). This framework for good practice played an important role in focusing attention on partnership working and was followed by the setting up of the Commission for the Future of the Voluntary Sector in Scotland that culminated in the publication of the Kemp Report (SCVO, 1997), and subsequently the development of a national Compact, similar to that in England emerging in the wake of the 1996 Deakin Report.

Notwithstanding the differences between the Scottish and English versions – a reflection of devolution and different local forms of governance – these national Compacts provided a similar framework of principles to guide and structure the relationship between the non-profit sector and the state (Craig et al, 2002; Osborne and McLaughlin, 2002). They are non-binding agreements entered into by the signatories, partners or their representatives that glean their legitimacy from the fact that they have been developed through consultation with the stakeholders (Morrison, 2000). They differ from previous initiatives in that they codify a set of responsibilities for *both* sides and in doing so draw on the idea of facilitating less top-down, more organic, partnership-type relationships, thus connecting to discourses of active citizenship, community building and community governance and the government's wider 'modernisation' agenda (Halfpenny and Reid, 2002).

In a devolved, Scottish context, Morrison (2000, p 125) claims that a 'special relationship' was encouraged by both sides, in part a result of the non-profit sector's perception of itself as oppositional to the Conservatives and in natural harmony with New Labour. New Labour has capitalised on those non-profits that share new Labour's values and arguably these organisations have been able to use the language of New

Labour to legitimise their own activities, particularly where they are called into question by service users and staff.

Launched in 1998 the Scottish and English Compacts drew on what Morrison (2000, p 115) called the 'language of recognition', expressed 'at a high level of generality' to construct a notion of shared principles and values. In essence they speak to the need for the government and its agencies to recognise and support non-profit sector independence and its activities, in part through the use of long-term funding to increase the sector's security, in return for high standards of governance and accountability from participating non-profits (particularly in relation to its use of government finance; see Halfpenny and Reid, 2002), and a commitment to recognise and promote good practice and inform and consult members, users and supporters. Lewis (2005) notes how Compacts worked to construct a shared public service ethos, which sought to bring together what may appear to be contradictory priorities and objectives, but also worked to enable government and state agencies to extend their tentacles further into the business of the non-profit sector *and* influence its self-governance. In formalising the principles of partnership in an apparently consensual way, Compacts secure for government a non-profit sector that is willing to regulate itself in very specific ways and utilise its autonomy in a 'responsible' manner, one that is defined principally by the state.

Indeed, Compacts, coupled with a continued reliance on service contracts (albeit now often referred to as 'service agreements'), work to promote cultural and organisational change at the level of individual non-profits, in part arising out of the need to ensure an organisational compatibility with the statutory organisations they are replacing (Deakin, 2001), but importantly also to ensure clear lines of accountability in relation to the finance they are accessing from the public purse.

However, before going on to explore what this cultural and organisational change might entail for those organisations increasingly involved in government-led partnerships, we should note that *national* Compacts, both in England and Scotland, are only part of the story. They offer a broad framework for partnership working involving statutory and non-profit actors but to make a real difference to everyday relationships and practices they need to be translated into *local* Compacts and implemented at the local authority level (Taylor and Bassi, 1998). In recognition of this, what emerged in the late 1990s was a number of working groups focusing on operationalising these national agreements at the local level. Nevertheless, it is this aspect of the Compact development process that has, to date, been slow and uneven. Codes of practice did begin to emerge in 2000, and in 2002 the Scottish Executive and the SCVO set up the Compact Review Group with responsibility for reviewing Compact implementation, yet, following slow progress at the local level, the Executive still felt the need to 'relaunch' Scottish Compacts in 2004 (Henderson, 2006).

The extent to which Compacts have been implemented, certainly across Scotland, is, then, still something of a moot point, but there is nevertheless clear evidence that New Labour is working hard to use partnerships, regulated by its own demands for increased accountability, to deliver its agenda, and has strongly encouraged would-be non-profit participants to become much more 'managerially minded' and accept a framework of government-defined 'good practice' that emphasises and reinforces 'economic rationality' (Morrison, 2000), even where this threatens to facilitate a shift away from their traditional 'voluntary' welfare ethos.

At this point we can return to the question of cultural and organisational change. Importantly the developments highlighted immediately above have not been accompanied by the introduction of 'new mechanisms for constraining and democratizing the new forms of public power' (Morrison, 2000, p 101). Rather, the focus has been on developing new methods of accountability and control including 'standard setting, monitoring and enforcement, inspection and oversight, adjudication of complaints and grievances, performance-related pay, indicators and targets, licensing and franchising, and benchmarking and audit' (Morrison, 2000, p 101) in the interests of maximising market efficiency. This seems to contradict the government's claims to be interested, at least equally, in the democratic values of participation and the potential for the non-profit sector to activate civil society. Indeed, rather ironically, in preparing sections of the non-profit sector for an increased role in service provision, New Labour has at one and the same time disempowered it in important ways. Essentially, as participating non-profits become more professionalised, better funded, more formally organised and more concerned with presenting their 'business-like' credentials in order to demonstrate themselves to be 'fit partners' (Ling, 2000) – not least by employing the 'language of risk and reward, choice, economic rationality, targeting, and output' (Morrison, 2000, p 109) – they become *less* able to deliver on the agenda of community governance. Crucial here is the marginalising of 'old' priorities, professional values and user-centredness. Taylor and Warburton (2003) lend support to this view arguing that government respondents in their research gave more legitimacy to the issue of 'top-down', fiscal and operational forms of accountability and managerialist strategies than 'bottom-up' accountability to the very people non-profit agencies claimed to represent. As such government policy relating to the non-profit sector is profoundly problematic.

In essence, an emergent, new breed of organisation is in evidence, one that is corporatist, hierarchical and bureaucratic, with a clear division of labour between managers and welfare professionals/volunteers, where passive citizenship is desirable and users are increasingly conceived of as 'consumers' of a service who are out 'there' (Fyfe and Milligan, 2003). These organisations then are being transformed with the effect of destabilising the assumed link between voluntarism and citizenship as relations associated with the state and statutory organisations come to displace old arrangements. Morrison (2000, pp 129-30) makes the point that:

> ... [s]tandards, guidelines and reporting mechanisms together will transform the ways in which at least some of the voluntary sector think about themselves and exercise choices within a newly constructed framework that reinforces economic forms of reasoning. What may be presented as increased autonomy, a chance to govern oneself, is in fact a reconfiguration of rationalities so that the self-interest of (parts of) the sector aligns with the interest of a state seeking to mobilize a reserve army of support effectively and on its own terms.

Indeed, under these circumstances the government's role is not to be one of the partners but rather to promote, set goals for and regulate partnerships, where necessary using funding as a lever and not just an incentive (Wyatt, 2002, p 175).

Looking at it from the perspective of non-profits, Lewis (2005) argues that the sector has not been given equal partnership status in relation to the setting and shaping of policy agendas. She suggests that even though some larger organisations have an elevated profile and an increased voice they are still operating within the 'templates' set and established by central government; while the government pays lip service to the sector's right to campaign, comment on and challenge government policy, in practice this is not tolerated (Craig et al, 1999; Taylor, 2001).

Therefore, while these kind of 'partnerships' are presented as a tool for getting stakeholders 'on board' and enlivening civil society, in reality what we are seeing is a growing culture of 'grant grabbing' as opposed to genuine partnership, which increases the potential for a separation of the organisation and its governing and managerial personnel from workers and service users who cannot square the new ways of working with the organisation's original mission and its claims to be value-driven. And, rather ironically, those non-profits that are *not* incorporated into the government's framework and are thus arguably more likely to be innovative and inclusive, are left out of the policy-making loop altogether.

So far this chapter has explored the impact of government agendas on the voluntary sector and highlighted some of the pressures participating non-profits are under and the consequences these have had for their modes of operation and cultural orientation. However, we need to take care not to construct the non-profit sector as a passive victim of government policy. While we have seen a growth in the state's control over the voluntary sector, the extent to which that is embraced or challenged, imposed or negotiated, reinterpreted and responded to, is crucial. As Deakin (2001, p 29) noted, the sector 'is not simply a spectator of change'. So before we turn our attention to the impact welfare 'modernisation' has had on welfare workers within the non-profit sector we must first acknowledge the possibilities and choices left open to these organisations.

## Non-profit organisations as active agents

Non-profit organisations have boards or voluntary governing bodies that are accountable for the organisation's activities, the implementation and integrity of its mission and its legitimacy in the eyes of internal and external stakeholder. As such their role is crucial in terms of steering and guiding the organisation and its managerial hierarchy and, crucially, negotiating over particular government agendas. Moreover, boards, along with the management hierarchy, also have a key role in delivering an accountability agenda to workers and service users, not just government bodies and financiers. This requires them to demonstrate a willingness and commitment to actively protect their organisational culture and welfare philosophy and hence develop a process of self-regulation to balance competing demands and thus maintain their organisational integrity. Miller (2002, p 555) noted that 'self-regulatory accountability' required an organisation 'to be constantly developing open relationships even when experiencing great discomfort, reinvesting in the process during times when one is being held to account and subjected to much criticism. A commitment to accountability must be at the heart of the organization, to be found in all aspects of its work, and central to its processes of governance'. He goes on to outline the main characteristics of self-regulatory organisations noting that the existence of policy documents is not sufficient to ensure this – they must be implemented. Moreover, the organisation must actively defend its mission statements and philosophy of care and foster a real partnership between its government bodies, senior management and workers – without an appreciation of their interdependence there can be no positive outcome.

However, should they choose to channel resources more into management, public relations (PR) and profile elevation, and the meeting of accountability and monitoring agendas set by government as opposed to other stakeholders – a trend already noted in some sections of the sector and which speaks to a capacity-building and organisational growth agenda (Harris, 2001a, 2001b) – increased tensions may well be created between the organisation, its management and board on the one hand, and its workers, volunteers and service users on the other, particularly where a gap is perceived to have opened up between the organisation's espoused values and those it applies in practice (Miller, 2002).

Therefore, while there is clearly the *potential* for non-profit organisations to deliver on community empowerment and active citizenship agendas, this cannot be realised simply by increasing the role of voluntary organisations in service provision (Fyfe and Milligan, 2003). These organisations must be empowered to maintain their own ethos and principles at one and the same time and not simply be subsumed into the agendas of government and state agencies. Clearly, the government is the source of much pressure, but voluntary sector organisations cannot hide behind 'victim status' – they are active participants and have a responsibility to staff and users to remain accountable to *all* of their stakeholders. And, as Scott and Russell (2001, p 61) note, if the government will not or cannot play its part 'it will be important that voluntary organisations reevaluate whether the contract culture is compatible with social values, public service, flexibility and reciprocity; and whether it is possible to reconcile the managerialist approaches associated with contracting with broad-based governance and community participation'. An unwillingness to do this makes them culpable in their own transformation, a transformation that is likely to result in a whole host of consequences including increased 'mission drift' (Halfpenny and Reid, 2002), the skewing of activity to meet government agencies' targets, a shift in the relationship between clients, professional workers and volunteers and in management and organisation structures as a result, in part, of commercialisation, and a downgrading of user involvement and consultation (Locke et al, 2001).

Under these circumstances, 'Short-term organisational growth may be achieved at the expense of long-term survival as an independent third sector organization' (Harris, 2001b, p 219).

Here we also see the possibility not only for the gap to grow between what Fyfe and Milligan (2003) call 'grassroots' and 'corporatist' organisations and Craig and Taylor (2002) term 'voluntary' and 'community' agencies, but also for one to open up between *participating* non-profits that are *active* in the partnership process – that is, willing to challenge and renegotiate government and state agency demands and to highlight the contradictory nature of a policy that seeks to transform non-profit organisations at the expense of those features that could potentially deliver for them in terms of a community governance agenda – and those that are not.

Having explored the policy context and analysed its impact on the non-profit sector, we can now turn our attention to the impact these developments are having on workers employed in the sector.

## Involuntary working? Worker perceptions

This section of the chapter builds on the work of Fyfe and Milligan (2003) that focused on criminal justice provision in Scotland and found evidence of non-profit transformation within a 'new' policy context. It presents data generated from the early stages of a research project that sought to explore the perceptions and experiences of workers employed in the non-profit criminal justice sector in Scotland by examining the perceptions of workers at the 'frontline' of service provision and, crucially, their *experiences* of organisational transformation in a 'partnership' context. To date very little research has focused on this aspect of voluntary organisation activity and transformation. And, while research into the impact of 'mainstreaming' third sector organisations on employment relations and human resources policies is beginning to emerge (see Cunningham, 1999; Hay et al, 2001; Palmer, 2003), there is still a need for more work in relation to the impact of change on managers and workers (Palmer, 2003). The research project drawn on here seeks to begin to address that need.

The project utilised a case study method that Scott et al (2000, p 2) argued would help to uncover dynamic and contradictory processes at work in non-profit agencies, taking the researcher beyond the simply descriptive by being 'explicitly concerned with explanatory issues and themes from the outset'. This 'more interpretive, issue-based approach ... driven by analytical themes' (Scott et al, 2000, p 2) focuses on an organisation, group or individual, bounded in terms of time and place, and while the data generated depends in part on who is involved in the study and their position within the organisation – demonstrating that data collection is not a 'purely technical affair' insofar as 'it is embedded in social relationships' (Scott et al, 2000, p 4) – the method was utilised here with the intention of capturing at least some of the relevant themes and issues and hence providing 'generalisable illustrations' (Scott et al, 2000, p 6).

Space precludes any detailed discussion of the preliminary findings of the research or presentation of primary qualitative data. However, it is possible to illustrate some of the main themes and issues raised in the focus groups by five employees of a non-profit partner organisation in a large criminal justice project in the west of Scotland.

## From innovation and service quality to standardisation and quantitative targets

Each of the respondents observed a profound shift in the priorities of senior managers within the project. They noted how in the early period of the project's life it was acknowledged by senior managers that there was no tried and tested formula for working with their very specific client group – serious and persistent young offenders who were having a high impact on their communities – and that there was an opportunity to set the agenda, develop new approaches as well as a commitment to innovative practice and to draw on the experience and professional judgement of a carefully selected team of largely professionally trained social workers. One respondent noted:

> 'In the beginning the senior management team were all saying "you're the people to do this job, you've got the experience, and you've got the ideas" and it was all very much "this can be something new, not just lifting things off the shelf and running them out to see if they work and going through the motions" ... it was very much like a new agenda, with us setting the agenda – being innovative and using our skills and experience to reach excluded difficult to reach offenders.' (Respondent 3)

However, over time the project's agenda became much more funder-driven, not only in terms of prioritising the meeting of *quantitative* targets but also through the application of particular ways of working – a trend that reflected what Newman and Mooney (2004) termed the elevation of a 'business ethos' and a prioritising of economic rationality over professional judgement as a basis for decision making sparked by the managerialisation of welfare services. In essence the project came under pressure to replicate the work of statutory agencies and workers were increasingly required to defend and justify the way they worked with and related to young people. In effect respondents reported that the project became less client and more target focused, which resulted in an obsession with statistics and a bureaucratisation of the project. The increase in monitoring, evaluation and hence paperwork experienced by the respondents reflected the shift towards an audit culture (Clarke et al, 2000). Moreover, as Kendall and Knapp (1996) noted, this often led to a focus on particular measurable outcomes and targets at the expense of *quality* outcome measures. Reflecting this, the respondents claimed that the work involved in the relationship building process increasingly came under scrutiny and important achievements were marginalised with a negative impact on the project and the perception of funders. Respondent 5 illustrated the point:

> 'I can understand that as purchasers you want to know how many people the service is working with and what quality the service is but it wasn't done in a way that would have been helpful ... it was all numbers based, there wasn't any detailed information asked for about what I see as positive changes amongst people ... whether they had more social skills or confidence, how much their offending had reduced, whether they had stopped offending altogether, whether they been prevented from being accommodated or imprisoned ... there was none of that unpicking of the work you had done and using that kind of evidence to support and acknowledge the achievements of staff working with an extremely difficult client group.'

Newman and Mooney (2004) claimed that professional care work was underpinned by a belief that the solving of social problems required the application of expert knowledge and judgement and the elevation of good client–professional relationships. Moreover, they suggested that such welfare work also involved 'emotional labour', a giving of real emotional responses and a management of the emotions of self and others. However, these are both areas of work that are difficult to quantify, and hence they can often be neglected and under-appreciated by those not working at the coalface who are driven by different agendas. So, in place of what can be a time-consuming relationship-building process, workers are increasingly under pressure to accept standardised tools, to compartmentalise work and standardise the time spent with young people, effectively moving away from the basic philosophy of working with individuals in a flexible, user-focused way that reflects their particular needs.

This 'practice standardisation' also increasingly involved the codification of professional knowledge into forms that could be utilised by lower-grade, non-professionally trained or untrained workers – a trend also noted by Newman and Mooney (2004). Several of the respondents noted this trend in relation to their own project. For example, talking about a training day he had recently been on, respondent 4 noted:

> 'The programme that was presented, we had to follow it through exactly how it was set out … you had the booklet with it all laid out in a certain order and you had to ask the questions or whatever using the pack, word for word … you didn't have any leeway to put your own slant on it, personalise it to the young person you knew and had been working with.'

Of course, the shift towards a greater codification of expert knowledge that creates inroads for non-professionally trained sections of the workforce also serves the purpose of being potentially more cost-effective, certainly in the long run. But there is perhaps something else at work here: clearly, if professional workers resist the imposition of what they deem to be bad practice and a threat to their self-regulation and professional judgement, vocalise their concerns about service quality, defend 'old' ways of working including the centrality of client–professional relationships and the principles of user-centred and individual needs-led service provision, often embodied in the organisation's own original mission statement, senior managers who are 'on board' with the *new* agendas may themselves come under pressure. Consequently, they may see benefit in marginalising those professional workers who are perceived to be a threat to the new arrangements and increasingly relying on less qualified, less highly skilled and less experienced personnel who are less likely to be attached to 'old' ways of working, making them a potentially more malleable workforce. In this scenario, the codification of expert knowledge is invaluable to the facilitation of cultural and practice change at the project level.

This top-down imposition of new priorities and working practices on the project workers also represented a challenge to the organisation's mission statement of the project for all of the respondents, giving rise to conflict, struggle and resistance. Of course, for some professionals there is scope to maintain their position within the organisation, even improve on it in salary and status terms, but only if they are willing to compromise their professional values and be subsumed into the new 'partnership ethos' in ways that reflect the agendas of senior managers. However, that is arguably a big compromise to make, not least when it requires an acceptance of the repositioning of the client group.

## From 'client-centred' to 'them and us'

As already noted, developments within the project impacted on the relationship between workers and service users, but they also impacted on the ways in which the latter were constructed. This is most aptly illustrated by the following contribution:

> 'It got to, in the end, where we went from us asking young people to come in, sit down, talk to staff, make themselves a cup of tea, to [the service manager] wanting a locked door with a wee reception hatch, you know ... we had to talk to clients through a wee hole in the wall ... it's like the social or the post office or something ... the project changed from being welcoming to young people to wanting to keep it like you know, you're a client and I'm the worker, you stand on that side and I'll sit here.' (Respondent 1)

As Scott et al (2000) argued, this kind of development reflected the ways in which new hierarchies, areas of demarcation and a more business-focused culture worked to disrupt service delivery, sometimes in the most fundamental of ways. This process could have real consequences for the supposed target group as noted by respondent 3:

> 'We weren't working with big numbers but with people who were causing a lot of damage – you know, they were stealing a lot of cars and they were getting involved in a lot of petty crime or violent crime, so initially it was really about focusing on the difficult ones, building relationships with them. But then it shifted and it just became, well the criteria that we used pretty much went out of the window ... you were under pressure to offer a service to everyone who was punted your way at the expense of the target group. Then it really was just about numbers.'

Respondent 2 added:

> 'Over a period of time the focus became more on hard
> outcomes, in terms of numbers not individuals. But how
> can you measure the distance a person has travelled in terms
> of what they've done with yourselves at the project ... so
> you know we lost sight of what the project was actually
> set up to do.'

## The division between senior management and frontline employees

Each of the respondents also commented on the growing gap between project workers and the practice team manager on the one hand, and the senior management team, from the service manager upwards, on the other. Respondent 2, for example, commented on the way senior managers marginalised individuals seen to be 'off message', especially where they conveyed unwelcome news about the impact of developments on workers and their relationships with their clients:

> 'As the practice team manager if there are issues coming up
> from the team I have got a responsibility to feed that back to
> the organisational hierarchy. And I think on most occasions
> they felt I was being like some sort of fifth columnist – they
> weren't happy with what I was actually telling them ... that
> team members were genuinely concerned about the way
> the project was going and the focus of it.' (Respondent 2)

Moreover, the respondents highlighted the ways in which recent developments had impacted on the priorities and principles of the organisation to such an extent that workers could barely recognise the organisation they had originally come to work for. For example, respondent 2 noted that:

> 'In recent applications [the organisation] was building in
> money for an assistant director's post which has nothing
> directly to do with the project. That way there is always
> money feeding into keeping the managerial core of
> the organisation alive and they will take on a poorly
> funded project, make a low bid, knowing they will get a
> management fee for that project for its two years existence.

> Effectively the project may never achieve any of its aims, but the management fee keeps [the organisation] in the game. Basically, they are all plundering each other's specialisms in order to bring money in – and the service users are not even in the picture.'

Another respondent noted how this involved a shift away from the organisation's stated philosophy of care, U-turns about policies that were suddenly 'politically in vogue' and ultimately 'the prostituting of themselves to whoever will fund them and keep the management team in business for another year' (respondent 1).

Here we see how new priorities gave rise to mission drift that in turn created further tensions between frontline staff, committed to working with hard-to-reach individuals, and senior management, keen to progress the organisation financially, with all the associated benefits that this brings for them.

## Resisting mission shift and the elevation of quantity over quality

Despite the pressure on workers to accept top-down direction, even where it put service quality and the organisation's original mission at risk, the respondents in this case study sought to challenge changing working practices and the 'new' priorities of the non-profit organisation and its senior managers through general discussion with the senior management team, through team meetings and in supervision with the practice team manager, and through memos and reports sent from the coalface upwards. The respondents also highlighted how they had sought meetings with a range of individual managers to discuss concerns raised in writing but had not succeeded in getting either any or an adequate response, or in some cases, even minutes of the meetings that did take place:

> 'The workers and team leader within the project tried hard to address the issues raised, without any guidance from management ... I was never clear about what senior managers were doing about the low level of referrals, how they were marketing the project and what their expectations were and yet we were not allowed to engage with the funders or courts directly ourselves as a team of professional, experienced workers – despite this being normal practice elsewhere. So we would send information up, in fact I wrote

a number of memos with my colleagues about what we'd been doing, how we had been trying to address things and what other initiatives might be constructive but I was never clear that they actually got to where they were going and generally we didn't get responses to our communications. In fact I met with one senior manager and I asked him about a particular set of communications relating to the work we'd been doing and he made out that he hadn't got any of them.' (Respondent 5)

Nevertheless they continued their efforts to enter into dialogue, defend the principle of a user-centred philosophy of care and encourage a degree of self-reflection by the organisational hierarchy, despite there being no evidence that they were being listened or responded to. For the respondents, there seemed to be a lack of self-regulatory accountability within the organisation – policies and procedures were in place but were simply not followed:

'I think senior management found it very hard to listen to constructive criticism and to responses that they didn't like – they found it difficult to respond to and just fobbed people off. I mean an example would be about the representation of ethnic minorities and the management's view that we needed to target greater numbers and that the way to do that was to take more referrals of people with particular names – when people said let's look at the statistics in the context of the numbers going through court and so on, we weren't allowed to present evidence and they wouldn't enter into any kind of discussion, even when people were raising the fact that their claims and methodologies were racist and went against organisational and professional good practice.' (Respondent 3)

Miller (2002, p 555) argued that self-regulatory accountability required an organisation 'to be constantly developing open relationships even when experiencing great discomfort, reinvesting in the process during times when one is being held to account and subjected to much criticism'. However, in contrast to this approach, the case study organisation's response to workers expressing their concerns and calling for more accountability was to enable a culture of bullying and victimisation to develop whereby 'troublesome' individuals could be marginalised. Miller (2004, p 130) talked about how New Labour displayed a 'low level of trust in those professionals on whom its policies depend', but this also seems to be a relevant observation regarding the attitude of the organisation case-studied here towards its own, handpicked staff.

Indeed, all of the respondents commented on the types of methods used to enforce unwelcome change including the adoption of a 'memo culture', the bypassing of normal practices and procedures and group 'confrontations' that involved the devaluing of individual workers, unsubstantiated accusations and assertions and a closing off of any discussion, debate and negotiation. For example, respondent 3 noted that:

> 'When the new service manager was appointed, unbeknown to any of the project team, the practice manager was out of the loop and then after that information wasn't coming to us directly, through him, because they didn't trust him, but rather through one of the partner organisation's managers or in a memo from the new service manager – never face-to-face or in a team meeting.'

This trend is captured by Scott et al (2000, p 35) who wrote, 'vertical subdivisions between service areas and between core functions, together with an increasing number of horizontal layers in the management hierarchy, have given rise to a degree of fragmentation of the organization', which can have the effect of undermining 'mutual support, information flows, and responsiveness to clients'.

## A culture of bullying and victimisation?

All of the respondents in this early part of the study highlighted a growing culture of bullying, victimisation and scapegoating that affected all of the project's employees to some extent, although the workers who were employed by one of the partner organisations seemed to be specifically targeted.

In some cases statistics were reworked and reinterpreted in order to blame workers for the project's poor performance in terms of its numerical targets. In others individuals were subjected to 'garden leave' – a status not referred to in the organisation's own policy and procedure documents but which consisted of two members of staff being escorted from the premises, without warning or explanation, for an unspecified period of time until they were recalled to work at a later date, again without explanation.

The respondents also reported how what was termed an 'investigation' into the project was used as a smokescreen for the further bullying and harassment of individual workers – a divide and rule strategy in relation to the team. As respondent 5 noted:

> 'It became a very difficult and a very unhealthy place to work ... and I felt that when things weren't maybe going the way that senior management wanted them to go that they targeted certain individuals within the project and took up a bullying, intimidating strategy whereby they would come down and tell us we were doing a bad job constantly but not tell you what you needed to do to fix it. They also never once acknowledged the things that we were doing very well. It was a constant – and I mean this went on for months – hammering of project staff about the things that they felt were problematic and accepting no responsibility themselves.'

Interestingly, this same respondent went on to highlight that despite accusing the staff team of bad practice senior management never once accepted the logic that as a consequence they should suspend the service in the interests of service users.

In the wake of these developments, four members of staff left the project, their positions having been made untenable. One member of staff went off on long-term sick leave suffering severe stress, having been given the work of absent colleagues without negotiation, explanation or support, and was later made redundant. Three members of the staff team were put through various disciplinary procedures (one after the individual concerned had left the project some months before), two of which ultimately either came to nothing or resulted in a formal warning later being withdrawn on the grounds that it was illegitimate. One member of staff was under pressure to accept redeployment in another project and eventually, after a long period of harassment, took out a grievance against the service manager. Four of his five specific complaints were 'upheld' but he was never given any information about the outcome of the process and continued to be managed and supervised by the manager in question, despite the worker's formal protestations.

The respondents also highlighted how the 'investigation' involved the interviewing of all staff by senior managers, both from their own and the partner organisation, who formally taped the sessions. Two respondents reported being under pressure to attend for interview without union representation. All of the respondents felt intimidated, were asked leading questions and in some cases were asked to speculate on events that they had not been party to in any way. Despite being told that they would receive copies of their interview tapes, none of the interviewees ever received one and when this was challenged the organisation claimed that the tape recorder had broken. However, they were all eventually given copies of what were called 'minutes' of these interviews, although in all cases they were skeletal and bore little or no resemblance to the actual interview – something that was implicitly accepted by senior managers, one of whom admitted that the responses of different interviewees had been 'mixed up'.

Interestingly, respondents gave examples of where workers employed by the *partner* organisation actually defended their fellow workers in the face of this bullying and misrepresentation – despite neither they nor their own partner organisation being under 'investigation'. However, they were subsequently reprimanded by their own managers for their actions.

On leaving the project three members of staff wrote formal letters to the chief executive of the non-profit organisation, with copies going to various other stakeholders including the members of the board of governors. However, the detailed issues that were outlined and the questions posed – including concerns about racist practice and data protection issues covered by the law – were never addressed in any of the three cases. Respondent 5 commented:

> 'Before I left there was a focus on getting things down on paper. Because people were being singled out and bullied you wrote things as memos and formally asked for meetings as well as making comments in minuted meetings.... I wanted it documented, what we had tried to do, how we had engaged in the process and our views on why things had changed as well as the context in which we were trying to work ... but it was all ignored just as our "exit" letters to the organisation's hierarchy were ultimately ignored.'

Another initiated correspondence with senior managers and one of the organisation's regional directors while still in post and then later, having left the organisation and initiated a tribunal process, received correspondence from representatives of the organisation and was offered a sum of money. This was turned down in favour of pursuing the case; however, the tribunal was ultimately abandoned due to a lack of trade union support – it accepted that there had been 'wrong-doing' and that there was a case to answer but felt that it was not worth the union's while to pursue it on the grounds that the compensation offered was likely to be minimal given that the individual had found alternative employment. There was no recognition by the union of the member's desire to pursue his case from a position of principle, in order to glean formal recognition of that 'wrong-doing' and challenge particular practices within the organisation.

One respondent captured the mood:

> 'I think that they were all for driving us out ... and I think that they didn't realise that we wouldn't just go, and wouldn't just bow our heads and walk out of the door as soon as they threw some false accusations at us. The fact that we stayed there and argued every single point that they raised and we tried to go through procedures that were their procedures, that they weren't following ... they couldn't keep up with that.' (Respondent 3)

Another noted how one of the now senior managers that had highlighted the quality of the project staff team at the beginning of its life was later to regret the decision to pick such an experienced and professional, user-centred team:

> 'That in the end came back to bite him – when he started throwing his weight about, people weren't lacking in confidence and ... had the dedication and the knowledge to argue back and he didn't like it....' (Respondent 1)

Here we see a tension between the need to employ quality 'units' of human capital to facilitate the delivery of a quality, value-driven, user-centred service on the one hand, and the need to secure a malleable workforce that would turn a blind eye to mission shift, for example, on the other. Again, while Miller (2004) highlighted quite rightly the tendency for New Labour to want only 'managed participation', and the involvement of only controllable, predictable service users, it could also be argued that some participating non-profits have a similar wish list when it comes to their employees – something that may in part be driven by the need to 'self-censor' in the face of funders' demands.

## Conclusions

The material in the last section of this chapter illustrates many of the trends and tendencies, highlighted in the literature, that have emerged as a consequence of the new relationship between a section of the non-profit sector, the government and state agencies, from an employee perspective. It suggests that the reactions of at least some individual non-profits has resulted in a 'top-down' challenge to professional power, autonomy and judgement that is discursive, material and territorial (Newman and Mooney, 2004). Moreover, it supports the claims by many commentating on the place of the non-profit sector in New Labour's 'modernisation' and 'national renewal' strategy that focus on the gap between the rhetoric and reality of partnership, community governance and active citizen participation. Importantly, this chapter has sought to highlight the ways in which workers as active participants in these agendas are at risk where they engage in different forms of resistance and do not acquiesce to the more powerful agendas of both government and non-profit organisations, themselves concerned to build a particular type of 'capacity' and retain their position in the 'new' welfare hierarchy.

### Further sources

Milligan, C. and Conradson, D. (2006) *Landscapes of voluntarism*, Bristol: The Policy Press.

Charity Commission (2007) *Stand and deliver: The future of charities delivering public services*, Liverpool: Charity Commission.

The Scottish and National Council for Voluntary Organisations both have useful websites: www.scvo.org.uk and www.ncvo-vol.org.uk

The Joseph Rowntree Foundation website is also a good source of research, reports and policy analysis: www.jrf.org.uk

### References

Cabinet Office (1999) *Modernising government*, Cm 4310, London: The Stationery Office.

Clarke, J., Gewirtz, S., Hughes, G. and Humphrey, J. (2000) 'Guarding the public interest? Auditing public services', in J. Clarke, S. Gewirtz and E. McLaughlin (eds) *New managerialism, new welfare?*, London: Sage Publications, pp 250-66.

Craig, G. and Manthorpe, J. (1999) 'Unequal partners? Local government reorganization and the voluntary sector', *Social Policy and Administration*, vol 3, no 1, pp 55-72.

Craig, G. and Taylor, M. (2002) 'Dangerous liaisons: local government and the voluntary and community sectors', in C. Glendinning, M. Powell and K. Rummery (eds) *Partnerships, New Labour and the governance of welfare*, Bristol: The Policy Press, pp 131-48.

Craig, G., Taylor, M., Szanto, C. and Wilkinson, M. (1999) *Developing local Compacts: Relationships between local public sector bodies and the voluntary and community sectors*, Bristol: The Policy Press.

Craig, G., Taylor, M., Wilkinson, M. and Bloor, K. with Monro, S. and Syed, A. (2002) *Contract or trust? The role of Compacts in local governance*, Bristol: The Policy Press.

Cunningham, I. (1999) 'Human resource management in the voluntary sector: challenges and opportunities', *Public Money and Management*, vol 19, pp 19-25.

Deakin, N. (2001) 'Public policy, social policy and voluntary organisations', in M. Harris and C. Rochester (eds) *Voluntary organizations and social policy in Britain: Perspectives on change and choice*, Basingstoke: Palgrave, pp 21-36.

Fyfe, N. and Milligan, C. (2003) 'Space, citizenship and voluntarism: critical reflections on the voluntary welfare sector in Glasgow', *Environment and Planning*, vol 35, pp 269-86.

Glendinning, C., Powell, M. and Rummery, K. (eds) (2002) *Partnerships, New Labour and the governance of welfare*, Bristol: The Policy Press.

Halfpenny, P. and Reid, M. (2002) 'Research on the voluntary sector: an overview', *Policy & Politics*, vol 30, no 4, pp 533-50.

Harris, M. (2001a) 'Boards: just subsidiaries of the state?', in M. Harris and C. Rochester (eds) *Voluntary organizations and social policy in Britain: Perspectives on change and choice*, Basingstoke: Palgrave, pp 171-84.

Harris, M. (2001b) 'Voluntary organisations in a changing social policy environment', in M. Harris and C. Rochester (eds) *Voluntary organizations and social policy in Britain: Perspectives on change and choice*, Basingstoke: Palgrave, pp 213-28.

Harris, M., Rochester, C. and Halfpenny, P. (2001) 'Voluntary organisations and social policy: twenty years of change', in M. Harris and C. Rochester (eds) *Voluntary organizations and social policy in Britain: Perspectives on change and choice*, Basingstoke: Palgrave, pp 1-20.

Hay, G., Beattie, R., Livingstone, R. and Munro, P. (2001) 'Change, HRM and the voluntary sector', *Employee Relations*, vol 23, no 3, pp 240-55.

Henderson, B. (2006) *Review of local Compacts in Scotland*, Research Findings No 25/2006 (www.scotland.gov.uk/socialresearch).

Kendall, J. (2000) 'The mainstreaming of the third sector into public policy in England in the late 1990: whys and wherefores', *Policy & Politics*, vol 28, no 4, pp 541-62.

Kendall, J. and Knapp, M. (1996) *The voluntary sector in the UK*, Manchester: Manchester University Press.

Leat, D. (1996) 'Are voluntary organizations accountable?', in D. Billis and M. Harris (eds) *Voluntary agencies: Challenges of organization and management*, Basingstoke: Macmillan, pp 61-79.

Lewis, J. (1995) *Voluntary sector, the state and social work in Britain*, London: Elgar.

Lewis, J. (1996) 'What does contracting do to voluntary agencies?', in D. Billis and M. Harris (eds) *Voluntary agencies: Challenges of organization and management*, Basingstoke: Macmillan, pp 98-112.

Lewis, J. (1999) 'Reviewing the relationship between the voluntary sector and the state in Britain in the 1990s', *Voluntas*, vol 10, no 3, pp 255-70.

Lewis, J. (2005) 'New Labour's approach to the voluntary sector: independence and the meaning of partnership', *Social Policy and Society*, vol 4, no 2, pp 121-31.

Ling, T. (2000) 'Unpacking partnership: the case of health care', in J. Clarke, S. Gewirtz and E. McLaughlin (eds) *New managerialism, new welfare?*, London: Sage Publications, pp 82-101.

Locke, M., Robson, P. and Howlett, S. (2001) 'Users: at the centre or the sidelines?', in M. Harris and C. Rochester (eds) *Voluntary organizations and social policy in Britain: Perspectives on change and choice*, Basingstoke: Palgrave, pp 199-212.

Miller, C. (2002) 'Towards a self-regulatory form of accountability in the voluntary sector', *Policy & Politics*, vol 30, no 4, pp 551-66.

Miller, C. (2004) *Producing welfare: A modern agenda*, Basingstoke: Palgrave.

Morrison, J. (2000) 'The government-voluntary sector Compacts: governance, governmentality and civil society', *Journal of Law and Society*, vol 27, no 1, pp 98-132.

NCVO (National Council for Voluntary Organisations) (2004) *The size and scope of the UK voluntary sector: NCVO's UK voluntary sector almanac 2004*, London: NCVO (www.ncvo-vol.org.uk/press/briefings. asp?id=826).

Newman, J. (2001) *Modernising governance: New Labour, policy and society*, London: Sage Publications.

Newman, J. and Mooney, G. (2004) 'Managing personal lives: Doing welfare work', in G. Mooney (ed) *Work: Personal lives and social welfare*, Bristol: The Policy Press, pp 39-72.

Osborne, S.P. and McLaughlin, K. (2002) 'Trends and issues in the implementation of local "voluntary sector compacts" in England', *Public Money and Management*, January–March, pp 55-63.

Palmer, G. (2003) 'Employee relations in the voluntary sector', Paper presented to the British Universities Industrial Relations Association Annual Conference, Leeds University Business School, 3-5 July.

Powell, J. (1999) 'Contract management and community care: a negotiated process', *British Journal of Social Work*, vol 29, pp 861-75.

SCVO (Scottish Council for Voluntary Organisations) (1997) *The Report of the Commission on the Future of the Voluntary Sector in Scotland* (Kemp Report), Edinburgh: SCVO.

Scott, D.W. and Russell, L. (2001) 'Contracting: the experiences of service delivery agencies', in M. Harris and C. Rochester (eds) *Voluntary organizations and social policy in Britain: Perspectives on change and choice*, Basingstoke: Palgrave, pp 49-63.

Scott, D.W., Alcock, P., Russell, L. and Macmillan, R. (2000) *Moving pictures: Realities of voluntary action*, Bristol: The Policy Press.

Scottish Executive (2003) Scottish Compact baseline review (www.scottishexecutive.gov.uk/Publications/2003/08/17485/22801).

Taylor, M. (2001) 'Partnership: insiders and outsiders', in M. Harris and C. Rochester (eds) *Voluntary organizations and social policy in Britain: Perspectives on change and choice*, Basingstoke: Palgrave, pp 94-107.

Taylor, M. and Bassi, A. (1998) 'Unpacking the state: the implications for the third sector of changing relationships between national and local government', *Voluntas*, vol 9, no 2, pp 113-36.

Taylor, M. and Warburton, D. (2003) 'Legitimacy and the role of UK third sector organisations in the policy process', *Voluntas*, vol 14, no 3, pp 321-38.

Wolch, J.R. (1990) *The shadow state: Government and voluntary sector in transition*, New York, NY: The Foundation Centre.

Wyatt, M. (2002) 'Partnership in health and social care: the implications of government guidance in the 1990s in England with particular reference to voluntary organisations', *Policy & Politics*, vol 30, no 2, pp 167-82.

# TWELVE

# Beyond New Labour: work and resistance in the 'new' welfare state

*Alex Law and Gerry Mooney*

Modernising leftists can, or should, have a clear idea of the kind of society they are seeking to create. It is one whose economy is competitive in the global marketplace, but which remains cohesive, inclusive and egalitarian. Bringing into being such a society means running with the tide of the great social changes of our era – not just the emergence of the knowledge economy, but the impact of globalisation and of rising individualism. (Giddens, 2003, p 38)

Many would argue that the hegemony of neoliberalism is demonstrated precisely by the fact that its policies survived the electoral defeat of the parties that inaugurated it. (Callinicos, 2001, p 7)

Other chapters in this volume have examined specific dimensions of restructured welfare work. Here we return to reflect on larger questions around the managerialist regimes of 'strenuous welfarism'. Our conception of strenuous welfarism attempts to capture the new ascetic work regime that often operates through 'control at a distance' to intensify individual effort and raise 'productivity' overall (see Chapter Two). In this chapter, we reconsider the intellectual underpinnings and genesis of strenuous welfarism in Third Way thinking and New Labour 'modernisation' (see Chapters One and Two). We then use this opportunity to reflect on the internal modulation of strenuous welfarism as it emerged in the workplace case studies in this book. In response to more flexibly intensive work regimes, workers 'exit', leaving their employer or even the sector altogether; or they stay 'loyal' to the organisation and the profession through the internalisation of the service ethos and managerial norms; or, finally, they engage in overt and covert forms of resistance, in the process confronting the tensions symptomatic of social neoliberalism. We then speculate about new tendencies and dynamics emerging from worker discontent with strenuous welfarism. A space is opening up for the sectional struggles of workers to reach out to other constituencies such as user groups, grassroots campaigns, new social movements and other political allies that wish to support and expand public services. These new social solidarities are also indicators of the way that class is being re-composed, not as a passive process but through dynamic altercations with New Labour's project for strenuous welfarism and the decomposition of collectivities.

## Social neoliberalism: a hatful of hollow

At one time recognisable as a social theorist of considerable repute, today Anthony Giddens has little difficulty in eliding together the quite distinct, although interrelated phenomena of *economy* and *society*. In the opening quotation to the chapter above he oscillates between global determinism and individual agency. In one breath 'modernising leftists' are told that they are 'seeking to create' a society premised on a world competitive economy. In the next breath, modernisers are not 'seeking to create' anything at all but are instead 'running with the tide of ... great social changes'. These 'social changes' are pre-given in the form of the 'knowledge economy', globalisation and individualism. Third Way welfare state 'modernisation' attempts to reconcile what was long considered by 'leftist' social democracy as irreconcilable antipodes: social justice and the market, collectivism and individualism. Giddens (2000, p 4) was concerned that neoliberal reforms, while 'necessary acts of modernisation', pulled apart the bonds of social cohesion. Therefore the Third Way was not the continuation of neoliberalism but an alternative political philosophy entirely (Giddens, 2000, p 32). On the contrary, we view the Third Way as the continuation of neoliberalism by other, more socialised means, hence 'social neoliberalism', with the accent firmly on social integration and networks as a national platform to help smooth out the effectiveness of neoliberal markets. In a typical Giddensian formulation, markets not only *constrain* social actors by creating profound structural inequalities but they also *enable* them in various socially desirable ways by permitting social mobility and personal growth. Which is just as well since the embrace of a competitive market ethos is demanded at every level of society, in descending order from the scale of the entire national economy to regions, cities and neighbourhoods through, ultimately, to the level of individuals themselves. Self-capitalisation through an entrepreneurial subjecthood is an essential component of Third Way ideology as Peter Bain and Phil Taylor argued in Chapter Three. Yet, despite the waves of 'creative destruction' wrought by global market forces, social cohesion, inclusion and equality are not only desirable but also dependent on the self-same disruptive, alienating and unequal forces of competitive individualism.

Giddens' form of 'social neoliberalism' does not advance an equality of wealth distribution and the other desirable social and personal capabilities that come with it. Instead, it seeks to ensure an equality of opportunity to enable individuals to compete and to remove arbitrary barriers in order to allow natural talent to flourish. In contrast, hard-line neoliberals like Hayek (1944) refused to share in the illusion that the market and social justice were compatible. Markets spontaneously produce inequality as their unintended consequence and because unequal outcomes are not intended they cannot, on naked neoliberal grounds, be considered 'unjust'. Therefore the state's welfare role ought to be set at a minimal level and any grand pre-planned egalitarian outcomes abandoned for the sake of individual liberty. Whatever Hayek's perverse logic and arbitrary prioritisation of atomised individuals, it is in this peculiar conjuncture of desirable and necessary economic, personal and social states where the Third Way departs from the naked neoliberal programme for reducing state welfare to a bare minimum for paupers and other unfortunates only.

New Labour, like the previous Conservative governments, is always more pragmatic in practice than the abstract constructs found in economic theories of neoliberalism. Third Way thinking performs the invaluable ideological service of positing a pragmatic intellectual rationale that, whatever hopes are entertained of a just social world, there is simply no alternative to the economic primacy of the market. While such privileging of economic necessity might make unreconstructed Marxists blush, nevertheless, the hegemony of neoliberal determinism identified by Callinicos in the quote above is unmistakable. For Pierre Bourdieu (1998), such determinism masks the extent to which the pragmatism of neoliberals is attempting to actively construct a reactionary utopia by preparing the ground ideologically for the very conditions of market dependency that they claim are already established social facts about the world. Market solutions are mobilised by social neoliberals as a 'logical machine', which, as Bourdieu (1998) argued, relentlessly constructs a utopian ideal in reality by reducing public services to the abstract verities of homo economicus endlessly choosing between alternative commodities (and alternative values) in the marketplace.

It is widely recognised that this project has its roots in the thought of Hayek and Milton Friedman. Friedman in particular exerted considerable influence in the implantation of 'the neoliberal project for a reactionary utopia'. Less well known is that the 'neoliberal utopia' is also rooted in that 'other 9/11', the physical destruction of socialists and trade unionists in Santiago and the forced dismantling of the welfare state in Chile that followed the coup of 11 September 1973. In the early 1970s the democratic socialist government of Salvador Allende introduced some very modest reforms to extend the Chilean welfare state, which suffered repeated fiscal crises. Before the coup a group of CIA-financed economists at the Catholic University of Chile and the University of Chicago, hence known as the 'Chicago Boys', had been trained in the monetarist economics of Friedman. The Chicago Boys developed a 'modernisation' programme for privatising public services and creating market institutions should the military come to power. After Pinochet's bloody coup Chile embarked on the world's first national neoliberal experiment of widespread privatisation. The fact that neoliberal market freedom for individuals depended on an ultra-authoritarian state was not a paradox lost on the Chicago Boys, who saw authoritarian rule as more 'efficient' than the 'inefficiency' of democratic institutions. 'Impure politics' had been replaced by 'pure economics'. Reductions in the social spending of the state bureaucracy hit welfare sectors hardest and a tidal wave of privatisations (437 of the 507 state enterprises were privatised) engulfed the social sectors of the state (Borzutzky, 1991). 'Modernisations' were undertaken to reduce the role of the state in welfare and to increase that of the market, transforming social security, health and education, while introducing laws to limit the independent power of professional bodies. In the process, trade unions and collective bargaining were eliminated in order to purify the labour market from artificial frictions.

Clearly, a liberal–democracy like the UK is not the same as Chile, under a military dictatorship. Yet, the kind of 'naked neoliberalism' found in Pinochet's Chile has a direct lineage to the wholesale privatisation of all state assets (with the exception of oil) in Iraq under US and UK occupation in 2003, along with severe restrictions placed on trade unions (Harvey, 2005). The fact that neoliberal reform in the UK on the basis of ideas first implemented in Chile took root more deeply and much earlier than in places like France, where *dirigisme* was still seen as the solution to managing industrial change, is in part due to the way that the welfare state was identified in the 1970s by influential Hayekian thinkers like Bacon and Eltis (1976) as part of a wider malaise of declining economic competitiveness (Kus, 2006).

In this view, what Bacon and Eltis (1976) called the 'marketed sector', where commodities were produced for sale in the market, was being increasingly 'crowded out' of investment opportunities by the 'non-marketed sector', above all the welfare state, which depends on transfers of revenue rather than profit making. Hence the solution for declining national economic competitiveness involved the neoliberal remedy of reducing the public sector to release more capital and labour to the 'marketed sector' and to transfer as much economic activity from the 'non-marketed' to the 'marketed' sector as possible through policies like privatisation. In such ways, greater scope would be created for fostering profit-seeking activities which, it was assumed, would lead to a drive to reduce production and distribution costs and improve economic efficiency, and thus national competitiveness overall.

Pinochet's costly experiment thus became a benchmark first for Thatcher in the UK and Reagan in the US, where 'not for the first time, a brutal experiment carried out in the periphery became a model for the formulation of policies in the centre' (Harvey, 2005, p 9). The process begun in Chile continues to unravel its way through the UK welfare state. Without the 'shock and awe' impact of naked neoliberalism, 'social neoliberalism', nevertheless, continues to evince the same relentless mantra of market efficiency and attempts to mould welfare institutions in its marketised image. A further difference from neoliberal Chile is that despite following Conservative spending limits in its first term, public spending under New Labour grew, not dramatically but by around £40 billion or 3%, from 40% to 43% of GDP (gross domestic product), with 2% of this rise generated by rising income tax revenues (although not an increase in the rate of direct taxation). Most of this spending was directed to health, from 4.5% of GDP to 6.5%, and education, from 4.5% to 5.5% (Hirsch, 2007). So, in fact, there has been a modest rise in public spending in the UK under New Labour, quite unlike the vengeful destruction of public services in Chile.

Three decades later such ideas have moved from the margins to the centre ground to define the 'non-marketed' welfare sector in Britain as an ongoing source of the inefficient use of economic resources. Some of the intellectual and political framework for this was discussed in Chapters One and Two. There we also registered some of the limits and contradictions of transforming the welfare sector along the lines of the 'marketed sector', above all the problems of pseudo-markets, managerialism, indeterminate labour power, and overt and covert forms of worker resistance. Furthermore, as the case study chapters in this book illustrate, the construction of such a neoliberal utopia continually runs up against intrinsic barriers in the sphere of the workplace. New Labour's programme of 'modernisation' sought to address itself to what it saw as the shortcomings of previous Conservative governments' management of public policy and public service organisations (see Chapter One). Nonetheless, New Labour continued and deepened the Conservative focus on tackling the micro-foundations of X-inefficiency by restructuring organisations and managerial regimes. As Newman (2001, pp 57-8) summarises:

> The strengthening of managerialism took place in a particular context: that of a strong focus on organisational, rather than system, efficiency. The unit of measurement and control, reflected in government performance indicators, Citizen's Charters and league tables, became the individual school, not the LEA [local education authority]; the individual hospital, not the NHS; the local government service, not the local authority.

This created a centripetal–centrifugal tension in the centralisation of command coupled with institutional fragmentation. New Labour's plans for 'joined-up government' and a greater role for the voluntary sector (see Chapter Eleven) emphasised the discourse of networks and partnership, but a discourse underpinned by a tougher regulatory regime. Regulation was not intended as a substitute for marketisation and managerialism. Instead it was viewed as a supporting bulwark for increasing efficiencies at a micro-organisational level.

Generic managerial solutions imported from commercial business models continued the process begun under Thatcher: 'modernisation continued the attack on the "producer dominance" associated with monopoly forms of provision, and sought to create new forms of accountability to users and local stakeholders' (Newman, 2001, p 83). But the delivery of welfare services by a seemingly ever diverse assortment and form of provider is restricting the scope for and nature of state welfare through what post-Fordist theorists term the 'hollowing-out' of the state. This foregrounds our concern to redress the missing dimension of labour in the political economy of welfare, particularly within the context of social neoliberalism. Such developments have given rise to claims that a distinctive form of state has emerged, alternatively termed the 'post-Fordist welfare state', 'the workfare state', 'the managerial state', 'the contractual state' and 'the new market state' (see Burrows and Loader, 1994; Clarke, 2004). We want to emphasise the embeddedness of the welfare state within capitalist social relations and institutions: work in the welfare state is premised on waged labour and value relations. In this way we want to emphasise that state welfare is a crucial part of the capitalist economy, a sector of it, rather than as something completely separate and only externally related to it. The shape of welfare services are therefore profoundly dependent on recent shifts in state, economy and society that have come to be known as neoliberalism.

The issues that have been highlighted and explored by all the contributors to this collection are ones that are still unfolding, developing and likely to remain active for the immediate future. By the time this book is published Gordon Brown will have replaced Tony Blair as Prime Minister. But, as we argued in Chapter One in particular, a view shared by all of the contributors to this book, we are very sceptical that things will be radically different under a Brown-led government. Beyond changes in personnel, the issues and questions that are raised in this collection are likely to out-live Brown and New Labour. From the outset we have been at pains to stress that the impact of New Labour's welfare reform and public sector modernisation agendas, and the neoliberal-inspired market and managerial drives that underpin it, are uneven, partial and far from absolute. We are minded to distinguish between the rhetoric of reform and modernisation and, to borrow a term more often now used in relation to social neoliberalism, 'actually existing' reform and modernisation. The claims made by the government, politicians and policy makers are often at odds with emerging realities. However, these caveats do not preclude us from re-emphasising here some of the main themes that have emerged from the substantive case studies in this book. Nor do they prevent us from identifying the broad thrust of government policies and how these are impacting on public service delivery.

## Inside the 'hidden abode' of welfare work

New Labour's neoliberal agenda is having a profound impact on public sector workers and on the clients ('customers') of the new welfare state. What we called in Chapter Two 'strenuous welfarism' in the form of flexible work intensification and working time extension, proceduralisation and commodification are clear and developing trends affecting different areas of public service and welfare work. Across the entire welfare industry new forms of managerial practice, human resource management (HRM), accounting and regulatory procedures have been developed in an effort to win 'control of the frontline' for managers and employers. This also raises the 'other' dimension that we wish to re-emphasise: resistance and struggle at the point of delivery by both welfare providers and users. The rhetoric and practice of welfare reform and modernisation struggles to shape new public sector and welfare structures, practices and cultures in the face of determined opposition from both workers and service users (see Chapter One for an overview). Managerial control is never complete; it is deeply contested. As the preceding chapters amply testify these 'collisions' are an increasingly important element of the unfolding terrain of public and welfare provision in the UK today.

Too often the analysis of neoliberal welfarism, in both its naked neoliberal version and its social neoliberal version, restricts itself to observable regularities in the market or the pronouncements of public policy. Important though such work undoubtedly is, the purpose of this book is to attempt to partly redress the balance by opening up the 'black box' of welfare work processes, welfare labour, industrial relations and organisational regimes. As Peter Bain and Phil Taylor pointed out in Chapter Three, Third Way theorists like Giddens, juggling market inequalities with equal opportunities, limit themselves to what Marx (1976, p 280) called 'a very Eden of the innate rights of man'. The socially minded neoliberal of Marx's day, the 'free-trader *vulgaris*', was hidebound to 'the exclusive realm of Freedom, Equality, Property and Bentham'. 'Freedom', because individual sellers and buyers of labour power freely enter into a contractual relationship; 'Equality', because the employment contract represents an exchange between equals; 'Property', because they each exchange what they own; and 'Bentham', because, as Marx (1976, p 280) put it, 'each looks only to his own advantage ... each pays heed to himself only, and no one worries about the others'. By remaining at the level of 'this noisy sphere, where everything takes place on the surface and in full view of everyone' (Marx, 1976, p 279), the parallels between the 'free-trader *vulgaris*' and neoliberal apologetics from Hayek to Giddens are manifest.

Contributors to this collection have invited us to think at a level beneath the 'very Eden' of public policy and market activity. Although welfare work and public services generally are often carried out in full view of the public, such work *qua* work is like the purloined letter, in that the underlying social relations are obscured. The chapters in this book have descended into this 'hidden abode'. There, they found that the neoliberal vision of the entrepreneurial self is transformed from an Edenic utopia, where everything returns to a splendid equilibrium of mutual benefits, into a workplace purgatory of strained, flexibilised bureau-professionalism. Insecure marketised conditions and managerialist authority in the workplace mutually condition each other. A simple empirical description of the labour processes of various providers of welfare services would therefore tell us little about the context under which this occurs – teaching a child to read differs qualitatively depending whether it is done at the kitchen table by a parent or in an overcrowded PFI (private finance initiative) classroom by a qualified but harassed teacher, as Henry Maitles shows in the case of the teaching labour process (Chapter Six).

Even in the non-profit sector, as Lynne Poole (Chapter Eleven) highlighted, similar pressures from the centre to demonstrate market efficiency bear down on the more responsive, civic objectives of non-profit organisations. Such organisations are beginning to resemble the hierarchical, managerialist bureau-professional chain of command and responsibility found throughout the state sector (Cunningham, 2001). In the process, Poole shows how this attempt to enrol 'voluntary' workers behind managerialism utilises a range of measures from discursive scripts to physical intimidation and bullying. Workers in this sector tend to identify strongly with the values of the organisation, something that it was thought might inhibit union recruitment (Cunningham, 2000). Yet, as managerialism encroaches further into the sector a lacuna opens up between the control and domination exercised over workers and the organisation's espoused values of benevolence and compassion (for example, 'equality', 'caring', 'support', 'advocacy', 'dignity', 'fairness', 'respect' and so on) directed at users and the public. As one worker for a charity that campaigns on disability rights put it: 'There are quite strange anomalies [between] the organisation fighting for human and civil rights for disabled people, and some of the ways they see ordinary people and workers' rights' (quoted in Simms, 2007, p 124). Even in such an unpromising environment as the not-for-profit sector, which has over 600,000 workers and is expanding, trade unions are able to call on the discrepancies between humane goals and degraded workplace conditions to mount successful recruitment and recognition drives among employees (although not among volunteers, who have no contract of employment or legal recognition as a bargaining unit).

So it has been necessary for each chapter to establish the marketised conditions under which welfare workers are engaged as paid labour. Marketisation is reinforced by centralised command and control at a distance. Centralised pressures for efficiency savings are endemic throughout the welfare state, nowhere more so than in public administration, as Tricia McCafferty and Gerry Mooney describe in the case of benefit workers in the Department for Work and Pensions (Chapter Ten). This brings into sharp relief the implications for the state employment relationship of New Labour's 'modernisation' (Chapter

One). While government departments were expected to shed tens of thousands of jobs the same level of provision was to be maintained. This could only mean that work reorganisation would equip each remaining worker with a capacity to produce a greater output. But, as even efficiency theorists like Leibenstein understood, there are intrinsic limits to the quality of the service being produced when the quantity of inputs declines so drastically (see Chapter Two). As Chapter Ten, for example, reports, the incessant managerialist demand for greater efficiency is a siren call for 'more and more with less and less'. How much further can the welfare state be 'hollowed-out', its structures 'flattened', its organisation made 'leaner', and its labour consumed more intensively and extensively, without public services risking widespread disillusion in their institutional legitimacy? This process may actually increase the calls for displaced welfarist solutions of privatisation, marketisation and public–private partnerships (PPPs).

The mutual conditioning of the external environment and the internal work regime is given clear expression by the various ways in which 'displaced welfarism' shifts capital and labour from the 'non-marketed' public sector to the 'marketed' private sector (see Chapters One and Two). A central finding that emerged throughout the book is that 'displaced welfarism' and 'strenuous welfarism' mutually determine each other. In the NHS, as Sally Ruane demonstrated in Chapter Four, PFI hospital schemes and outsourcing contests have led to pressures being applied on the internal organisation of work and the terms and conditions under which health workers sell their labour power. The periodic changing of employer and the continual shifting of priorities and targets undermines workplace norms of reliability, trust and service. Similarly, league tables for school performance add significant pressures for teachers such that, as Henry Maitles shows (in Chapter Six), severe problems of retaining qualified teaching staff are being felt in the sector. Teachers become demoralised that they cannot teach effectively because of time and resource constraints and embark on exit strategies from the profession. Just as school teaching needs a certain slack in the working day for effective, stimulating learning to take place, so nursery nursing needs porosity during working time to play with and attend to infant development and safety. Yet, as Gerry Mooney and Tricia McCafferty illustrate in Chapter Eight, New Labour's goal of increasing nursery places to free up mothers for economic activity elsewhere means that nursery workers have been showered with additional and more skilled tasks – what the chapter calls 'functional flexploitation'. The added burden of so-called 'upskilling' tends to result in the loss of the 'free' time necessary for unstructured nurse–child interaction. Universities have similarly been subject to the structuring regime of audit mania and other published measuring devices, as Alex Law and Hazel Work noted in Chapter Seven. A creeping bureaucratisation of teaching and research is consolidating a hierarchy of institutions in competition with each other for student enrolments, which determines the size of central funding. It is also stimulating labour market churn, with excessive workloads caused by non-core administrative duties and high staff–student ratios encouraging more mobile academics to scour the labour market for improved conditions (although not always pay) at an alternative institution.

Under displaced welfarism not only labour power but also capital assets are more intensively sweated. Working space has been redesigned in PFI new-builds and managerialist capital projects alike. With cost-minimisation often a top priority, the result can be the use of inferior materials, built to minimum standards. What is known as 'sick building syndrome' has deleterious implications for public service workers' health and safety as workspaces resemble ones more familiar to commercial call centres than healthcare or education. Indeed, as Peter Bain and Phil Taylor illustrate in the case of the emergency services and Tricia McCafferty and Gerry Mooney for the huge investment in information and communication technology (ICT) in the Department for Work and Pensions' call centres, or 'contact centres', these have deepened the rationalisation process. Here the loss of local offices and face-to-face interaction negatively affects access to benefit services for the poor and for elderly people. In terms of meeting the needs of users it is counterproductive. Work space is made functionally cost-efficient as more workers are located within smaller areas, with open-plan offices steadily extending to colleges and universities, in part facilitated by greater reliance on ICT (see Chapter Seven). As highlighted in several chapters, health workers and higher education (HE) staff report that the more functional reorganisation of space results in higher levels of sickness and absenteeism.

## Voice, loyalty or exit

This may be understood in terms of institutional choices of 'voice, loyalty or exit' (Hirschman, 1970). Staff 'loyalty' is eroded due to unequal treatment and the rupturing of the moral economy of effort (see Chapter Two). Workers face two other options: to 'exit' the organisation or exercise 'voice'. With the exit option, staff turnover increases and overall staffing levels decrease (see Chapters Four, Five and Seven). The result is a depletion of organisational knowledge, tacit ways of getting things done, with the fewer experienced staff that are left straining to cope with meeting user needs and performance targets. With the 'voice' option, workers make their views known, undertake various overt forms of resistance, typically through trade union bargaining, culminating in industrial action. For those that remain in organisations 'loyalty' is often a poor way of conceiving their long service. Almost every chapter in this book made some reference to the idea of 'loyalty' in the form of a service obligation still current among nurses, teachers, lecturers, social workers and nursery nurses. As these chapters also showed, such 'loyalty' has been sorely tested by the vicissitudes of strenuous welfarism. But in situations where voice cannot be exercised through overt resistance the outcome is not simply obedient fidelity to organisational goals.

Strenuous welfarism places strain on the values and belief in public service that welfare professionals traditionally exhibit. This was brought out with particular salience in Michael Lavalette's discussion of social work (Chapter Nine). Social work as an occupation has at times attracted idealistic people by its vocational, care-centred promise to ease personal suffering and alleviate social need. Yet, this is counterbalanced with the radical critique of social work as a profession that controls and polices the weak on behalf of the powerful, recognising that welfare in its widest sense is rarely benign. In the current conjuncture of neoliberal managerialism and the impossible demands of moral policing, Lavalette argues that social workers have to endure the anguish of contradictory pressures. For him, the exercise of workers' voice is necessary to redress the dilemmas of a tormented profession. Such resources of hope are found in collective organisations, above all trade unions, but also in professional bodies and social movements. Lavalette advocates a new kind of professionalism, one that takes up the values of the social movements as its own, including issues of justice, equality, freedom and social solidarity. Gerry Mooney and Tricia McCafferty argue for something similar in the case of joint protests by nursery workers and parents (Chapter Eight). There is a wider lesson here for other welfare professions, welfare users and social movements on the need to develop a joint space for defending and enriching welfare relations through restoring the priority of use value over exchange value. We will develop this important dimension further towards the end of this chapter.

Resistance to managerial encroachments and the declining value of wages is taking overt form, sometimes predictably, sometimes surprisingly (see Chapter One). What is noticeable is the depth of the enmity within the public service workforce to managerialism. This has recently been expressed in a burst of militancy rarely seen for nearly 30 years. In the so-called 'winter of discontent' of 1978, public sector strikes were blamed for heralding the advent of Thatcherite neoliberalism. The contrast with today's forms of overt resistance, after decades of the neoliberal experiment, is striking (see Chapter Three). Trade union action in the welfare sector is typically justified not as the self-interested actions of a privileged section of the working class of neoliberal lore but as one of defending the quality of public services. When nurses take strike action popular support is almost automatic and near-universal, based on the high standing that the nursing profession continues to enjoy in the popular imagination. Similarly, the nursery nurses strike in Scotland galvanised widespread support (see Chapter Eight). On the other hand, workers who are seen as policing the benefits or services of the poor will struggle to enjoy similar levels of sympathy, although as Lavalette argues, even then solidarity action may still be possible. Traditionally well-organised groups of workers like civil servants have also engaged in significant strike action in recent years over pay, conditions at work, pensions and cuts in services (Chapter Ten). Here workers need to primarily rely on their own organisational strength in collective bargaining: the rhetorical appeal to 'wait until public opinion is right' is a favoured tactic of the union official intent on stalling. Similarly, the lecturers' strike of 2006 failed in its aims at least partly because it was widely enough believed that students rather than bureau-managers were being harmed by the action.

Resistance in the form of a tenacious but muted voice can take covert or individualised forms, such as Merton's 'trained incapacity', downright bloody-minded obstruction and sabotage, or other coping strategies. However, there are also inherent structural limits to strenuous welfarism. This arises, as Chapter Two argued, from the indeterminate character of labour power, and the specific context-bound knowledge and practice in many sites of welfare work. In the nursing labour process, Peter Kennedy and Carole A. Kennedy emphasised (Chapter Five) that while work intensification was being widely felt on the ward, further management attempts to more fully exercise detailed control were in vain. However, they also note that worker 'loyalty' may be a result of the internalisation of organisational norms as workers become self-disciplining 'docile bodies'. Any idea of the service ethos in welfare work as an unvarnished 'good thing' perhaps needs to consider its contradictory nature – commitment or compliance – and the extent to which employers rely on workers' extra-contractual dedication, both intensively in trying to cope with too many, sometimes conflicting tasks, as in HE and nursery work (Chapters Seven and Eight), and in the extension of the working day through unpaid overtime (Chapters Five and Seven). Yet, as Chapter Two noted, these contradictions result in an impossible managerial effort to cope with perpetual failure. On the one hand, commitment suffers under the duress of external controls imposed by strenuous welfarism. On the other hand, compliance inhibits workers' usefulness as serviceable agents to cope with the day-to-day exigencies of overcoming organisational limits and to respond creatively and empathetically to meet user needs.

## The shape of things to come?

While it is difficult to predict with any degree of certainty the future direction of the welfare state in the UK, we have more than enough evidence to begin to develop an informed picture of the likely trends and the shape of things to come. We are reminded once more of the important distinction between the welfare state and state welfare, recognising that much of what is still generally referred to as state welfare is not produced by the state as such with more space being created for other forms of provision by a multitude of providers. New Labour's valorisation of the consumer will remain central to the ongoing programme of welfare reforms; not least that such a figure is central to the government's vision of a 'modern' welfare state, underpinning new organisational and cultural logics (see Vidler and Clarke, 2005). New Labour has sought to 'sell' such a vision on the grounds that it will deliver 'better' services and more customer-orientated services:

> Public services ... have to be refocused around the needs of the patients, the pupils, the passengers and the general public rather than those who provide the services. (Blair, quoted in Introduction to Office of Public Services Reform, 2002, p 8)

> I am not talking about modest further reorganisation but something quite different and more fundamental. We are proposing to put an entirely different dynamic in place to drive our public services: one where the service will be driven not by the government or by the managers but by the user – the patient, the pupil and the law abiding citizen. (Blair, 2004)

Such thinking informs much of the rhetoric that accompanies announcements of 'modernisation' that feature across the different sites of welfare provision explored in this book, from the education sector through to healthcare, pre-school provision and social work.

However, it is clear that the government is seeking to develop this much further, in no small part through its 'personalisation' agenda. Accorded government approval thanks to the inclusion of a foreword by the Minister for School Standards, Charles Leadbetter's *Personalisation through participation: A new script for public services* (2004) points to the future direction and shape of government thinking in this respect:

> Privatisation was a simple idea: putting public assets into private ownership would create more powerful incentives for managers to deliver greater efficiency and innovation. Personalisation is just as simple: by putting users at the heart of services, enabling them to become participants in the design and delivery, services will be more effective by mobilising millions of people as co-producers of the public goods they value. (Leadbetter, 2004, p 19)

Leadbetter draws a distinction between 'shallow personalisation', 'a programme to apply a lick of new paint to fading public services' (p 20), and 'deep personalisation' where

> ... dependent users become consumers and commissioners, and eventually co-producers and designers. Their participation, knowledge and responsibility increases. (Leadbetter, 2004, p 24)

The overriding emphasis in Leadbetter's argument is on the individual user as an active participant in the production of services. Against 'dependency' on state welfare he emphasised responsibility and how personalisation could create a 'new script' for public services. There is little sense that workers play an active role in mediating these scripts, save perhaps as call centre workers responding to individual enquiries. Indeed, one of the examples Leadbetter highlighted as a good example of a responsive service was Liverpool Direct, discussed critically by Michael Lavalette in Chapter Nine in this volume (see also Ferguson, 2007).

Personalisation is now informing important areas of government policy making, taking the emphasis on the individual as consumer to a new level but also working to legitimate in the process further marketisation. Perhaps not surprisingly it allows for a greater role for private providers and firms in the development of more personalised services. This is at odds with the sense of 'bottom-up' involvement as advanced over the past two decades by user movements. It is also at odds with other evidence about the state of provision in the key area of welfare today. In a report published in January 2007, for example, the Commission for Social Care Inspection for England (CSCI, 2007) claimed that the current social care system was 'failing older people' as a result of a decline in provision. The Commission warned that 70% of local authorities are now limiting home care services to people who are so frail they need help to get out of bed or who cannot cook a hot meal for themselves. Those who are deemed to have more 'moderate' difficulties, such as mobility problems, have to rely on family, friends or fund private care themselves. Once more there is a massive gulf between rhetoric, here in terms of personalisation, and the realities of provision on the frontline. For us there is little disagreement that service users should be involved along with workers in designing and producing good-quality services that provide equally for all in need, services that are not driven by overriding concerns to maximise 'efficiency' or to cheapen costs.

As this book was nearing completion in early 2007, two apparently unrelated events took place that for us helped to reinforce what this book is all about. On Monday, 22 January 2007, one of Scotland's largest after-school care and nursery providers, One Plus, announced that it was being wound up following mounting debts and the failure to secure additional funding from the Scottish Executive in Edinburgh. One Plus provided after-school care for around 10,000 children in Glasgow, supporting many single parents in the process, and employed 600 people, all of whom were to lose their jobs (*The Herald*, 22 and 23 January 2007). Just over a week later, on Wednesday, 31 January, around 250,000 civil service workers in the PCS participated in a one-day strike. For one day, the action seriously disrupted work in tax collection offices (at the busiest time of year for tax returns), courts, museums, art galleries and other public services. The strikers had a number of targets in their sights: pay and conditions, compulsory redundancies, privatisation of services and the increasing use of private sector consultants by the government (*The Guardian*, 1 February 2007; PCS press release, 31 January 2007, at www.pcs.org.uk; *Socialist Worker*, 3 February 2007). Other days of action are set to follow.

In different ways staff at One Plus and civil servants, in PCS and in other unions, provide services for some of the most disadvantaged groups in UK society today. One of the One Plus workers who demonstrated on a march in Glasgow on 27 January 2007 commented:

> One Plus was about so much more than just childcare. We offered a whole range of crucial social services for parents,

including mentoring and educational support. For children who have started counselling, we've opened up a Pandora's Box, and just abandoned them, and that's a dangerous thing to do. (Quoted in Dalgarno, 2007)

Such concerns are reflected in a number of the case studies in this book. In the chapters on nurses, nursery workers, benefits officers and social workers in particular, what emerges is that the world of the public sector/welfare worker and the world of the welfare 'consumer' or client are not necessarily conflicting worlds. As we noted above, public service workers claim that they have the interests of service users at heart, even when they are at the forefront of implementing New Labour public policies. It is also now widely recognised that welfare workers in health, education, social services, housing and so on often face physical assault and abuse from welfare users. Indeed, abuse from service users or their families was a key reason that trade unions were able to recruit successfully in the not-for-profit sector. As Melanie Simms (2007, p 126) found in her study into trade union activism in the not-for-profit sector, union organisers 'pushed managers to clarify the procedures for protecting workers from such an abuse, and again this served to demonstrate the power of collective action to (potential) members'.

In recent years, and again, while wishing to avoid minimising the importance of such a development, we recognise that this is uneven and partial, there has been something of a merging of the concerns of public sector workers and their unions and the demands of service users and welfare clients. There are a growing number of examples we can use here to illustrate this point. PCS run a high-profile 'public services not private profit' campaign (see pcs.org.uk) while UNISON (www.unison.org.uk) have fought in particular against PFI/PPP. Both have involved non-union members and users groups as well as the wider public. Keep Our NHS Public (www.keepournhspublic.com) brings together NHS workers, unions and NHS service users. In other areas of welfare provision, for instance council housing, organisations such as Defend Council Housing (www.dch.org.uk) have also mobilised tenants and public sector unions in defence of state provision of affordable housing to rent (see DCH, 2006). 'Privatisation', in all its guises, has worked to re-energise debates around health and other public services over the past decade (see Keep Our NHS Public, 2006) and this has given rise to a large number of more localised campaigns and organisations that fight to prevent hospital closures or reductions in health and other public services.

There is a further dimension to this. Together with the Conservatives before them, New Labour have inadvertently repoliticised the whole question of welfare and public sector provision in a multitude of ways. One of the key aspects of this, as was highlighted in Sally Ruane's chapter (Chapter Four), is that the increasing use of PPP/PFI forms of investment in welfare, along with the increasing penetration of welfare provision by the market, often through large multinational firms, has brought the question of 'profits from illness' (the activists' rendering of PFI) centre stage. Capital-driven and for-profit forms of provision have become highly unpopular. It has led to the re-emergence of political unionism, thereby challenging in the process the apparent 'division' that has existed in recent decades between a concern with 'bread and butter' issues such as pay and conditions on the one hand, and more 'political' issues on the other, such as fighting privatisation or cuts in welfare provision. Such a divide, which was often more apparent than real, and which tended to express the mediating function of the trade union bureaucracy more than ordinary members on 'the frontline', now looks seriously dated and redundant in the face of New Labour's political agenda of the past decade. Union-sponsored campaigns are making direct links between pay and conditions to the importance of good-quality services for those in need; between a well-funded and free at the point of delivery NHS and issues of taxation and pensions; and, in a few instances, between 'cut-backs' and service withdrawals alongside massive expenditure on wars in Iraq, Afghanistan and elsewhere. Campaigns to Make Poverty History, to achieve global social justice and for sustainability are often drawn into opposition to public sector modernisation. New Labour is being challenged 'head on' here: its social and economic agenda is now profoundly contested. The challenge here is also to the Third Way project itself and, if not in the sense meant by John Clarke, there is also often a conscious resistance to the 'dissolving of the public realm' that lies at the heart of neoliberalism (Clarke, 2004).

Such campaigns frequently bring together the 'producers' and 'consumers' of welfare in ways that are far removed from claims of an unbridgeable gulf between the demands of each. Among New Labour politicians and for many policy makers and academics, the idea that public service workers may take action to defend both their jobs as well as services to a wide spectrum of UK society including the most impoverished is something that is all too readily ignored or otherwise marginalised. It also overlooks the point that public sector workers and their families are themselves consumers of welfare. In another sense the growing campaigns of resistance to New Labour's public sector modernisation and welfare reforms also illustrate that far from being 'passive recipients of welfare', clients and users can and do take action to both defend and fight for public service provision – that is, state-provided public service provision.

The significance of the struggles that have taken place across the public and welfare sectors since New Labour came to power in 1997 should not be underestimated, although they have all too often been neglected in the social policy literature. Against the general downturn in strike activity and in other forms of 'industrial action' during the past 10-15 years, as highlighted by Peter Bain and Phil Taylor in Chapter Three, the re-emergence of widespread, large-scale and continuing action in the public sector shows oft-repeated assumptions and claims that labour would no longer struggle or resist in the 'new' conditions of the early 21st century to be very wide of the mark. This is not to be taken that we are implying that there is a return to the heady days of the 1970s and 1980s but simply to counter the general rejection of the capacity of labour to resist that has been a stock in trade for much of academic and wider commentary in recent years (see also Dunn, 2004).

Throughout this book different forms of resistance and types of struggles have been explored, taking place in the varied sites that comprise the complex division of labour that characterises the welfare and public service industries today. Of course, sectionalism and division remains a trenchant problem, and there are narrow forms of bureau-professionalism that operate social closure manoeuvres to exclude or relegate other groups of workers. But amidst the struggles against the neoliberal and Third Way onslaughts on UK public and welfare services, such insular practices are being challenged. Against the myriad of 'end of class' or 'death of class' proclamations of the past few decades (for a critical discussion, see Ferguson et al, 2002), public service workers in the UK comprise a key section of the working class today.

## What is to be done?

One of the many objectives that we set ourselves for this book was to redress the neglect of welfare workers and welfare work in accounts of industrial relations and workplace activity, in the sociology of work and in much of academic social policy analysis and commentary. In different ways across this collection the contributors have drawn from industrial relations and work organisation literature, from the sociology of work and organisations, from labour process theories and, of course, from social policy. While we have not collectively produced a neat, one-size-fits-all synthesis, the collected case studies point to some fruitful ways in which we can gain a more informed understanding of the multiple impacts of New Labour welfare reforms, of neoliberalism 'on the ground', of resistance to such developments, and how these are impacting on the contested terrain of the new welfare 'settlement' that the government is struggling to impose.

In other important ways there is an emerging research agenda here: we feel that a transdisciplinary approach can provide the basis for further work in this area, and not just in the UK context. There is a desperate need for a comparative and transnational study of welfare work and welfare workers, and in particular for state worker resistance to actually existing neoliberalism in different national contexts, building on important examinations of neoliberalism, globalisation, consumption and welfare (see, for instance, Whitfield, 2001; Fine, 2002; Kiely, 2005; Smith, 2006). Over the past decade or so there have been notable episodes of public sector workers taking action in France, Germany, South Africa, Portugal, Canada, Brazil, New Zealand and elsewhere. Important and pioneering work has been done in recent years on 'global care chains' and how these are now working to service public welfare provision in different countries (see, for example, Hochschild, 2001; Yeates, 2005). In such ways the working class are being reconfigured, regionally, nationally and inter- or transnationally, a 'working class … enriched with greater numbers of women workers, workers from ethnic minorities and a new wave of migrant workers who are also entering the workforce' (Smith, 2007, p 66). Less attention has been paid, however, to the resistance and struggles of migrant labour. In the US on 1 May 2006, migrant workers mobilised through their diverse networks and trade unions 'A Day without Immigrants', hitting core areas of US industry, commerce and care work from Los Angeles to New York. In London in late 2006 cleaners working for investment bank Goldman Sachs, most of whom were migrant workers, organised against low pay and poor working conditions. Elsewhere in the UK unions are starting to organise among new migrant workers arriving from Eastern Europe, some employed in the welfare sector. There is also the thorny problem of restitution from the UK welfare state where they recruit medical professionals from Africa and elsewhere to staff the NHS, leaving behind a labour market vacuum in the country of origin (Mackintosh et al, 2006). This provides for new and exciting opportunities for valuable research work to be undertaken.

This is not, however, a call for 'just any kind' of approach or for some kind of impartial or supposedly 'balanced' account of these issues (if indeed such an account was possible). The general approach taken in this book is from a political economy standpoint – but again, not just any political economy. This book is avowedly pro-labour. Most of the authors contributing here share a Marxist perspective, a perspective that celebrates struggle and resistance, an approach that views social collectivities re-cohering as a class through collective action. With some important exceptions (see, for example, Lavalette and Mooney, 2000; Mooney, 2000; Ferguson et al; 2002; Farnsworth, 2004, 2005) class has largely dropped from view in social policy analysis. By this we mean class as agency, class as resistance. Rarely are workers placed at the centre of analysis. However, our understanding of the impacts of neoliberalism on welfare provision in different national and transnational contexts, of diverse forms of welfare and public services 'reforms' and 'modernisations', is seriously compromised when the workers on whose labour welfare is so dependent are noticeably absent from the concerns of a major scholarly discipline like social policy.

There is, finally, a key message in *New Labour/hard labour?*. Against much of the gloomy prognosis that pervades the discussion and analysis of neoliberalism and of New Labour there are different ways of thinking about the potential opportunities for the future. Certainly, as our contributors have noted, there is demoralisation among many categories of welfare workers. This is expressed in many ways, not least by high levels of workplace stress, sickness, absenteeism and other forms of worker refusal to engage or participate with the new scripts of managerialism and self-capitalisation (some of which may be seen as forms of resistance). With the intensification of work under the regime of strenuous welfarism, there is most definitely much *hard labour*! But on the other hand, against neoliberalism's core drive to corrode and erode solidarity (Lorenz, 2005), new forms of solidarity are emerging, new examples of resistance unfolding – locally, nationally and transnationally. We do not wish to accord these with significance that may not be realised, nor attribute to them meanings that may not develop along predetermined paths. But, at the same time, we can identify some emerging tendencies that we wish to register: welfare workers continue to resist the machine-like market logic driving the neoliberal project.

## References

Bacon, R. and Eltis, W. (1976) *Britain's economic problem: Too few producers*, London: Macmillan.

Blair, T. (2004) Speech on public services delivered at Guys and St Thomas' Hospital, London, 23 June (http://news.bbc.co.uk).

Borzutzky, S. (1991) 'The Chicago Boys, social security and welfare in Chile', in H. Glennerster and J. Midgley (eds) *The radical Right and the welfare state: An international assessment*, Hemel Hempstead: Harvester Wheatsheaf, pp 79-99.

Bourdieu, P. (1998) 'The essence of neo-liberalism', *Le Monde Diplomatique*, December.

Burrows, R. and Loader, B. (eds) (1994) *Towards a post-Fordist welfare state*, London: Routledge.

Callinicos, A. (2001) *Against the Third Way*, Cambridge: Polity Press.

Clarke, J. (2004) 'Dissolving the public realm? The logics and limits of neoliberalism', *Journal of Social Policy*, vol 33, no 1, pp 27-48.

CSCI (Commission for Social Care Inspection) (2007) *The state of social care in England 2005-06*, London: CSCI.

Cunningham, I. (2000) 'Prospects for union growth in the UK voluntary sector', *Industrial Relations Journal*, vol 31, no 3, pp 192-239.

Cunningham, I. (2001) 'Sweet charity! Managing employee commitment in the UK voluntary sector', *Employee Relations*, vol 23, no 3, pp 226-39.

Dalgarno, P. (2007) 'Protesters demand help after childcare firm folds', *Sunday Herald*, 28 January.

DCH (Defend Council Housing) (2006) *The case for council housing in 21st century Britain*, London: DCH.

Dunn, B. (2004) *Global restructuring and the power of labour*, London: Palgrave Macmillan.

Farnsworth, K. (2004) *Corporate power and social policy in a global economy: British welfare under the influence*, Bristol: The Policy Press.

Farnsworth, K. (2005) 'International class conflict and social policy', *Social Policy and Society*, vol 4, no 2, pp 217-26.

Ferguson, I. (2007) 'Increasing user choice or privatizing risk? The antinomies of personalization', *British Journal of Social Work*, vol 37, no 3, pp 387-403.

Ferguson, I., Lavalette, M. and Mooney, G. (2002) *Rethinking welfare*, London: Sage Publications.

Fine, B. (2002) *The world of consumption*, London: Routledge.

Giddens, A. (2000) *The Third Way and its critics*, Cambridge: Polity Press.

Giddens, A. (2003) 'The challenge of renewal', *Progressive Politics*, vol 1, no 1, pp 36-9.

Harvey, D. (2005) *A brief history of neoliberalism*, Oxford: Oxford University Press.

Hayek, F.A. (1944) *The road to serfdom*, London: George Routledge and Sons.

---

Hirsch, D. (2007) 'The swansong has a sting', *New Statesman*, 26 March, p 14.

Hirschman, A.O. (1970) *Exit, voice and loyalty: Responses to decline in firms, organizations and states*, Cambridge, MA: Harvard University Press.

Hochschild, A. (2001) 'Global care chains and emotional surplus value', in W. Hutton and A. Giddens (eds) *On the edge: Living with global capitalism*, London: Verso, pp 130-46.

Keep Our NHS Public (2006) *The 'patchwork privatisation' of our health service: A users guide* (www.keepournhspublic.com).

Kiely, R. (2005) *Empire in the age of globalisation: US hegemony and neoliberal disorder*, London: Pluto Press.

Kus, B. (2006) 'Neoliberalism, institutional change and the welfare state: the case of Britain and France', *International Journal of Comparative Sociology*, vol 47, no 6, pp 488-525.

Lavalette, M. and Mooney, G. (eds) (2000) *Class struggles and social welfare*, London: Routledge.

Leadbetter, C. (2004) *Personalisation through participation: A new script for public services*, London: Demos.

Levitas, R. (2005) *Inclusive society? Social exclusion and New Labour* (2nd edn), London: Palgrave.

Lorenz, W. (2005) 'Social work and a new social order – challenging neoliberalism's erosion of solidarity', *Social Work and Society*, vol 3, no 1, pp 93-101.

Mackintosh, M., Raghuram, P. and Henry, L. (2006) 'A perverse subsidy: African trained nurses and doctors in the NHS', *Soundings*, vol 34, pp 103-13.

Marx, K. (1976) *Capital: A critique of political economy, Volume one*, Harmondsworth: Penguin Books.

Mooney, G. (2000) 'Class and social policy', in G. Lewis, S. Gewirtz and J. Clarke (eds) *Rethinking social policy*, London: Sage Publications, pp 156-70.

Newman, J. (2001) *Modernising governance: New Labour, policy and society*, London: Sage Publications.

Office of Public Services Reform (2002) *Reforming our public services: Principles into practice*, London: Office of Public Services Reform.

Simms, M. (2007) 'Managed activism: two union organising campaigns in the not-for-profit sector', *Industrial Relations Journal*, vol 38, no 2, pp 119-35.

Smith, M. (2007) 'The shape of the working class', *International Socialism*, vol 113, Winter, pp 49-70.

Smith, T. (2006) *Globalisation: A systematic Marxian account*, Leiden: Brill.

Vidler, E. and Clarke, J. (2005) 'Creating citizen-consumers: New Labour and the remaking of public services', *Public Policy and Administration*, vol 20, no 2, pp 19-37.

Whitfield, D. (2001) *Public services or corporate welfare: Rethinking the nation state in the global economy*, London: Pluto Press.

Yeates, N. (2005) 'A global political economy of care', *Social Policy and Society*, vol 4, no 2, pp 227-34.

# Index